FOOTBALL, FAST FRIENDS, AND SMALL TOWNS

FOOTBALL, FAST FRIENDS, AND SMALL TOWNS

A Memoir Straight from a Broken Oklahoma Heart

Steve Love

Football, Fast Friends, and Small Towns: A Memoir Straight from a Broken Oklahoma Heart

For information about this title or to order other books and/or electronic media, contact the publisher:

Hawk Bookworks
P.O. Box 400
Uniontown, OH 44685
stevelovewriter.com
stephenlove222@yahoo.com

Library of Congress Control Number: 2020912646

ISBNs:
978-1-7351227-2-4 (hardcover)
978-1-7351227-0-0 (softcover)
978-1-7351227-1-7 (eBook)

Printed in the United States of America

Cover and Interior design: 1106 Design

For KB Berry, Bucky Buck, and Charles Dugger—teammates and friends—and to all the others in the Class of 1964 who allowed me to feel a part of Nowata even after I wasn't.

Also by Steve Love

The Indomitable Don Plusquellic (*2016*)
How a Controversial Mayor Quarterbacked Akron's Comeback

The Holden Arboretum (*2002*)

Stan Hywet Hall and Gardens (*2000*)

Wheels of Fortune (*1999*, David Giffels, co-author)
The Story of Rubber in Akron

The Golden Dream (*1997*, Gerry Faust and Steve Love)

CONTENTS

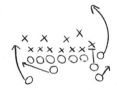

INTRODUCTION

This work began not as memoir but as a construct of essays intended to reveal quarterback attributes beyond throwing and running, qualities too often underappreciated or unrecognized. It was to have included quarterbacks of all stripes, high school to professional. That book must wait. At the fountainhead of this trickle of exceptionalism stood, in my mind, a quarterback whose name not even the most ardent and knowledgeable football fan is likely to have known—Kenneth Beryl Berry. That is a loss, one I hoped to rectify. KB was my high school quarterback, the youngest brother of another Berry quarterback who had inspired all us boys.

As I laid the groundwork, the backstory to introduce KB Berry, one of the many quarterbacks I have known in the ways people come to know them—as failed player, admirer of the game, and, in my case, sports columnist and excavator of the forgotten—the story morphed into more than the drama of KB, quarterback. It took on a life of its own, one about a small town in Oklahoma, a town like many in which people love football and boys who play the game that can create common cause and give purpose to a community it would not otherwise have. It became KB's story and that of Steve Davis, another small-town Oklahoman who quarterbacked the University of Oklahoma to national championships. It became mine as well.

The other quarterbacks with equally admirable qualities and stories might understand this turn of events. Many of their lives were not straight lines to glory, either. As I assayed the way forward, one word at a time, some sure, others as shaky as one of the newborn calves my veterinarian father let me help him birth when I was a boy, one phrase kept recurring in my mind. Originally a Walt Whitman poem, "O Captain! My Captain!" it was touchingly and tellingly reprised in a 1989 Academy Award-winning movie, *Dead Poets Society.* An unorthodox English teacher (John Keating, played by Robin Williams) encouraged his students to "seize the day"—*carpe diem*—and "make your lives extraordinary." It did not work out well for everyone.

Such mixed outcomes are not limited to movies. Sometimes a person seizes the day, and other times the day gets the best of him. It happens everywhere, in small towns and large, even to the most exceptional among us—our quarterbacks, "captain, my captain." That became the story, KB's and mine, and this book evolved into something unplanned, taking a trajectory that follows the paths we took to arrive at the place we have ended up.

My hope is to return to the other quarterbacks to whom this book might be considered an unintended prequel. As you will discover, however, I have been known to fumble, stumble, and bumble, which is not unlike a go-to description—"rumblin', bumblin', stumblin'"—the great Chris Berman once used to explain quarterback and other football follies to devotees of the ESPN *Sunday NFL Countdown* program he anchored. Boomer had a way with words and a delivery that seized listeners. KB Berry, quarterback and captain, had some Boomer in him.

Some of it resulted from our hometown, Nowata, Oklahoma, which I must admit to seeing through rose-colored glasses fogged by time. Those who remained in Nowata or returned later see more clearly. Bucky Buck, another teammate and friend, once confessed today's Nowata could make him sad. "Nowata is not exactly a rose garden," he said. "But this is home." The home we knew, the home that is, for good and bad.

Even diminished, hometowns continue to be places that have a hold on our hearts, weaker, perhaps, yet strong enough to remain unbroken. "'Home is where the heart is,' I heard a wise man say," Bucky reminded me, wisely. That will not change. Sacred memories and the hope of a homecoming sustain us. As Bucky put it, "Hope is the typology of heaven." And . . . Nowata.

A SMALL-TOWN BACKYARD QUARTERBACK

When Mama blew her whistle, it meant *Game Over.* Forget who had the ball, what down it was, or which team was leading. Mama's whistle was final. No ifs, ands, or Hail Marys. Her whistle, a 1950s means of communication, predated smartphones by decades; it did not waste words. Even if this whistle-blower was not an official, everyone understood Mama ruled our backyard games, as much Oklahoma small-town authority figure as any football coach.

Mama knew football as surely as she knew when dinner was ready and that her little quarterback had better head for home as if it were the end zone.

The players could hear Mama's metal or plastic whistle a block away, which is where kids in my Nowata neighborhood usually played. Nowata, a town of four thousand or so, is in the northeast corner of the state, twenty miles south of Coffeyville, Kansas, where Mama grew up and the Dalton Gang went down. If I did not want to end up like the Daltons—or worse, on the wrong end of Daddy's razor strop—I had to grab my football and leg it home. We usually played with my football, which explains why I was the quarterback. I would have left the ball for others to finish the game, but, when someone left, it often created uneven sides. Game over.

Seventy-plus years later, I still hear the shrill echo of Mama's whistle, a nostalgic blast more welcome in memory than it was before our game had been settled. I cannot remember how old I was when our neighborhood games began. It seems as if we were born playing football, basketball, or baseball—especially football—and as often as not in yards at the sides of our modest houses as in those in back of the small lots. When I visit Nowata now—Mama and Daddy are buried there—it seems as if the yards have shrunk even further. Once, there might have been enough room to play in my yard if my father's animal hospital and my mother's prodigious plantings—flowers, shrubs, trees—had not eaten up so much of what could have been a small football field. Hedges and the street marked out-of-bounds. With three or four to a team, we did not require enormous spaces. We ourselves were on the small side.

The Love home on Cedar Street in Nowata, Oklahoma. Taken in 2017, this photo reveals a house no longer sided with thick green shingles and absent the yard the author knew from 1946 to 1962, one so abundant with shrubs, flower gardens, and trees a boy could hardly find a strip of turf large enough for a neighborhood football game.

Backyard games went on all over Nowata, which, like most in Oklahoma, was a football town, the community rallying around the game and schools that served as its locus. I did not fully understand the scope and depth of our shared obsession until I began elementary school in 1952 and discovered that almost all the boys—and the occasional tomboy—had neighborhood games that we melded on a playground, more dirt and chat than grass. Because ranches and farms dotted Nowata County, semi-famous and semi-prosperous for one of the world's largest shallow-well oil fields, a number of my teammates lived in the country. Section lines and mileposts served as markers rather than city blocks, giving broader meaning to "next-door neighbor."

I understood this sooner than most "city boys," because my father, the veterinarian, would sometimes let me ride along when he visited ranches and farms to care for all manner of large animals that could not be brought to town to be treated at Dr. Clarence A. Love's animal hospital. Small-town vets made house calls, because their livelihoods depended more on ministering to cattle, horses, and other large animals than to dogs and cats. Small animals, particularly cats, did not generate the income their care does today. If a veterinarian had limited his practice to small animals in Nowata, he and his family would have starved.

My father found his way from Kansas State University's School of Veterinary Medicine to Nowata in 1942. He knew something of the town from growing up in neighboring Rogers County, where he played football for Chelsea High School, one of Nowata's rivals. He may even have known the correct spelling of the town's name—but maybe not. It should be "no-we-ata," an American Indian word from the Delaware language meaning "welcome." There are multiple stories of how it came to be bastardized into "Nowata." One of them might even be true.

When I was growing up, the most prominent story had a sign painter misspelling the name on the downtown depot in 1889 for what was then the Kansas and Arkansas Valley Railroad. Its tracks traversed the town some three blocks west of our home at the corner of Cedar Street and Osage Avenue. The chugging, clanking, whistling trains became almost comforting, as familiar to my childhood as neighborhood football. The fact that the misspelling went uncorrected makes the story seem apocryphal, though not as much as the one in which a traveler who came upon a dried-up spring posted a warning for others: "No Wata." Even today, if I declare I'm from Nowata, the response is incredulous: *You mean the town has no water?*

In fact, Nowata County is rich with water, from farm ponds to creeks—pronounced *cricks*—to rivers and now the northernmost end of Oologah Lake, a U.S. Army Corps of Engineers water-conservation project begun in 1950 along the Verdigris River and completed hit-and-miss. A recreational asset for Nowata and Rogers counties, it is the primary water supply for Tulsa, fifty miles south of Nowata. The lake extends almost to Coody's Bluff (sometimes spelled without the apostrophe, which seems grammatically incorrect, since this was a place settled in 1828 by a Western Cherokee family named Coody).

Historically, Coody's Bluff may be best known for a cave alongside the Verdigris River that the Dalton Gang used as a hideout. Two Coody's Bluff men—Bill Rattlingourd and George "Bitter Creek" Newcomb—ran with the gang but were not present on October 5, 1892, when the Dalton brothers—Bob, Emmett, and Grat—quarterbacked simultaneous robbery attempts at the First National and Condon banks in their hometown of Coffeyville. They had help from Dick Broadwell and Bill Powers. The Daltons' play took a deadly turn when someone recognized the lawmen-turned-outlaws. As they worked the banks, townspeople took up weapons and lay in wait outside. The resultant shootout killed everyone in the gang but Emmett, as well as four townspeople. Only after spending fourteen years of a life sentence in prison was Emmett, who had been seriously wounded, paroled. The missing Coody's Bluff gang members must not have taken the lesson. Rattlingourd was killed in 1895, Newcomb in 1896.

Good, law-abiding people lived in and around Coody's Bluff in my youth. The Berrys, Roy and Jewel, their four boys and four girls, may have been the finest of the fine. In the early 1950s, they had a place off a county road a quarter mile east of the Verdigris River bridge on U.S. Highway 60 and a quarter mile north. I don't know if my father doctored the cattle they kept, but, if so, he must have noticed the yard fenced off from them. In the southeast corner of the yard stood a basketball goal, metal rim affixed to a backboard made of lumber and attached to a small, cut-tree upright. Perhaps the basketball goal gave Daddy the idea for the fancier sheet-metal backboard welded onto a pole stanchion and erected for me at the end of a concrete slab that once served as Daddy's exercise pens for hospitalized dogs.

Though we didn't know it then, Kenneth Beryl "KB" Berry, youngest of the Berry brothers, would become not only my quarterback—schoolyard to high school—but also one of my better friends. At a time I was learning in town to shoot a treasured basketball I had won, KB was doing the same in the country. "My memory is he used [the goal]," his brother Chuck said, "but not as much as me and my friends." Chuck was four years older and KB's competition for "court" time since Gene, the oldest brother, was working, and Warren, whom his dad nicknamed "Rooster" because he crowed like one, was in high school in Nowata, already a star on one of its more memorable football teams. I began watching the Ironmen when I was nine months old. Football-loving Mama made sure we attended every game, home and away. She taught me to love the Ironmen, but it was hardly an exclusive affair.

The Roy and Jewel Berry Family (center, in their wedding photo): (From top, clockwise) Gene, Margie, Warren, Erville, Helen, Charles (Chuck), Kenneth (KB), and Janice. [*Photo courtesy the Berry Family*]

On football Friday nights, when the Ironmen played an out-of-town game, Nowata shut down tighter than a happy tick on a sad old dog. A caravan of cars hit the road and made passing on narrow, two-lane highways impossible. We followed the taillights of cars bearing Nowata County license tags, all bound for a Verdigris Valley Conference game in Pawhuska or Pryor, Vinita or Miami [pronounced *My-AM-ah*], Tahlequah, Claremore or Broken Arrow. When the caravan drew close to one of these towns, almost all larger than Nowata, we looked for the Friday Night Lights and pointed the car in their direction. If the team played at home, Mama, Daddy, and I would be early to our reserved seats, car parked in the driveway or on the yard of a friend's house across from Ironmen Memorial Stadium.

For a reason I did not understand when I was a child and still don't, the reserved seats, which cost extra, were in the east stands across the field from larger ones with the Nowata bench in front and press box at the top. My parents paid more to be seated on the 50-yard-line with other "big-spenders," all surrounded by the visiting team's fans. Talk about perilous. Most of the Nowata kids sat on the home side of the field. Some of them, including the irrepressible Bucky Buck, at halftime would run onto the field near one end zone or the other, imitating the "big boys" or improvising what the players should do when the second half got underway.

KB and Bucky became friends before we began elementary school in 1952. They had an advantage I lacked—older brothers in KB's case and an extended family renowned for its athleticism in Bucky's. Whereas I was an only child, Bucky and KB would tag along with the big football players in their families and reap the benefits. Rooster Berry would let KB and Bucky throw and kick the football around with him and Bucky's uncles, Wilbur and Dewey, notable athletes, reputed hell-raisers, and guys you wanted on your side in a fight.

"The older boys in Nowata always helped us along," Bucky said. "We thought [that] someday we would be like KB's brothers and my uncles." This belief went beyond KB and Bucky. If not articulated, it was nonetheless a Nowata tradition. Today, it is often referred to as "paying it forward." "The younger kids," Bucky said, "were happy just to be learning from the bigger boys. Down through time, the older kids tried to help the younger ones because they knew that, someday, those younger ones would be Ironmen—and football was King in Oklahoma."

With no older brothers or uncles to inspire and teach me, I relied on neighbors, particularly Gerald Wayne Anderson, whose name in the mouths of us Okies ran together with a twang: *Gerrralwayne.* He was three years older and also lived on Cedar Street in the house nearest what was then the National Guard Armory. Gerrralwayne occasionally played neighborhood football, but baseball was his sport, a summer game, not one played as a high school spring sport.

Gerrralwayne tried to mold me into a semblance of the excellent catcher he was, and the fact that the effort failed was no fault of his. He could not only *handle* the most difficult position on the field but also *teach* it. The only thing he could not do was make me comfortable behind the plate, bat whooshing inches in front of a catcher's mask that felt like inadequate protection. I blinked, literally. I caught a few games but realized I preferred to play in front of the bat rather than behind it. I became an all-star infielder at various levels of what amounted to Nowata's little league, playing on teams with KB, Bucky, Charles Dugger, and the phenomenal pitching Jordan Brothers, Ray and Billy. If only I had been able to hit as well as I could field and throw.

I did have the advantage of living near Nowata's ballpark, which was across the street from the National Guard Armory. When the carnival visited town, its small midway and a few rides would pop up between Cedar Street and the unfenced sea of grass that was the outfield. As well and hard as I thought I could throw a baseball, I never could knock down all of the milk bottles to win the largest stuffed prize. It took time to understand the game was rigged, the bottles bottom-weighted to make it nearly impossible to knock them all down, no matter how hard you threw. It was a good lesson about others' deceit and the depth of my naiveté, which may have included believing one of the legendary feats attributed to Bucky's Uncle Dewey.

"I saw him hit one *out* of the old baseball field," Bucky said. "Hit the *roof* of the old armory." I don't know how many feet the ball traveled, but it would have been a proverbial mile, a distance I cannot imagine even our childhood hero Mickey Mantle, another small-town Oklahoman, from Commerce, attaining. But Bucky, proud member of the Delaware Nation, as talented at performing ceremonial dances as he was at carrying a football and stopping foes who tried, did not lie. His dad, Henry Lawrence "HL" Buck, would not have tolerated it.

The Bucks, HL and the uncles, toughened up Bucky, as did neighborhood football games, especially when he and his buddies ventured beyond their neighborhood. It would have been difficult to define KB's neighborhood in the country, and, after he moved to town at about age eleven, he, unlike me, lived in several different houses. Bucky had no difficulty defining his neighborhood. More than sixty years after those games, he could still rattle off the streets that set off what he considered its boundaries and the kids who made up his "hood"—the Hathcoats, Hickses, Peytons, and Kitchersides, principally. Like all of us, they played not just football but baseball, basketball, kick the can, "whatever was in season."

Bucky defined the northern boundary of his neighborhood by a Nowata landmark: Campbell Hill. The steepest street in town, East Cherokee Avenue, ran along the north side of the Campbell Hotel and would be blocked off to traffic on those occasions that it snowed enough to turn it into Nowata's best sledding. Since the street was brick, like many of the town's oldest, it required a "substantial" snow to make it safe. Even then, sledders had to take care not to overshoot the bottom of the hill, lest they find themselves sled-to-bumper with a car. At the top of Cherokee, Nowata's main drag dead-ended into Hickory. Bucky lived four blocks south on Hickory at its intersection with Wettack, the "neighborhood" southern boundary. It was bordered on the west by Mississippi Street and on the east by Pecan Street.

As we grew older, more adventurous, and won our parents' trust, we expanded our neighborhoods, first on bicycles and eventually with motorized transportation such as my pink Cushman Eagle motor scooter. In the 1950s, pink may have been an odd color for a guy, but no one yet associated it with being gay. In fact, the word "gay" had an entirely different connotation. It meant "bright, lively, full of good cheer"; it did not define sexuality, which we knew nothing about in the fall of 1952.

Our world, which is to say, neighborhoods, expanded when we got to know not only classmates in our homeroom but also those in two other homerooms of first-graders. Three or four rooms per grade was typical: Small town. Small school. Friendships began alphabetically. One teacher taught those whose surnames began with one of the first letters of the alphabet; the second taught my group, who had last names with middle letters; the third took the rest. Until late in our elementary education or junior high, when we began to have classes by subject and changed classrooms, I never had class with KB, Bucky, or Charles Dugger, or with Ralph Wood or Joy Whitson, two of my neighbors. Even so, Charles Dugger and I formed a bond through Scouting, summer baseball, and Cushmans that has lasted a lifetime. The first common meeting ground, though, was recess. We went outside and played—hard. "No computer games or Gameboys," as Bucky liked to say. "We *were* the gameboys."

This may mystify those who have never lived in the confined and confining universe of a small town. All we had was one another. We didn't communicate by text messages on a smartphone. We talked to each other, sometimes too loudly, as we stared into the face of the person we had knocked down during a schoolyard game. "We always played ball at school," Bucky said. "We couldn't wait for recess." In fact, we didn't wait. Planning began on the sly in class, not the easiest thing when you did not share a classroom with some of those you wanted on your team. After a few games, though, everyone knew everyone else, who could play which position, and who you wanted to pick for your team. "We chose up sides long before recess," Bucky remembered. Choosing sides *during* recess wasted precious minutes.

"KB was the quarterback," Bucky said, "because he could handle the ball and knew where to send everyone." The plays came out of KB's head, learned at home and from watching brother Rooster on the field. "He was our little leader," Bucky said. "We were little followers." It was a different time, a simpler time that hammered home the sense of place I still feel, my place. But even then, Nowata had started down a long, craggy path of steep decline. Later, Larry McMurtry's stark yet wonderful setting of the 1971 movie *The Last Picture Show* [Thalia, Texas, about 80 miles from his hometown of Archer City] would remind me of the less-dusty Nowata that gave us the gift of closeness and offered self-conscious glimpses of hope.

Some places a person learns to love over time. Some, a person is born to love. I was born to love Nowata, and that love was consummated on a cold, November night in 1953 watching Rooster Berry, our little leader's big brother and his undefeated team. I do not remember specifics from the many earlier games Mama and Daddy had taken me to, but I do remember this one because it was the Ironmen's first state playoff game of my young life.

To reach the playoffs, the Ironmen had to defeat a team that had been their nemesis and would continue to be until the Claremore Zebras outgrew the Verdigris Valley in the mid-1960s and were classified with larger schools. The 1953 Ironmen had looked like a juggernaut through the first four games, the only challenge coming from Labette County Community High School in Altamont, Kansas, a straight shot up U.S. 169 beyond Coffeyville and east a few miles. After scoring 52, 34, and 28 points in victories over Chelsea, Vinita, and Pawhuska, the offense, with Rooster guiding the team and adding key runs, had to claw for 13. It was enough.

The defense, particularly the line, proved a bulwark Altamont could not penetrate. It gained only 33 yards rushing and 60 passing. This set up the home-field showdown with a Claremore that looked as if it would give the winner the right to represent District 8-A in playoffs Nowata had not seen since 1946, the year I was born and so don't remember that first game I attended. Unlike the current playoff structure of the Oklahoma High School Activities Association, in which four teams from each district in nine classifications (Class C to 6A-I) qualify, only one team per district qualified in four classifications (C to 2A; Nowata played in Class A, the second-largest high schools. In 2020, Nowata was 2A, sixth of nine size classifications.)

Verdigris Valley coaches had predicted Claremore would win District 8-A. They underestimated Assistant Coach Bill O'Neil's ability to innovate and remold Nowata lines depleted by graduation. Opponents, including Claremore, found it all but impossible to score. After a Zebra fumble, Rooster Berry orchestrated an 11-play drive during which he "mixed his plays beautifully," the *Nowata Daily Star* reported. Harold Wood's 6-yard pass to flanker Allan Gordon proved all the points Nowata needed. The defense shut out the Zebras, using a ploy contrived by O'Neil and Coach John Brown. Bill Rush played defensive tackle, and, despite weighing only 150 pounds, defensive back Jerold Wood became an end. It was magic.

In six of nine victories, including the final three, Nowata shut out its opponent or allowed only one touchdown. When, after Claremore, Broken Arrow interrupted the spell with a 13–13 halftime tie, Rooster

Berry turned it to dust with an uncommon play for a single-wing team: a quarterback 40-yard sneak that produced for a 19–13 advantage which Richard Bloom (154 yards on 21 carries) capped with a 57-yard run for a 25–13 victory.

What was special about this lead-up to playing host to Poteau in the Class A playoffs is the fact our Ironmen were not distant, unapproachable college or professional players. They were big guys a second-grader could see and even talk to, if he dared walk to the red-brick building next door to the elementary school. KB Berry was even luckier. Every day he found himself with the Ironman quarterback. I couldn't imagine how that felt. I envied KB, and even more so when I came to know the Berrys well enough to think of them as a second family.

Warren "Rooster" Berry, Nowata Ironman football and basketball star from 1951 to 1953. He was voted Most Athletic Boy. [*Nowata High School yearbook photo*]

Rooster Berry was one of nine seniors on that memorable 1953 team, Nowata's first undefeated Verdigris Valley champion since 1942. He played a key role in John Brown's early success at Nowata, where he became coach in 1950 after Tulsa high school football and becoming a three-sport star at Warrensburg (Missouri) State Teachers College. He began coaching at his alma mater before moving on to Missouri and Texas high schools. After a 4–3–1 start in Nowata, his teams grew progressively better: 7–1–1 in 1951; 8–1–1 in '52; and then, the undefeated champions of '53 that had Nowatans holding their collective breath over the possibilities. Could these Ironmen win a state championship? The unbeaten 1942 team had lost to Bristow 14–7 in the first round of the playoffs. Would Brown make a difference?

He could be a tough coach, I learned during his final season in 1960, when we freshmen became varsity raw meat and blocking dummies. Brown was old school, adhering to unenlightened dictums such as no water during practice (take a salt pill) and requiring proof of manhood, sometimes with the instructive Oklahoma Drill invented by Sooner legend Bud Wilkinson and other times with The Circle, which must have been conceived by the Marquis de Sade. Whereas the Oklahoma Drill required an offensive blocker to go one-on-one with a defender and beat him lest a ball-carrier suffer a violent smack-down, The Circle bordered on cruelty. Players formed a circle around a teammate. Those on The Circle came at the victim one after the other, as coaches called names or numbers. It was a human demolition derby. It was about hitting, not tackling—hitting as hard as possible, with a running start at a sitting duck. If the man in the middle survived, it was with hand skills and strength—jerking charging bulls past him and to the ground—or using brute force, forearms, and even fists. Anyone with a grudge against a teammate drooled when the coaches commanded "Circle up." It was payback time.

I never faced the 1953 players in The Circle. It might have altered my perception of them and my face (face masks were minimalist in those days). They were undeniably a tough bunch, and I could not wait to see what they did in the playoffs. The senior backfield, supplemented by sophomore Francis Chair with wingback Jim Taylor injured, was not only fast but also deceptive, using the single wing's spinner plays and reverses. Rooster Berry was a key. "In Berry, Coach Brown has a boy who can do just about everything," the *Nowata Daily Star* noted. "He was the best blocker on the squad, a good runner (363 yards in 45 tries for an 8.7 average) and called signals, besides being a good defensive player." No wonder we idolized Rooster.

As good as the '53 Ironmen had become, Poteau had lost only one regular-season game in Sherman Floyd's four years as coach. And these unbeaten Pirates were his best, averaging 49.5 points per game to Nowata's 28.2. They were bigger than the Ironmen, including reserve end JC Holton, who would return to Nowata to teach me algebra in junior high.

Game night brought blanket weather, cold enough to demand heavy ones to supplement coats. I think it was the first time my parents let me drink coffee. I didn't like the taste but welcomed the warmth. Nothing, however, could take the chill off the fact that, after leading 21–20 at the half, the Ironmen could not continue to match Poteau's speed and the offense it fueled. All of Nowata and half of Poteau—a crowd of 5,500—watched the usually reliable Ironmen running attack sputter (115 yards). Throwing more than usual (11) led to almost as many interceptions (3) as completions (5 for 45 yards), not to mention a lost fumble.

Most of Nowata's yards came on a 92-yard first-half kickoff return by Richard Bloom. He had picked up a rare Rooster Berry fumble at the Nowata 8-yard line and scored the only TD runback of the season. Berry rectified his mistake when the conversion snap went awry and he scooped it up and ran in the ball he had intended to kick. But even a seven-year-old could see that, despite such magical moments, including three fumble recoveries and a blocked punt, Poteau had turned into an irresistible force against moveable Nowata objects in a 33–21 victory.

The loss did not discourage us wannabe Ironmen or diminish schoolyard games in which we emulated Rooster Berry and teammates. Rooster moved on to the basketball court, where he led the Verdigris Valley in scoring and was named to the all-conference team before going on to great success at Northeastern A&M Junior College (NEO) in Miami and ultimately Northeastern State University in

Tahlequah. At NEO Berry became one of the uncommon winners of eight letters in four sports—football, basketball, baseball, and track.

Soon, KB and I added more football to our lives. Youth football began in elementary school, complete with uniforms, pads, and the opportunity to try the field for real at Ironman Memorial Stadium. That's how serious Nowata was about the game. Like KB, leader and quarterback, I had a natural, if less-glamorous, position in this more organized version. Natural, because my father taught me to snap the ball for a single-wing offense, as he had.

It was a process: Explain. Demonstrate. Observe and critique the raw center. Make corrections. Do it again. Practice. Practice. Practice. Centering a football is a skill devalued not only by the virtual disappearance of the single wing but also by the less-precise demands of the direct-snap shotgun and pistol quarterbacks, who mostly throw the football rather than run it. The snap has become more a no-look flip of the ball into the vicinity of the quarterback rather than the precise spinning of the ball described by Ken Keuffel, longtime coach of the single wing and author of *Winning Single Wing Football: A Simplified Guide for the Football Coach.* Keuffel sought centers with particular physical characteristics and skills, especially inexperienced ones he found in high school but even those at Indiana's Wabash College.

Keuffel considered center "the first position you must provide for in a single wing offense." I might have felt important if I had not known none of my teammates wanted to play the position. The reason: the center must snap the ball precisely—and *then* execute his block. A pinpoint snap required the center to keep his head down and look between his legs at his tailback and fullback as he delivered the ball. If the center failed, the play failed.

Because of these demands, Keuffel, unlike my coaches, expected centers to "carry out only limited blocking assignments." My coaches demanded more. If I had played for Keuffel, I could have met his foremost expectation—good snapping. My father taught and stressed precise snapping—in other words, do it as he had: put the ball where coach's demand and back's preference intersected. The technique I learned differed from Keuffel's but worked after I had snapped the ball for hours at targets on exterior walls of the garage or animal hospital. Football and walls, not to mention the center, suffered visible wear and tear.

When I began playing center, and through junior high, I also met Keuffel's physical criteria for a "good-sized boy" who was the "steady, persevering type," willing to practice diligently, even off-season. He believed that his centers, who played only offense, did not have to be more than "an average athlete" and "need not be fast." Early on I considered myself a slightly above-average athlete: Good center and linebacker with some speed. The coaches ran me against the backs and receivers during sprints. I won my share. What I would come to realize, though, is that where a player ranks in the athleticism hierarchy depends on the competition. Small schools have fewer players than large ones. It's easier to look good. What became clear, however, from youth football to my sophomore year in high school, is that, by seventh or eighth grade, I had stopped growing—and never restarted. Once a larger lineman, I became a smaller back, like KB. How do you play center when you are hardly bigger than your small QB?

This concerned me, and two older cousins, larger linemen, hammered home the point when, in practice one day, playing out of position, they lined up over me, one on each of my shoulders—good, tough offensive linemen turned dual noseguards bent on destruction. Their battering felt personal. Was it something I had done or said? Could have been the latter. When I was chosen for Scouting's Order of the Arrow (OA) honor organization, I was informed that my (Indian) name would be "Talking Bird." It was not meant as a compliment.

If the beatdown from my cousins occurred under today's scrutiny of football's inherent dangers, I might have come away worried I had suffered a concussion. It caused me to question not so much the game as myself. Such feelings aren't unique. In his compelling book *Why Football Matters: My Education in the Game*, Mark Edmundson shares his travails of transforming himself from a boy he thought too soft for the game into one tough enough not only to earn a uniform but also to contribute to a winning team.

Edmundson's topic bowled me over, as did Steve Almond's *Against Football: One Fan's Reluctant Manifesto.* What sounded like counterpoint to Edmundson instead revealed an authorial kinship: Both men love the game and appreciate what it gave them, yet each, in different ways, acknowledge the losses that football can inflict.

For Almond, his losses, and potential of loss others might suffer, led him to address the elephant on the field—the game's inherent dangers heretofore unrecognized or ignored. For Edmundson, while he wore the fear of contact on his jersey sleeve even as he overcame it, his most feared losses are existential, more of the soul than what might happen to him in his well-padded uniform. Edmundson spent time in that uniform staring into a mirror and talking himself into having the courage he needed to face off against "the real football players."

"I'm grateful for the character football helped me to build," Edmundson writes. "I've needed it to progress in my profession [University of Virginia English professor], to publish my books, and to take care of my family. But my football-based character has probably come at a cost. Maybe I stanched the most imaginative and life-loving parts of myself by embracing character and identity as much as I did back there in high school staring into that mirror. I was a high-school semi-loser, sure. But I was a dreamy boy, a thoughtful one and not a dunce. I wonder what would have happened if I had said 'No' to character and identity and climbing the ladder and the rest. Suppose I'd chucked the uniform and gone home and picked up a book."

If I were to respond cynically, I would suggest there might have been no football book on his résumé. But I am too appreciative of his insight to engage in cynicism. Edmundson obviously picked up more than a few books, as well as degrees at Bennington College [B.A.] and Yale University [Ph.D.]. And he did not have to forgo those satisfying tackles for his team.

Because his manifesto is a variation on the theme of football's dangers—real and potentially devastating—Almond explains how and why he ignored them until he no longer could. Injured during a pickup game in high school, his shoulder joint popping in and out of its socket, he writes, "It never occurred to me stop playing." He goes on to explain: "Much of this was the invincible idiot joy of youth. But there is something about football that elicits this behavior. You know you might get hurt playing. That's part of why you play, to see what you're made of, how you take a hit, to see what happens when your courage meets real hazard."

When Almond, a Raiders fan, was eleven years old, one of his Oakland heroes, defensive back Jack "The Assassin" Tatum, crushed New England receiver Darryl Stingley during a pre-season game. "I knew I was supposed to feel bad for Stingley," Almond remembered thinking, "and I did in some, minor dutiful way. Mostly I was proud of Tatum, of the destructive capacities central to his identity." Courage had met hazard, and Stingley was rendered a quadriplegic, as a national TV audience watched. Almond is honest enough to acknowledge the fear he had, the fear that abides with me now—that the game of football could be outlawed.

After I became a sportswriter and columnist, I worked for several Knight-Ridder newspapers, including the *Miami Herald*, where I wrote about the Dolphins. Hall of Fame linebacker Nick Buoniconti had retired the year before I arrived, but what he had meant to the team was forever. Just as he affected the Dolphins' fate, Buoniconti became the embodiment of the game, on and off the field, a man who said what we do not want to hear yet cannot ignore. To reduce the risk of long-term harm to brains not fully formed, Buoniconti urged that parents not allow children to play football until high school. Almond goes further, suggesting those younger than sixteen be limited to flag football. He wants high schools to eventually "drop football altogether."

While my memories, rose-colored though they may be, prevent me from agreeing with Almond, I share his desire to weigh and address the value and danger of football. I cannot get Buoniconti out of my mind, both the player he was—undersized but Hall-of-Fame smart and tough—and the man and father to a son paralyzed by the game even before his own fatal damage became a cautionary tale.

After a helmet-first tackle in 1985 turned Citadel linebacker Marc Buoniconti into a quadriplegic, his father co-founded the Miami Project to Cure Paralysis and became the force behind the Buoniconti Fund that by 2017 had generated more than $450 million to support research by some 300 scientists seeking the cure for paralysis—Marc's and that of so many others. SL Price described in *Sports Illustrated* the blessing and toll of Nick Buoniconti's effort.

By the time Price wrote about Nick Buoniconti in May 2017, Nick himself had become one of the faces of another of football's great dangers, chronic traumatic encephalopathy (CTE), a degenerative brain disease. Price documented the cost Buoniconti paid for the game he loved and played so well: dementia, in the form of memory loss, mood instability, and chronic debilitating pain. He told Price: "I feel lost. I feel like a child."

Almond and Edmundson, like so many others, were drawn to football, even understanding its potential to inflict loss, because of something they gained from the game—a deep and shared relationship with their fathers. The game brought together the sons and fathers, as it did Nick Buoniconti and his sons. The two authors offered similar explanations of what originally drew them to football. Edmundson: "My football education began with my father. Of how many other boys in America, past and present, is that true?" It was true of Almond, who admitted his love for the Raiders was only part of it. "Mostly," he wrote, "I just wanted to be close to my dad. That's why most boys take up with sports." A Football Mama can have the same effect.

The Loves, 1948: Colleen, Stevie, age 2, and Clarence. [*Photo courtesy the author*]

Mama knew how much I loved football: Almost as much as she did. It may have pained her to blow her whistle to halt our neighborhood games and bring me home, but she blew it anyway. If a coach could stop play with his whistle, she could do it with hers. She was competitive, too. We both liked to enter the *Nowata Daily Star* contest to predict the winners of college and high school games. The current version offered by the *Star*, now a weekly, is built around advertising, each game incorporated into an ad. There are fewer games on which to pick the outcome, and time has inflated the winner's reward to a still-modest $25. The money never mattered as much as recognition for your football knowledge.

I swear I remember winning the weekly contest, but that may be wishful thinking. I did stumble across one small success on the newspaper's microfilmed pages of 1961, my sophomore season, in the Nowata County Public Library. I won $2 for finishing fourth one sorry week in October. I missed six games. I'm not sure how many we were picking, but six of us tied for first place, a tie broken based on net yards gained in that week's Oklahoma game. Not much to brag about, especially given that Mama had finished second a couple of weeks earlier with only two incorrect. She won $5. She taught me more than football, of course, in particular, how to treat others. She had an unforgettable teacher's aide in this endeavor.

Because of her ability—she had a master's in mathematics from Pittsburg (Kansas) State College when most women had no college degree—Mama shepherded the business side of my father's veterinary practice. A couple of days a week, she had household help from Ida Mae Williams. At least I *think* Ida Mae's surname was "Williams." My uncertainty results from never referring to her as "Mrs. Williams." Ida Mae told me that, if I was "Stevie," she was "Ida Mae," and that is the only name I knew growing up. Ida Mae was more family member than someone hired to clean, do laundry, make lunch, and help with chores that didn't fit into Mama's workday.

Mama and Ida Mae became fast friends. She was like my second mother. I had a front-row seat to observe how they treated each other with binding kindness. I could no more have talked back to Ida Mae than I would have to Mama. I took my cue from these two strong women. Their mutual respect grew into affection and, I think, love.

I *know* Ida Mae loved me. She showed it every day, even when she had to nudge me back onto the straight and narrow or refused to save me from my lazier self. Sometimes I put off my chores: cleaning dog cages in the animal hospital or those our pets occupied off the garage, mowing the lawn, taking out the trash, or, especially, tidying up the tornadic-like mess I could make of my room.

"Ida Mae," I'd plead, "would you help me?"

With a smile and gentle-but-firm voice, she'd reply: "Stevie, your mama pays me to help her, not to do the chores she has given you. They're your responsibility."

"Just this once, Ida Mae." (I thought whining might work. It could wear down Mama.)

That's when Ida Mae rolled her eyes as if examining her head to see if she might have lost her mind or perhaps misplaced it in our small, modest house. She did not have to say another word. My co-coach, she taught me responsibility as surely as Mama.

I don't know if this sort of relationship was common. Oklahoma may not be geographically the South, but, in the late 1940s and the '50s, its norms and attitudes were unmistakably Southern. Nowata was segregated, and Ida Mae was black. Mama and Ida Mae showed me that skin pigmentation meant nothing to them. Ida Mae was Ida Mae. It was that simple. In a time of prejudice and racial pressures, Mama was having none of either. She judged a person on the quality of her character, not the color of her skin. When segregation finally ended in Nowata, after the Supreme Court's *Brown v. Board of Education* decision, my class was the first to be integrated, as we moved into junior high in the late '50s. This provoked no great alarm in our house, which always had been integrated. The courts had finally caught up.

Not everyone in Nowata found this righteous societal shift acceptable. Even today, prejudice and inequality remain. I used the word "black" to describe Ida Mae. I could have chosen "African-American." Ida Mae would not have used either word. She would have described herself as "a Negro" or, perhaps, "colored." Both were commonly used. Whites often called the neighborhoods where blacks lived "colored town." In Oklahoma and elsewhere in the South, some folks substituted "Negra" for "Negro." Is it variation or subtly disrespectful? I prefer "person of color." A broader description than "skin tones," it is more inclusive; multiple races fall under its umbrella. And the N-word, the one used from ignorance and a desire to hurt? I heard it in Nowata, a place of many good people and some racists. Incidents that occurred during junior high school carved away at my naïve hope that everyone shared a belief in equality.

When our new classmates from Lincoln, Nowata's segregated black school, joined us for seventh grade, I knew I was going to like Clarence Smith. Smitty was tall, for our age, and thin—what we called "wiry." He looked like the athlete he was, a running back/receiver—wing back in our single wing—who possessed such graceful strides and speed that it was difficult to appreciate how fast he was until he had effortlessly glided beyond your hopelessly flailing attempt at a tackle. He may have been even better on the basketball court, though that seems impossible.

Smitty earned appreciation for what he brought to our teams, for how much better he made his new teammates. That is not, however, how he won my undying respect. That occurred one day on the schoolyard—an indelible moment that seemed inevitable in those early years of integration, a moment part racism, part bullying, and all clarifying.

I knew there was going to be trouble. Word had spread fast. When Smitty tugged on leather gloves to protect his hands before meeting the white kid who had been picking on another of our classmates, the fight was unavoidable. Everyone came running. Smitty said little. The bully who had targeted a weaker black kid may not have understood the consequence of his behavior. He knew, though, when he looked into Smitty's eyes. The fight was short. Smitty's fists were a blur, his reach keeping him out of harm's way. I don't think the bully touched him. Some onlookers may have appreciated the rush violence can bring. What I admired was the act of love. It sent a loud, clear message not simply about race but about standing up for a friend. More than a schoolyard fight between belligerents, the moment informed our understanding of friendship. Smitty would have fought for *any* friend, even his white center on the football team.

Color mattered to others in Nowata. After Daddy had my basketball goal built and we poured concrete and set it in place, it allowed me not only to share the goal and small concrete "court" but also to put in hours alone shooting the *special* basketball I mentioned. When I was nine years old and in the third grade, I had entered a mini-essay contest that Wilkinson, University of Oklahoma football coach, sponsored on his TV show. I looked forward to the show almost as much as *The Lone Ranger*, *Sky King*, *Sergeant Preston*, and radio broadcasts of Sooner football. I don't recall what I wrote, but the topic was "Good Sportsmanship," and I won a "top-grade" basketball—which I wore out. I was proud of my first writing award but disappointed and confused. Why did Bud Wilkinson give me a basketball instead of a football? Was he trying to tell me something?

By the time Smitty, KB, Bucky, Mike Whistler, and I were teammates on our junior high school basketball team, my respect for Clarence Smith had grown as high as the top of the backboard, which I thought Smitty might be able to touch. The school did not provide practice gear. We wore what we had, and, when we scrimmaged, it became "shirts and skins" to differentiate the teams. At one practice, Smitty did not have a shirt. When our coach, Wiley Armstrong, who also served as our football coach and high school football assistant, changed up the sides, I tossed Smitty my T-shirt. I could see from the look on his face that he was not sure he should put it on. We were feeling our way through integration, still new to each other. I thought I knew what he was thinking. We would be working hard on the court, sweating torrents. The T-shirt would get soaked. By the end of practice, we all smelled like a pile of dirty, musty laundry. "Don't worry about it," I told him. I figured he might not have liked the smell of my shirt when he put it on. Shared sweat. Different. All odoriferous. He laughed. Another bond.

Smitty may have shared my T-shirt, but neither he nor any other black could share the community swimming pool. Such remnants of discrimination remained. Other vestiges were less obvious but no less real, as Smitty and I discovered. Nowata was a typical small town. Everyone knew everyone else and liked nothing more than to stick their noses into others' business. Whatever I did, especially if someone considered it wrong, would get back to my parents—especially to Mama, with her rich network of friends—often before I got home to tell them myself. Basketball practice must have run late, and I offered Smitty a ride. He lived in the north end of town, where most blacks had their homes; I lived in the south.

We hopped on my Cushman Eagle—the white kid, the black kid, and the pink motor scooter. It must have been a sight. We barreled through downtown, shortest route to Smitty's. Didn't think twice about it. It was just one friend giving another a lift home. Apparently, someone found integrated motor-scootering offensive and phoned Mama. Big mistake.

She listened to what the person had seen: me going to the black section of town—Ida Mae lived there, too—with this black kid.

"So?" Mama replied to the tattletale.

"I don't think he should be doing that."

"Doing what?" Mama shot back. "Giving a teammate and friend a ride home?"

"Uh . . ."

"'Uh,' nothing. I know what you're saying and why. You oppose integration. You don't think my son should be friends with Clarence Smith. I think he should. He doesn't see color. He sees someone he likes, and he treats him as he would any friend, regardless of color."

"But . . ."

"No 'buts.' My son did the right thing. I'm proud of him. Now, goodbye."

And that was that. Leave it to Mama. She had a way with words.

Even Mama, though, did not have words to respond to those coming from our car radio that summer of 1957. We were returning from a Love family reunion in Lake City, Colorado. The radio must have been tuned to a Bartlesville station, because Nowata did not have one. The news report concerned a fatal automobile accident between Nowata and Bartlesville on U.S. Highway 60 near Hogshooter Creek. Warren Berry had been killed in a two-car crash in which six others were injured. Rooster was twenty years old.

He had been a passenger in a car driven by Buddy Riner, friend and teammate from the 1953 state playoff team. Riner had been a junior lineman with a knack for creating turnovers. Warren had been the senior team leader—the quarterback example to younger brother KB, who was almost eleven. What would I say to KB? And how? Nothing would be enough.

Friendships mean everything in a small town, for better and sometimes worse. Riner had been driving a late-model Oldsmobile. He suffered only minor injuries but was hospitalized in Bartlesville with "severe shock," according to the *Nowata Daily Star*. The Oklahoma Highway Patrol reported Riner had been attempting to pass a car on a hill when a third car appeared from the other direction. Riner steered left, toward the bar ditch, but the oncoming car, carrying five people from rural Coffeyville, crashed head-on into the right side of Riner's Oldsmobile, ripping it apart and hurling Warren Berry to the pavement. He died at 9:50 p.m., June 29, in Bartlesville's Washington County Memorial Hospital from severe shock and internal injuries.

The driver of the car Riner was attempting to pass fled without talking to officers. That driver and Riner, according to Chuck Berry, Warren's brother, were apparently engaged in a race that turned deadly. Riner was charged with first-degree manslaughter and served about a year in prison for actions that resulted in the death of his friend, who would have been a senior that fall at Northeastern State College, where he played football and basketball. Riner's full sentence included living with the knowledge of what he had done, the pain he had caused.

Warren Berry, whom the *Nowata Daily Star*'s Dave Johnson proclaimed "the *Star*'s All-Star" after his senior season, had gone on to become an all-around athlete, first at Northeastern A&M, a Miami junior college, and then at Northeastern State in Tahlequah. He had scored the team's winning touchdown in a 14–7 Mineral Bowl victory following his junior season in 1956. Johnson described Rooster as "strictly a team player" who "proved to be an elusive and hard-running back" but spent much of his time "out in front throwing the blocks." Because he was the quarterback—blocking back in the single-wing—that was Rooster's job, that and calling the plays. Coach John Brown gave "him full rein in guiding the team on the field," and Rooster Berry, more than anyone, was responsible for the fact that the Ironmen "probably had more teamwork and [fewer] individual standouts than any unbeaten team in these parts."

I delivered the newspaper that both honored Warren Berry and brought to the community's doorsteps the worst news it must bear. I may have been only 11 years old, but no one had to tell me what

Rooster meant to Nowata and that the family's loss was everyone's loss. When the now-weekly *Nowata Star* was a daily, I lived to deliver the newspaper almost as much as to play football. In some ways, the paperboys were a team just as the Ironmen were. Almost from the time I could ride a bicycle, I trailed after Gene Lewis or his substitute carrier on the paper route that included my neighborhood. It turned out to be sound strategy for future employment—the beginning of a lifetime in journalism, if you care to stretch the image.

First as a substitute on Route 4 and then as "owner" when Gene Lewis gave it up in the later stages of his high school basketball career, I forged bonds with other carriers, most of whom I already knew—none better than Charles Dugger. Charles and I were closer than some of my other teammates because we also shared Scouting, from Cubs to Explorers. Much of that time, Jack Dugger, Charles's father, served as our Scoutmaster. I spent as much of my early years growing up at the Duggers'—Jack and Estelle, and Charles's younger brother Tom—as I would later come to haunt the Berry home. Both families, and the Whistlers, too, since they let me tag along with Mike to out-of-town basketball games in which his older brother Doug starred, probably thought I didn't have a home. Untrue. What I didn't have were siblings.

Charles and I rose together through the ranks until we reached Eagle Scout. I feared he was going to leave me behind, though, when it came decision-time for Order of the Arrow (OA), a Scouting honor. I knew he would be chosen. He represented everything a Scout should. I was less certain OA members who made the decision whom to invite to join them felt the same about me. On the summer-camp night when Scouts stood lined up on the grounds of Camp Cherokee, backs to the OA members in their Native-American regalia, I feared I would not feel the tap of the chosen on my shoulder. When it finally came, I was as much relieved as happy.

Being a member of this honor organization, with its Native-American influences, had a tangential effect. When my parents and extended family shared with me my ancestry, they told me it did not include Native Americans. That seemed odd. My family had a long history in what, before statehood, had been Indian Territory. Oklahoma is home to 38 federally recognized Native tribes. Was I the only Oklahoman with no Indian blood? I wanted to know. Years later, a similar and more important personal quest seized the national political stage.

Elizabeth Warren, U.S. Senator from Massachusetts, who sought the 2020 Democratic presidential nomination, became an early target for President Donald Trump. Because she was an Oklahoman and claimed Native-American ancestry, based on family stories, Trump challenged and ridiculed her with one of the infamous nicknames he slaps on people he does not like and/or are political opponents. With a smirk, he labeled Warren "Pocahontas." The attack got under her skin, and she sought an appropriate response.

Warren tried to validate her family's stories with a DNA test, which exacerbated the ridicule. The result indicated she had a smidgen of Native-American blood but not enough for tribal membership. This presented Trump an excuse to redouble his typically gentle attacks. Despite this—and thinking I should know with greater certainty whether or not I might also be a smidgeon Native American—I sent a saliva sample to AncestryDNA.

The ethnicity estimates from my DNA test suggested my pre-American ancestors were not native but likely from England, Wales, and Northwestern Europe (79 percent probability), Ireland and Scotland (19 percent), and Finland (2 percent). Disappointed but not surprised, Oklahoma—especially Nowata—remains deep in my heart, even if it pumps no Indian blood. The only "tribe" I am entitled to claim is the Order of the Arrow, and it seemed to have admitted me reluctantly.

Just as OA had its rituals, there were those associated with delivering the *Nowata Daily Star*. Before the evening papers were printed, we often dropped by Chubb Dodge's soda shop up the alley from the newspaper office, with its flatbed press in back and a wire cage "room" in which the carriers could fold their papers into a tri-corner star ideal for throwing. A newspaper of only four to eight pages made "star" folds possible most days.

"We all complained if we had to fold an eight-pager," Charles Dugger remembered. "The number of pages seemed to always be the first thing we asked when we arrived." Shared complaints, like the drudgery of searing two-a-day pre-season football practices, forged individuals into a team—even at the newspaper. We would go up the alley to play pinball on a machine in the back of Chubb's or down the alley to the pool hall to shoot a game.

The game—pinball, pool, snooker—was less important than the camaraderie of the paper carriers, on good days, sitting outside in the alley on concrete footers that protruded from the buildings, talking and folding away on our papers. "[I remember] the time spent with the other carriers being a great experience," Charles said. Bucky Buck worked a route on Hickory Street, and he would "usually meet Johnny Allen [his delivery partner] up on Campbell Hill and "fly on our route, with delivery of the most newsworthy source in Nowata County."

Bucky and the rest of us became artisans of varied throws used to achieve particular results. I suppose since our extracurricular lives were spent throwing one ball or another—footballs, basketballs, baseballs—it was inevitable we would apply these skills to delivery of the newspaper. "I was adept at several varieties of deliveries," Bucky said. "Of course, best at the overhand." It was a motion used in all our sports. "Then," Bucky continued, "there was the underhand flip that kind of floated like a knuckleball until it landed flat on the porch."

This motion came with a warning. "Do not mix with the underhand spinner," Bucky said. This could produce erratic results—papers missing porches and ending up on roofs or breaking windows. "Necessity," Bucky said, "was the prime reason for the type of throw . . . in rain, snow, and wind."

If the mechanics of a precisely thrown newspaper became an art form, in-person bill collecting from customers could be a nightmare—or dream. "Collections could be painful," Charles Dugger said, "but a great learning experience." We were little businessmen, who bought our product from the producer and distributed it to our customers. We knocked on doors and got paid, or didn't, returning until there was a resolution. "We had to make decisions," Charles said. "How long do we let the customers go without paying?" If we determined they could not pay, we had to choose whether to give them one of our "extra" newspapers. Our decisions depended on circumstances. We had to pay for the papers regardless. In a small town like Nowata, we knew our customers and often attended school with their children. This helped us differentiate deadbeats from those who deserved a hand—at least for a while—and forced us to decide what kind of person *we* wanted to be.

I had one of the larger routes in number of papers I delivered, but Charles had two routes, one in his neighborhood near the Nowata water tower that rose up from the highest point in the city and another that took in downtown stores—before they disappeared—and extended south on Elm Street. The latter he delivered on a Cushman Eagle (gray, not pink). The two routes gave him twice the number of collections and possible complaints, called "kicks." If a customer called to complain that he had not received his paper, it did not matter to the person in the business office why this might have occurred (often another family member picked up the paper without the complainant knowing). The kick stood. Lesson: Business can be cruel.

It also had its surprises. One startled me to the point of disbelief. I want to describe my memory of it as a hormonal delusion. I will admit that perhaps I *thought* I saw more than I actually did. When I knocked on the door of a house one block over and another block down from where I lived, the subscriber's daughter and a girl who lived across the street from me must have seen me coming. They opened the door, but only enough for a limited view.

These two girls were a couple of years older than me, and to say they were memorably attractive would be a gross understatement. They were beautiful, and they were wearing pretty much nothing except birthday suits. I think they were playing the best prank of my life on me, maybe willing to barter a better look by opening the door further if I would count the bill paid in full. I might have suggested I would do so for the rest of my paperboy life if collecting continued to be like this, but I was dumbstruck. I just stared. After a minute, they laughed—at me, not with me. I turned, mouth agape, got back on my bike, and pedaled away. I do believe I paid the bill that month and thought it a good bargain.

As stimulating as the sight was that surprising collection day—it did not recur—what I found equally memorable and more believable was the vision on Friday nights in the late 1950s of a fully uniformed and equally fast Chuck Berry setting sail for an end zone on Ironman Memorial Field. Because he played tailback, or halfback in an occasional T-formation, Chuck, by the end of his sophomore season, was not only showing the promise of living up to the large legacy of his late brother Rooster but also doing so in difficult circumstances only months after Rooster's death had stunned Nowata. He would never play for a team as successful as the one Rooster quarterbacked, but Chuck's running possessed a singularity that, entering my teens, I could appreciate in ways a seven-year-old could not the subtleties of Rooster's play.

Chuck Berry hinted at his excellence as a sophomore and, for the next two seasons, fulfilled the Berry promise and expanded on it. His quickness through the line and fluidity and speed on the outside made carry after carry memorable. He had a particular knack, an almost ghostlike essence, after he fielded a punt. One second, he was right there in front of a potential tackler, the next he had disappeared from sight, a wisp of smoke in the night. He set a Nowata season record for punt-return touchdowns—50, 80, and 63 yards, the 80-yarder another record for longest that was tied by the younger of the Nash brothers, Phillip, in 1964.

Time and again, Chuck took over a game and dominated it, as those of us who were coming behind him, especially KB and the rest of the Class of 1964, marveled at and tried to figure out how he performed such inexplicable football feats. Could we ever do that? In a 36–6 1958 homecoming rout of Pawhuska, Chuck gained 226 yards on only 10 carries, scoring from 89 and 38 yards and, oh yeah, throwing for two more touchdowns. Such exploits became commonplace. In a 28–14 victory over Broken Arrow, it was 18 carries for 263 yards, including a TD run of 60 yards and a 51-yard set-up to the Broken Arrow 11-yard line, from where he finished the job. Against Pryor, one of the better Verdigris Valley teams, Chuck scored all 20 points for a tie, including runs of 26 and 63 yards, one of two of that length, this a stunning diagonal slice across the field. For good measure, he intercepted a pass.

As good as Chuck Berry was, Nowata could not do better than 3–2–2 in conference play, although the Ironmen did tie co-champions Miami and Pryor and finished 5–3–2 overall. Berry scored 14 of the team's 34 touchdowns, his 96 total points 60 more than the runner-up. He was chosen Nowata's football athlete of the year, a prelude to All-Verdigris Valley honors as a senior, a season he capped with four touchdowns, including one of 85 yards; he provided 28 of Nowata's

34 points in a victory over Miami. Yet, with a 3–6–1 record at a small school, Chuck had scant chance for the statewide recognition that flowed to Norman's Jay Wilkinson.

Whether because the Norman High School quarterback's famous father once had given me a basketball or I simply appreciated the excellence of Jay Wilkinson's all-around play, I followed his senior season closely in the state's metropolitan newspapers—*The World* and *The Tribune* in Tulsa and *The Daily Oklahoman* in Oklahoma City. His iconic father made it impossible to ignore Jay. The sports media began to heap superlatives on him—"superb all-around play," "wizardry," and "flashy"—when, as a sophomore, he joined fullback brother Pat in Norman's backfield. By the conclusion of his prep career, Wilkinson not only had become an All-Stater but also had won State Player of the Year honors to go with lesser and greater ones, including multiple All-American. He demonstrated similar ability in basketball, taking Norman to a state championship in 1958, his junior season. (Maybe Bud gave his son one of those basketballs he awarded his essay-contest winners.) Jay did know disappointment, however. His football team lost the 1959 championship 16–14 to Oklahoma City Northwest.

The unrelenting attention paid to his son once prompted Bud Wilkinson to observe, "It would be a great help if he was named Jay Smith—it would be a great help to *him*." The preeminent question in Oklahoma concerned whether Jay would choose to play for his father at OU or attend college elsewhere. As the pressure mounted, even in those days, before recruiting turned into a season-unto-itself, Bud Wilkinson made one thing clear, from his perspective: "The only consideration we will have will be to do what is best for Jay's education."

For his son, the decision proved more complex. Jay loved his father, whom he described with great warmth in two books. Anyone who reads *Dear Jay, Love Dad: Bud Wilkinson's Letters to His Son* will recognize the love Bud felt for his sons. Jay acknowledged in *Bud Wilkinson: An Intimate Portrait of an American Legend* that he "had the athletic skills to play for Oklahoma." He also noted he and his brother had been "reared believing we would go away to school, be on our own, and get out from under Dad's shadow." When the moment arrived, it "proved to be one of the most painful decisions" Jay Wilkinson ever made.

In a poignant scene, Bud Wilkinson entered Jay's room and found him face down on his bed. When Bud wrapped his arm around his son's shoulders, Jay burst into tears. "I think I should go to Duke," he said of the school he had chosen from among five he visited. "I really want to play for you, but I think it would be better for me to be on my own." Bud rubbed his son's back as Jay "cried uncontrollably." But, as his father's letters to Jay at Duke and graduate school eloquently attest, Bud's son may have been on his own but was never alone.

At Duke, Jay Wilkinson escaped neither his famous football name nor its pressure. When he faced challenges on and off the field, his father's letters, often seven pages, lifted him as surely as his teaching and words elevated his Sooners. They "assured me that I was appreciated for who I was, not what I accomplished," Jay wrote. The son accomplished much—becoming a consensus All-American, even as he was moved from one position to another like the key chess piece on the field of play. Bud's letters were more philosophy of life than football X's and O's. They strengthened Jay's resolve when he found himself adrift concerning his long-term future and faced with challenging academic work made more difficult by "lack of direction." Whereas my well-meaning father could come off as a self-aggrandizing know-it-all—he did know a lot—Bud Wilkinson, who reached unreachable heights as a coach, appeared much humbler.

As I attempted to negotiate my own adolescent and athletic traumas, I might have benefitted from Wilkinson's gentle guidance.

It is easy to see why Jay Wilkinson describes his relationship with his father as a lifelong friendship. If my relationship with my father fell short of the Wilkinsonian ideal, the same can be said of short-circuited connections. I've always wondered what heights Chuck Berry might have reached athletically if he had played for Wilkinson at Oklahoma. Could Wilkinson have helped Chuck fulfill his promise? Chuck did receive a letter of interest from Eddie Crowder, Wilkinson assistant and future successful head coach at Colorado. Instead of Oklahoma, Chuck ended up at Fort Scott (Kansas) Junior College, which had been through hard football times, leading to a new coach, Howard Mahanes.

Chuck Berry became two-time captain of the Greyhounds and during his second season helped them to complete a turnaround that brought a conference championship. This, eventually, led to Mahanes' induction into the Fort Scott Athletic Hall of Fame, a case of player helping coach. "I don't have many regrets in life," Chuck said, "but one of them is that my alcoholism shortened my football career." Chuck did not go on to play for a four-year college: "I will never know how the ending of the story could have been."

What Chuck does know—what he taught me—is that there can be life after football, even if sometimes it does not feel that way. He not only achieved sobriety but also helped others start and hold to the path of recovery. "I am grateful I have that to replace what might have been," he said. His passion for football—and what it inspired in his younger brother and me—was nonetheless unforgettable. Chuck found in a lifetime of helping others, including working with Habitat for Humanity and assisting in Hurricane Katrina disaster relief, a deeper, more lasting passion. Football was Chuck Berry's first mountain to climb, a concept David Brooks has described in his *New York Times* column and more deeply in the book *The Second Mountain: The Quest for a Moral Life*.

On their first mountain, people strive to succeed in "individualistic, meritocratic" ways. Even team players like Chuck Berry derive ego satisfaction from excelling personally. The people whom Brooks most admires are those who move on to a second mountain, often as a result of being "broken open" and finding "bigger desires" of the heart and soul that allow them to "live in loving connection to others" and to be of service. This is what Chuck found after alcoholism had broken him open. On his life's second mountain, he discovered a higher, clearer, more satisfying version of himself.

In the scorching summer heat of 1961, KB, Bucky, Charles, Smitty, and I, with our teammates, started up that first mountain we had seen in the distance since we were small and our football heroes loomed so large. We followed the footsteps of Rooster and Chuck Berry, Bucky Buck's uncles, and other once-starry-eyed Nowata boys. We were going to be Ironmen.

ON BECOMING AN IRONMAN

The 1961 Nowata football season began with hope and trepidation, the latter an unease among new varsity players that threatened to hollow out our childhood passion for the game and long-held dream of becoming an Ironman. The uncharted can border on fear. Doubt eviscerates confidence. Could we sophomores do this? We were so young, and so much was new—new building, new locker room, new coach, even new positions.

When we reported for pre-season practice on Monday, August 14, Coach Dick Noble and assistant Wiley Armstrong greeted 42 boys, a number that grew to 48 for two-a-day practices. Only 16 lettermen returned from Coach John Brown's final team. The would-be Ironmen lacked varsity experience: 22 sophomores, 19 juniors, 7 seniors. The sophomores had had success in junior high school; with few seniors, positions could be won.

Today's teams—even at smaller schools such as Nowata—use off-season programs to build strength and skills. We were on our own. There was no weight room. For most of us, lifting meant pitching bales onto a hay truck. My pre-sophomore-season lifting consisted of 50-pound bags of potatoes at an IGA grocery. I ran sporadically, not as routine. I was a busy boy.

This may have been the summer I decided to take the family car for a spin when Daddy was out of town, which he sometimes was as a veterinarian with the United States Department of Agriculture. Mama was also otherwise occupied and absent. It seemed harmless to go joy-riding, even if I was only 15 and did not have a driver's license. Daddy had been teaching me to drive—"steer" might be more accurate—from the time I could sit in his lap and see over the steering wheel. In my early teens, he let me take the wheel on gravel country roads. Gravel may not be the surest surface for an inexperienced driver, but ditches alongside the road were shallow and not too steep, trees few and mostly scrawny. Traffic was sparse. Small-town and country kids drove early.

These realities of life in and around Nowata did not include permission to take the car. I knew it was wrong. Even so, with a co-conspirator riding shotgun, I went tooling aimlessly around Nowata one evening in our Plymouth. (We always had Plymouths, purchased from Joe Titsworth, the local dealer Daddy frequented. He replaced his vehicles often, given the miles he put on them and the beatings they took on country roads when Daddy had been in private veterinary practice.) My plan worked flawlessly. We got that Plymouth back into the garage without incident before Mama returned. Self-satisfied, except for pangs of guilt for violating Mama's trust, I had proved myself a wild boy.

I should have known better. The next day, Mama confronted me. She blew a different kind of whistle on me than the one with which she stopped neighborhood football games. She asked the question I least wanted to hear: "Did you drive the car last night?" How to answer? Do I lie, compounding my problem? The cover-up, as I learned when I became a student of presidential shenanigans, is often worse than the crime. Or, do I 'fess up and fall on my sword? By this point, Daddy had more or less retired his razor strop as instrument of punishment, my parents having come to other means of showing their displeasure. None was worse than the disappointment in Mama's eyes.

"I cannot tell a lie," I said.

"Don't try to be funny," Mama replied.

This was a running joke. I was born on the same day as George Washington, future first president to whom the phrase was attributed—no doubt apocryphally—when as a youth he answered to whether or not he had chopped down a cherry tree.

"OK, I won't. I drove the car."

"Where did you drive—and why?" Mama demanded.

"Just around. Cruised town but avoided the streets where I might run into a cop. I know I shouldn't have taken the car."

"You don't have a driver's license," Mama reminded me. "You aren't sixteen."

"I know. I'm sorry. I won't do it again."

"You better not, mister," Mama said.

"Can I ask a question?"

"What?"

"How did you know I drove the car? I was careful to park it in the garage precisely as you had had it parked."

Mama sustained her stern look, but, secretly, I think, she wanted to smile about her super-sleuthing and maybe to lighten the moment.

"You can't pull anything over on me," she said. "When I parked in the garage, I happened to notice the mileage on the odometer." *Gotcha.*

"And you remembered it?"

"Of course," she said.

I knew what she meant. She was good with numbers. Better than good. Though not precisely mathematics, the former teacher had nonetheless given me a lesson in, if nothing else, the value of being aware of your surroundings and the information to be found there.

This recognition, properly applied, might have helped me better prepare for my first varsity football season. Even without benefit of today's Internet and instant access to information, such as the best way to train and condition for football, I could have found a training regimen if I had applied the effort I wasted on becoming a failed car thief.

I was not a good-enough athlete to skip this important step, especially when I had requested to move from single-wing center to the backfield. Since we did not yet know our new coach, Dick Noble, seeking his counsel was not a possibility. This does not explain why I did not go to Wiley Armstrong, who had coached our junior high teams for two years, including when I was good enough to play on both the eighth-grade and freshman teams. He was an approachable person, and any advice would have been better than none.

I hadn't thought critically about what being an Ironman meant, about the background of the name. I still do not know when and how it was chosen—Nowata was oil country, not mining or steelmaking—but I do know how it came to be attached to football teams. Vic Frolund, in 1980, wrote an explanation for "The Coffin Corner," a publication of the Professional Football Researchers Association, to which I belong. Frolund credited what Fielding H. "Hurry-Up" Yost's Michigan team had done in 1902 in the first Rose Bowl Game. In the Wolverines' 49–0 victory over Stanford, Yost never substituted. "Football games," Frolund explained, "were endurance contests back in those days, with no quarter asked and none given." Playing both offense and defense, competitors commonly stayed on the field for 60 minutes—or until carried off.

Chuck Berry recalled hearing that the first Nowata team had only three players. The coach told them they "would have to be Iron Men to survive." No one thought to apply "Iron Men" to the early players or teams until in 1926 Brown University earned the distinction by defeating Yale and Dartmouth in consecutive games without a substitution and then added Harvard to the list—though the starters played *only* 57 minutes. They were back to going all the way against Colgate in the season's last game, a 10–10 tie, their only blemish in ten games.

I wanted to be an Ironman, but if I had played in the old "Iron Men" days, I might have ended up like the substitutes on some of those early teams and played not at all. As it was, with teams in the early '60s using platoons of players on offense and defense, the opportunity to get on the field increased. Of course, those who worked out year-round, or at least during the summer before the season, enhanced their chances. High schools, especially in small towns, often had too few players to support two units. To increase the chance of winning, the best played two ways.

This necessitated becoming one of the better players, someone a coach could not limit to special teams or relegate to the bench. Report in the best condition. Understand that coaches who say, "You play like you practice" really are saying: "If you don't put effort into practice, you won't play in the games." As important as it was to prepare your body, it may have been even more important to get your mind right. This meant crushing and being crushed by your closest friends, not an appealing prospect. Yet some did not mind.

If KB Berry—by destiny, desire, and unselfish talents—was meant to be our leader and quarterback, Bucky Buck's goal was, like himself, straightforward. "I just wanted to run over somebody," Bucky said. "I wanted to be like Jimmy Brown or Jim Taylor." Power backs, both, and Pro Football Hall of Famers. Their style could be described as blunt force trauma; Bucky's, too. He was a natural-born fullback and a hard-nosed linebacker. He played no-sissies-allowed positions with unbridled glee.

When I played center, I loved blocking for Bucky. He made his offensive linemen look good. If they didn't make their blocks quickly and decisively, Bucky would run over them, along with the defender. It was no surprise what I had to contend with when I got my wish to move to the backfield. Bucky and I were competing for time at fullback, along with junior David Neely.

This was an unintended consequence of the move from center. I must have talked with Coach Noble about the change. It seemed ideal timing. Noble was new. He had no preconceptions about positions. He couldn't watch film from the previous season, because junior high games were not filmed, as I remember. I know I had never heard of a game film, much less seen one. He could, however, have talked with his assistant, Wiley Armstrong, who knew who among the sophomores had heart and would compete. Neither coach could know what kind of runner I would be. Neither did I. I had never been one.

Ironmen backs in 1961, including some of the usual suspects and friends: Charles Dugger (10), Steve Love (41), KB Berry (11), and Clarence Smith (32), sophomores all. [*Nowata High School yearbook photo*]

That should have concerned me. It didn't. I was young and dumb. I must have thought that if, as the center, I could outrun the fastest backs, receivers, and defenders, I would make a good running back. Think again. Becoming a single-wing running back meant learning new and different skills, digesting them, and applying them until they became second nature. Maybe this is why practices seemed long, mistakes frequent, successes illusory. Normally a good and quick study, I felt like a foreigner in the strange land of the backfield, where life was uphill.

More than direct advice and corrections encouraged me to get beyond my tentativeness. What I remember most was the coaches shouting "DON'T JUMP" at my friend and fellow back Charles Dugger. Charles was small and so quick he had earned the nickname "Tater Bug," perhaps not solely from his adventures on the football field. A wingback, he was as elusive as, well, a tater bug. He could run and catch and had been doing this since schoolyard days. Charles's predilection to take flight when about to be tackled alarmed the coaches. They preached feet on the ground and legs churning as the best way forward and living to run another play. Jumping left a back susceptible to catastrophic midair collisions with defensive missiles. I was no jumper.

My flaws were less life-threatening but no less damaging. On plays up the middle or off-tackle, I had to read the defense and blocking quicker, decide to go hellbent at the point of attack, allow the blocker another second with a strategic hesitation, or blow up the play and scoot outside. The latter options can make a fullback look silly or smart, usually silly. The better choice was to run hard where the play was intended, something I did not do well.

The learning curve proved steep. This meant I ended up on my back studying the sky or with a pile of inhumanity on me. I worked hard but had trouble cracking the code, much less the starting lineup.

In trying to recreate what must have been going through my mind, I can see a broader picture. I was a thoughtful boy more than one who proceeded on instinct and reaction. I embraced whys-and-wherefores when I should have thought less and run harder. I feared embarrassment more than the hits or injury. A boy who talked to himself a lot, I did a poor job of ginning up the will to succeed.

Mama could not have been proud of me. I was 15 years old, a less than fully formed person, but she would have told me: buckle your chinstrap and quit bellyaching. The progression from backyard to schoolyard to youth to junior high to varsity football raises the demands and alters the game. When you become an Ironman, you are no longer playing just for fun or for yourself. You're playing for the *team*, which comes with responsibility to teammates. Let them down, and you've let yourself down.

First, of course, you have to get into the game. My speed earned me a role on special teams, particularly kickoff coverage. Lining up outside, my job was to avoid blockers as I hurtled toward the return man. This was a place to begin, because I could tackle—even if this fact seemed ignored by our new coach, who gave me no time at linebacker. Did he recognize my struggles at fullback and not want to overload me? All I knew was that Bucky Buck had been named to start the first game against Chelsea—Daddy's high school. Playing a position at which he was an old hand gave Bucky an advantage, but he would have deserved to start anyway, as did KB Berry at quarterback and Clarence Smith at wingback. Sophomores dominated the backfield, and others found their way onto the defensive and offensive lines, where juniors opened the season, including Charles Driskill at center. He weighed 30 pounds more than me. It would have been difficult to win that job, even with superior snapping.

KB's ascendance at quarterback surprised no one, least of all his sophomore teammates. As he extended his leadership to a team of older players, I detected no doubters. He had an aura, not only athletically but also personally. He set an example with such an easy manner, even the older, more-experienced players accepted his leadership without question. Some players—Smitty at wingback and Richard Nash at tailback won respect with their athleticism. KB did it with a deeper, more innate quality. Yes, he was a Berry, and the name meant something. No one had forgotten Rooster's accomplishments and Chuck's excellence. KB was, as Bucky suggested, "our little leader," and he was growing up before our very eyes.

KB Berry, Nowata Ironman quarterback and leader, 1961 to 1963. [*Nowata High School yearbook photo*]

For our young team, with only three senior starters, Chelsea could not have been a more perfect first opponent. A smaller school back in the day, it lacked a history of success against Nowata, a non-conference foe. The Green Dragons were smaller in numbers and size, which allowed us to quickly build some confidence. Smitty ran as if the wind were always at his back. When Nash replaced senior Gary Lilburn at tailback, the onslaught hit another gear, as he scored on touchdown runs of 78, 84, 45, and 22 yards. On the latter, KB Berry, reminiscent of Rooster, the 1953 team's best blocker, provided Nash a one-man wall of safe passage.

As we expanded an 18–6 halftime lead, I replaced Bucky at fullback, and KB, showing faith in me, called our power-up-the-middle play—"391." Nothing fancy. Take a direct snap, fake a handoff left to the tailback, and bust up the middle behind the center and two guards, one of whom was a cousin who had practically beaten me to death in practice as a freshman. He could block, though, and I set up him and the others up front perfectly, if unintentionally.

Nerves jangling as the huddle broke, I hardly heard KB bark the snap count. I've never been certain whether the snap was too low or I mishandled it. In any case, with next-to-no fake but a hesitation that seemed to last forever, I launched into the heart of the line. No trying to be cute, no waiting for blocks. I hit the line hard—once I got going.

Nowata sophomore fullback Steve Love, 1961. [*Nowata High School yearbook photo*]

The line parted as if it were the Red Sea and Moses a blocker. (I never believed that story.) I saw miles and miles of green grass. Thinking something like *Run, Fool, Run*—I did.

And I kept running.

I was fast enough to have scored but not clever enough. Using my knowledge of math—Mama must have been smiling—I applied the shortest-distance-between-two-points-is-a-straight-line theory. I didn't look back, because, as Satchel Paige had warned, somebody might have been gaining on me. A more experienced runner would have better assessed who was where in the secondary and deviated from this straight line or made a stop-and-start move to let the pursuer overrun the tackle. Me? I was just happy to be motoring down the field.

I didn't quite make it. One of Chelsea's Dishman boys played the angle, coming at me from the side, and tackled me inside the 10-yard line after a gain of 40-some yards. Not Nash-like but a good first run that could have been great with a diagonal cut to the right-front corner of the end zone. I did score a two-point conversion later with the same play—in fact, with a harder run.

What I did not know—what none of us knew—is that with our 40–26 victory, we had hit our high-water mark, and the remainder of the season would feel as if we were drowning. Even so, football made my heart race—and football wasn't the only thing.

At a high school sock hop—an anachronism, I realize—I worked up the nerve to ask a new and *older* girl to dance. This came with the risk of embarrassment. Jayna was a junior, and junior women do not date sophomore boys, unless desperate. Her family had moved to Nowata from nearby Bartlesville. Since she was new to the school, I thought she may not have a boyfriend. To a girlfriendless boy, it seemed a risk worth taking. Another serious roadblock: she was beautiful, and I wasn't. Superficial? Sure. But we were teenagers, and what was high school if not a series of superficialities blocking the way to happiness?

Our dance went well, if not romantically. We talked. I didn't step on her feet, which would have been bad if I were wearing my football cleats but not so much at a sock hop. Before the conclusion of the evening, I asked if she would like to go out. This was a country too far for Jayna. She flattened me with a sweet technique my offensive linemen would have envied. Polite and kindhearted girl that she was, Jayna dropped the NO-bomb subtly. She didn't mention she didn't date "children" but instead proposed an alternative.

"I have a younger sister who is a freshman," Jayna said. "You two should meet."

Clever. Throw me off the scent by foisting me off on the poor, unsuspecting little sister. What could go wrong? Well, among other things: I could become a double-dumpee, without so much as a first date. I began to realize why no one thought of me as a ladies' man.

If I remember anything from life in Nowata, it should be meeting Jayna's sister. I don't. I must have been dumbstruck. Or, maybe, the lost moment is the culmination of the haunted last months of 1961 and the years that followed. Whatever the reason, the details are lost in the golden haze of that football fall and this new sensation ignited by little sister Ginger.

Ginger hit my heart like an attack. And it wasn't as if she were my first encounter with a girl. Kathy Radcliffe, who lived down the grassy alley behind my house, made the earliest impression on me. Because our mothers were friends, we knew each other almost from the moment she was born, the year after me. Mama would take me down the alley to Kathy's house to visit. She seemed sweet on Kathy and lavished her with attention. That must have stimulated my resentment. I can think of no other reason I would have bitten a chunk out of Kathy's arm when we were small. I was a green-eyed monster. So I bit her—and never lived it down. As appalled as Mama was by my act, she loved to tell the story.

Kathy must have remembered the incident, because when we were older and I asked her out, I don't think she had a good time. She seemed uncomfortable, purposely keeping me at arm's length. When I moved closer for a goodnight kiss, she acted as if she would rather have been bitten—or had been. I didn't get it. I had had my tetanus shot and had reached an age where I wanted to only nibble on girls, not leave teeth marks as forensic evidence against me.

Phyllis Hendricks, on the other hand, did not try to keep me at arm's length. She, too, was a year older. But in a happy hideaway from high school—the Nowata skating rink owned by Phyllis's parents—it didn't matter as much. Phyllis could roller skate better than I ran with the football; she was the beautiful star of the hardwood. When boys lined up to nervously reveal with whom they wanted to skate, a spotlight fell on the choice. I ended up with my arm around Phyllis's waist, my other hand holding hers, and we flowed around the floor as one. I considered the spotlight skate a gift from the gods.

Phyllis and I were pretty good together. I was a pest. Phyllis was the sweetheart on wheels.

Sadly, it isn't easy to build a deep, lasting relationship going in circles. In the end, Phyllis was, like Ginger's sister, an older woman. I never seemed to learn. I was drawn to the younger Janie Osborn in part because I had a crush on her red-haired sister, also older. Nyla was a senior when I was a freshman. I realized she was well beyond my reach, but, in mooning around for her at our church—and anywhere else I saw her—I came to appreciate Janie, whom I consider my first true girlfriend. I think this would have occurred even without Nyla as beautiful bait. Janie, I would come to believe, cared about me. She was pretty and smart and played a heart-stopping game of Spin the Bottle. What a gentler, sweeter time that was. But as in many male-female relationships, something must have gone wrong because by the time I met Ginger, Janie and I were no longer an item. It was a good life-lesson: misunderstandings may be an unavoidable reality of closeness, but the specifics often are lost with passing time—or by the next morning.

Some reality lasts, and that of our sophomore football season began to sink in after we had had our moment with overmatched Chelsea. We traveled to Cushing the following week, there to learn from ten returning seniors on Cushing's first unit what was required to succeed at this new level of the game. Dick Noble told the *Nowata Star* that his sophomores were improving daily. I doubted he meant me. What echoed in my mind each day was his dictum: "If you want to play ball," he would say, "*prove* to me you want to play ball." Proof began long before Friday nights. It started on the practice field. Noble worried that some of us inexperienced players did not know our assignments well enough and threatened to bench anyone with a lack of knowledge or focus. When he and Wiley Armstrong talked, you listened—or else.

I listened. I knew the plays, my responsibilities, and those of others. I had a mind for the game. But something was missing. Desire? Toughness? I didn't know. I had always succeeded on the field. What had changed? My coach? Position? Level of competition? Cushing showed us the reality of the latter. The Tigers were not only more experienced but also larger. Though our backs ran hard—I did not play much, so I don't count myself—we got manhandled. The only points we managed came when senior Gary Lilburn, all of 122 pounds, returned a punt 50 yards for a touchdown. We trailed 19–0 at the half, quickly gave up another touchdown in the third quarter, and Cushing rolled us, 26–6.

Bucky Buck, playing ahead of me at fullback, had run with an exemplary determination that met Noble's expectations. Bucky was establishing himself at our position. I did not know where this left me, but I accepted the reality that Bucky was playing better. If I could not get playing time, all that was left was learning and improving at practice. This required altering *how* I practiced—to view it as a daily opportunity rather than repetitive drudgery.

Vinita, our first Verdigris Valley opponent, presented the same problem as Cushing. The Hornets were more experienced. A fast but unsustainable start could not save us. After Clarence Smith hit senior Kenny Hewitt with a first-quarter touchdown pass, we put ourselves on the defensive. We committed too many penalties to overcome. Worse, Bucky suffered a season-ending injury, a double hernia. This might have been good for my prospects, but I did not want to gain as a result of Bucky's loss. He was my friend and made our team better.

When KB, I, and others visited Bucky in the hospital following surgery, he joked that they threw in a bonus circumcision at his dad's request. I was a jumbled mess of emotions. I worried about Bucky because I knew how much playing meant to him and that he would miss it. I don't think I was able to say anything that made him feel better. Bucky was thinking about the team and told me he was counting on me. Was I ready for a larger role? Ready or not, the *Nowata Star* reported I would be in the starting backfield at Pawhuska. Really?

I don't remember doing anything of consequence in another loss, 26–6. I ran too tentatively to satisfy even my standards, much less those of the coaches. It would be two games—a 0–0 tie with Tahlequah and a 32–14 trashing from Claremore—before I got another chance, in a non-conference game against Mama's alma mater, the Coffeyville High School Golden Tornado, a much larger school than Nowata.

If being an Ironman was proving difficult, what football meant in the scheme of things—even in football-crazy Nowata—was put in perspective by the death of Harvey Lilburn, my classmate and brother of senior teammate Gary Lilburn. Harvey, with whom I had played summer baseball, had struggled for two-and-a-half years against leukemia. Three of my four grandparents, including my beloved Ma, Mama's mother, had died during the 1950s. But Harvey's service at Benjamin Funeral Home marked the first I had attended for a classmate, someone my age. It was sobering and heartbreaking for Harvey's classmates and friends. Nowata teenagers, including many from the sophomore class, led in establishing the Harvey Lilburn Fund to defray the family's expenses from Harvey's illness. We were supported by all ages and segments of the community, reinforcing why I loved Nowata.

As we prepared for the Coffeyville game, turmoil tormented me. My parents had told me Daddy was considering a U.S. Department of Agriculture transfer to Northern California. The job had potential of leading to assistant director of a state, from which state directors were chosen. Unthinking, I said California sounded exciting. I came to regret that. Life-changing decisions shouldn't be left to a teenager, and this one wasn't. Had I opposed the move because I wanted to finish high school in Nowata, I am not sure how Daddy would have responded. Could he have waited two-and-a-half years for another opportunity?

As time passed and interviews occurred, the reality of a job offer loomed, and I understood that this would alter my life in ways I had not recognized. What I might gain from a new experience in Sacramento blurred, and I saw with stark clarity what I would lose—my place, the only home I had known, the friends I had grown up with and loved. I don't know how much this affected me as we readied ourselves, with a 1–4–1 record, for our seventh game. The coaches said either tailback/fullback David Neely or I would start at fullback; both of us would play, the one who performed best getting the most snaps.

When Coach Noble told me I was starting, KB offered encouragement and support. His successful transition to varsity quarterback, with a clear-eyed toughness, allowed him to retain his confidence even in the face of our struggles. I realized the remainder of my season would turn on this game. Do well and play. Stumble and be consigned not only to the bench but also to overcoming growing doubts about what I had to offer in future seasons. What had happened to the eighth-grade center good enough to play with the freshmen team, to the fullback who, on his first varsity carry, ran wild and free?

No one offered a road map for how to navigate my way on the field or off it. When the chips were down, I folded. I could feel myself tiptoeing to the line of scrimmage as if I were a cat burglar on little cat feet, hoping against hope to steal a few yards. Instead of blasting into the line, exerting my will, if only over my own self-doubt, I robbed myself of this opportunity that Bucky had paid for with his pain. I did not get many chances after that to conquer my tenuousness, to get into the flow and regain my confidence by cranking off a good run or two. The coaches showed little tolerance because I had not earned it. David Neely came into the game. I was through—and we lost 21–8, despite showing some dominance when Neely provided more help for Richard Nash and Smitty than I had. I let everyone down—most of all, myself. I could no more figure out my mess of a life than I could understand adolescent love.

The season slid further into the ditch when we could not finish three drives inside the 5-yard line at Pryor. Worse, a holding penalty cancelled our one touchdown, a 15 yard Richard Nash run that would have given us the opportunity to avoid a 7–0 loss. Even when the offense got untracked at Broken Arrow the following week—Nash scored four times—it was not enough. The defense allowed a season-high 48 points. It made me wonder if earlier I should have gone to Coach Noble or Coach Armstrong, who knew I had played well at linebacker in junior high and during "B-team" games, and asked for a chance to help on that side of the ball. By this time, though, I had undermined whatever belief my coaches might have had in me.

Two days before the season's November conclusion against Miami, my parents broke the news: Daddy had accepted the job in California. We would be moving in January between the end of the semester in Nowata and the beginning of one at my new school, Mira Loma, a one-year-old high school in the Sacramento suburbs. As we went through our final practices, I did so with a heavy heart. In the huddle, I looked into the eyes of teammates I would never have a chance to play beside again, never have an opportunity for self-redemption or to help prove we, as this team's foundation class, could be better than 1–8–1. You are what your record says you are, but I clung to the belief we could be more . . . and I wouldn't have the chance to be.

Basketball practice began immediately, with us football players joining Mike Whistler and others already working out with Coach Bill Shahan. In small-town schools, athletes more often than not played multiple sports. Moving on overnight from a forgettable record in a nevertheless unforgettable first varsity football season presented a fresh start—except for me.

When I told Coach Shahan I would be moving at the end of the semester, he seemed disappointed. I'm not sure Coach Noble shared the feeling. He had given me a chance, and I had not lived up to his expectations—or mine. Maybe I was overly sensitive to the responses that accompanied word I would be leaving Nowata; telling friends was difficult, but, when I told Coach Shahan, it prompted a straightforward, team-first reply. He explained he had looked forward to coaching me but had to devote his attention to those who would be there.

I don't know who felt worse, Coach or me. He said I could practice with the team but would get no time with the varsity and would be limited to providing opposition to the "B-team" starters, including Clarence Smith, Mike Whistler, and KB Berry, whose ball skills and quickness caught Shahan's eye early on and won him time with the varsity as well.

During my last week at Nowata, as I wrote in an essay for my first English course at my new school, "it seemed as if my whole world was folding in on me like a great blanket of fog." (I already was benefitting from the heightened writing demands at Mira Loma, but the material for the essay that received an "A" was hard won and painfully received.)

It had been difficult to walk the Nowata High School hallways knowing I was seeing friends for what might be the last time. I felt I had to memorize each and every face. I did not know how my friends felt—the exceptions being Charles, KB, Bucky, and, of course, Ginger, to whom I entrusted my innermost feelings—but I was to find out in a most unexpected way.

On what must have been my last Saturday night in the town where I was born and had lived for nearly 16 years, a couple of those friends dragged me to the former Rainbow Café on the edge of town, where they said there was a dance. As much as I loved to go to Teen Town, a floor above the Rexall Drug Store on the main drag, and to the

VFW Post to hear Rodney and the Blazers, the most popular area band, I did not feel like dancing.

When I walked into the Rainbow, everyone who was anyone in my life was there. A gigantic "Good Luck, Steve" banner, signed with heartfelt messages, hung from the wall. More gifts than I had ever seen and Mama threw some lavish birthday parties as I was growing up—covered tables. The kindness and generosity of spirit that filled that room made me want to cry—and I damned well did. How could I not? Teenagers, regardless of the era, do not easily display their true feelings about one another. But these teenagers risked doing so in a way I had never known and have never known since. The best and worst moments in my young life—maybe of my entire life—were the same moment. It hurt so good.

WHEN PAST AND PRESENT COLLIDE

Oklahomans had been loading up and heading for California since the Dust Bowl days. During the 1930s, drought famously choked the Great Plains, and clouds of once-good land, not rain, chased Oklahomans west. Their migration made the words of writer John Steinbeck famous and turned Oklahomans into Okies, a pejorative diminution of a proud people. The Loves—my paternal grandparents—were not Steinbeck's Joads. They moved years later and not from the Oklahoma Panhandle, epicenter of the Dust Bowl, but from Northeast Oklahoma—Green Country—to a small piece of land outside Bakersfield. Their search for a promised land was not so different from ours. Could wanderlust be hereditary?

My father wanted something else, something more. Me, I still wanted to be an Ironman. Though I relate Daddy's move—and it was *his* move—to the Dust Bowl migration, for me, a more apt comparison was the infamous Trail of Tears. Many from multiple Indian

Nations died when they were relocated by government coercion from their ancestral homelands in the southeastern United States to land considered less desirable but that I could not have loved more. The Cherokee Nation, which includes Nowata, lost more than 5,000.

Our journey west was less traumatic. We moved to a house with an orange tree and brick patio, covered by vine-draped, wooden latticework as our backyard. The house had a nice location on a quiet street with a peculiar-sounding name—Kerria Way. It was definitely an upgrade. (I think we paid $35,000 or so for it; Zillow reported that it sold for $245,000 in 2018 and estimated its worth at $295,811 a year later. *That's* California real estate.) The house was bigger (three bedrooms, bath-and-a-half) and newer (built in 1950) than what we left behind in Nowata. There was another difference. That was a home. *My home.* This was just a house.

Mama, I think, shared some of my feelings (misgivings?), but we both had resolved to try to make the best of our new situation. Daddy meant well. He usually did. He had talked to one of the football coaches when he preregistered me at Mira Loma High School. A teller of tales by inclination, Daddy fancied himself a latter-day Will Rogers, the famous Oklahoman Daddy once served as driver on occasions when Rogers returned to his birthplace near Oologah, a part of Indian Territory, where the humorist-actor-newspaper columnist was born in 1879.

Daddy, as was his wont, got carried away when talking, this time about me and my ability. This flaw usually crept into stories about himself. But this time, he described in glowing detail my first-ever carry in a varsity game and how I had thrilled the crowd with a long run that portended promise—promise unfulfilled the remainder of the season. He conveniently forgot to mention those considerable failures that eventually banished me to the bench. He should have realized he was creating outsized expectations too large for me.

I did not know until the following fall, when football practice began, what Daddy had done, but I learned that first spring semester at Mira Loma that, like Dorothy in *The Wizard of Oz,* I was in a strange new land, not Kansas, in her case, or Oklahoma, as in mine. If the essay I wrote about leaving home and friends gave me confidence that I might excel, other experiences in the classroom and in sports gave me pause. Spanish class opened my eyes (*abrí mis ojos*). What had been passable foreign-language competence in Oklahoma was laughable in a state where Spanish was the second language even then and sounded like the first for my new classmates.

Baseball, even the junior varsity, similarly convinced me I would not be moving up to the varsity with my better teammates the following spring. My new teammates had had the opportunity to play year-round, and it showed. They were more accomplished. As in Oklahoma, my sound defense proved a strength, but opposing pitchers quickly exposed shortcomings I had brought west with me. I played but, increasingly, as a late-innings defensive replacement. The greatest similarity between the game I knew in Oklahoma and the one I discovered in California turned out to be camaraderie among players. On the field, I felt a little less the outsider with the Oklahoma twang that everyone mistook for a "Southern accent." Some of those players—Dave Illig, Mike Alberghini, Barry Gildberg among them—even became friends.

While they seemed to like me well enough, Mike and Dave just might have been influenced by the fact their new teammate had a car and was happy to pick them up in the morning and give them a ride to school. For me, it cemented a connection, and, lost as I felt early on, each one became a lifeline from my isolation. Some of my loneliness was self-inflicted. Talking Bird—my Order of the Arrow alter ego—had resolved to talk less and listen more, to not be an obnoxious newcomer bulling his way into places and unwelcome relationships.

This did not mean I wasn't inquisitive. One of the differences I noticed was the unusual number of students with limbs in casts, especially legs. While I kept to myself my theory about the constant misidentification of my accent (my classmates had heard too few people from the deep South to know the difference between a Southern drawl and my twang), I asked a person supporting the plaster-of-paris industry how his leg came to be encased.

"Skiing accident," he explained.

"But I see so many kids in casts. Same cause?"

"Mostly," he said. "It's that time of year."

It was late January, early February. The Sierra Nevada Mountains were an easy drive from Sacramento. Everyone skied, it seemed. I decided to be an exception. I never tried it. Couldn't risk my great athletic career! Besides, I grew up on lakes. I water-skied. Seemed a better choice. Oklahoma lakes were flat. California's mountains were not. It was among my early geography lessons.

If it sounds as if I was adjusting well to my surroundings, that would not be entirely accurate. As I tried to find and strike the right balance to gain acceptance, my innermost thoughts centered on home—and I don't mean the house on Kerria Way. Though such thinking was an exercise in futility, I still reviewed what I might have done to reverse the course of events. I couldn't help it, then or now. My mind spun home-going scenarios until my head was a tangled web worthy of an industrious spider. (E.B. White's Charlotte?)

Some of my ideas should have been dismissed out of hand. Of course, I did not do so until I had tortured myself with them. Perhaps foremost was one in which I sought admission to Oklahoma Military Academy in Claremore, near Nowata. This would have sidestepped an eligibility requirement that an athlete must live with a parent. OMA would not have allowed Mama to accompany me, even if she had wanted to, which she wouldn't have. On the downside, neither would it have allowed me much, if any, contact with my girlfriend—did I even still have a girlfriend in Nowata?—and I would not have been with KB, Charles, Bucky, and the other teammates with whom I had grown up. Stupid idea of a desperate boy.

Those same athletic-eligibility rules would have prevented me from living with someone in Nowata to continue my education while my parents remained in California. Not even my uncle and aunt would have qualified, and both they and I—not to mention my helmet-whacking cousins—would have taken a pass on this solution.

My parents and I never discussed the only feasible solution: Mama and I could return to Nowata for two years, renting a place to live, while Daddy remained in California on his new job. Such a resolution might have brought me some happiness, but it would have been unfair to Mama. And, honestly, I neither deserved nor expected such sacrifice. Since I had not voiced a strong objection when Daddy broached the idea of California, I had no complaint coming. It was only the first, though most important, of a series of unhappy youthful mistakes.

Daddy became convinced that our less-than-idyllic co-existence began with the move. But he inexplicably and wrongly blamed a neighbor, an older woman who allowed me to accompany her to church—the wrong church, in Daddy's estimation. My Nowata girlfriend was Catholic, and I had decided converting to Catholicism could bring us closer. It didn't. What it did do was drive a wedge between Daddy and me. The odd thing is, he was not intolerant of others' beliefs. He was instead, I think, frustrated with my unhappiness and believed this religious misadventure added to it. What I resented, and unfairly, is that his transfer to a new steppingstone job proved futile.

My father's work impressed his superiors in California, and they recommended him for a nearly year-long training program in Baton Rouge, Louisiana. He and Mama moved there temporarily and got to attend the world's largest outdoor cocktail party, otherwise known as Louisiana State University football. I was in college by this time, isolated from details that were never discussed. Daddy had not been advanced to assistant director of a state. The problem? "Politics," a euphemism for what experience told me happened.

Daddy had an unwavering belief in himself and his strong opinions. He could be self-righteous and rub people the wrong way, as well as win over those receptive to his good work and clear vision. Bottom line: His future ended up in the hands of the former, and he neither tempered himself nor backed down. He ultimately found himself in a situation similar to that of a major in the armed services who is not promoted to lieutenant colonel. The consequence may not have been as dire as "up-or-out," but he chose to return to an assignment in Oklahoma City, where people who knew him and his ways were pleased to have him back. Except for the embarrassment of his failure, I always believed he was happier back home in Oklahoma.

I know I would have been happier in Oklahoma—and, for a few weeks during the summer following the move to California, I was. It was like going down the rabbit hole. But at least when Alice did this in Lewis Carroll's *Alice's Adventures in Wonderland*, she was able to ask the King for guidance. "Would you tell me, please, which way I ought to go from here?" To which the King responded: "That depends a good deal on where you want to get to." I knew where, and the Berrys, in a memorable act of kindness and generosity, made it possible.

I don't know how the Berrys came to invite me to stay with KB that summer of 1962 or what arrangement my parents might have made to cover the expense of having me in their home. Jan, KB's younger sister, was the only one of their other seven children still at home. Maybe Jewel and Roy missed having a houseful. What I do know is that it became both the happiest and saddest summer of my life.

My parents, particularly Mama, had instilled in me an independence they came to regret. That was my fault, particularly with regard to Mama. Though I needed her—and wanted her love and counsel—I, like many teenagers, did not show this demonstrably. If anything, this grew worse with age, an inexplicable and unforgiveable flaw. I hurt the person who loved me most, and she blamed herself for my excessive independent streak.

How independent was I? Consider my trip to Nowata. I was 16 and had had my driver's license for only four months, but I drove my Volkswagen Beetle convertible from Sacramento *home* to Nowata. I mapped out my route, determined overnight stops, and off I went, dutifully checking in with Mama along the way. [I just Googled *distancebetweencities.us* and discovered my northern route was a distance of about 1,775 miles.] I drove U.S. 80 through northern California, Nevada, Utah, Wyoming, a little of Nebraska, then south to hit U.S. 70 in Kansas, and into Oklahoma. Good thing I was not a new driver and knew where I was going without help of GPS. Looking at me, no one would have guessed how lost I was inside.

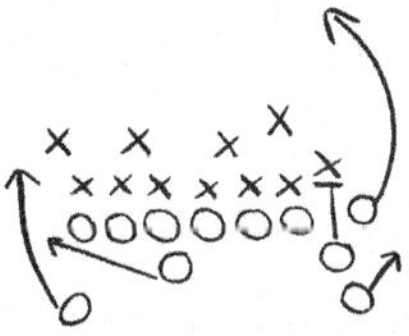

TORN BETWEEN TWO WORLDS

The Nowata I returned to in the summer of 1962 looked little different from the one I'd left only months before, but this could not have been further from the truth. I knew its streets and houses, especially those of my friends. They were imprinted on my mind—indelible, unchanged—this place where I was born, the one I knew better than anyplace in the world.

Time had not yet had its way with Nowata and those who lived there. It would, and when that happened, there would be no denying its ravages and consequences. Yet even at this stage, recognition was dawning, pangs of unavoidable truth I would live with, brought home by returning for reunions, funerals, reexaminations of the inescapable: I was a stranger.

This truth had not been so obvious when, one day in Sacramento, the mail included the *1962 Ironman*, the Nowata High School yearbook that, while not the last I would receive, was the only one in which I am more than an inscription. I had ordered the yearbook in the fall of '61; my forced exile to California had not eliminated photographic record of my presence. I had brought the previous yearbook with me on the move, because, even though my freshman class had not been physically present in the new high school building or acknowledged with individual photos, my teammates and I were included in the 1960 football-team photograph. That yearbook, without a single inscription, looks bare.

The same fate might have befallen my *1962 Ironman* had not one of my former sophomore classmates made sure my yearbook was signed. I never knew who was responsible, but I suspect it was one of the girls, since they were the more conscientious when it came to sentimental tasks and would have recognized what the signatures and inscriptions would mean to me. The '62 yearbook contains not only my sophomore photo but also team and individual photos from football and basketball. I also show up in "candids" taken in my Spanish and Plane Geometry classes (head down, as if problem solving). In retrospect, my inclusion among 27 Oklahoma Honor Society members spoke more to my future than athletics. KB Berry, my friend and quarterback, seemed to sense this. "I'm sure that, after you finish college," KB wrote in my yearbook, "you will really be a success, because a guy with a brain like yours can hardly fail."

On the same yearbook page with KB's too-generous inscription, my former math teacher, JC Holton, had a different take on my brain and the person it was making of me: "To my student [who] thought he knew more than his teacher did," he wrote. Fortunately, the yearbook and my homecoming were filled with warmer greetings than Mr. Holton's, including an invitation from Janie Osborn to visit her, which I did after listening to a warning from KB regarding the consequences of re-establishing my relationship with Ginger, my girlfriend.

"You may have to fight for her," he said, meaning *literally* fight for her. "She has been going out with [someone]." KB told me who. He also had practical advice, born of growing up with brothers. "DO NOT," he said, "let him get in the first punch. First punch usually wins."

KB would have offered this advice to any friend, especially one he thought enough of to share his bed with. The Berrys' house was small. There was no spare bedroom for guests, and KB's room had only one bed. Brothers shared beds in those days. We were like brothers; he knew I had no brothers to teach me to fight. So he became my corner man during a memorable summer. "This is going to be a *real* summer," is how he put it. "A swinging time."

We had *chosen* to make it what KB promised—with parental acquiescence and more than a touch of understanding and love. Mine permitted this test of my independence and ability to behave appropriately, if not always maturely. KB's folks took a deeper plunge. Jewel and Roy made me feel like one of their own, not a visitor. They made this look easier and more natural than it was. KB's younger sister, Jan, and Helen, his older sister closest in age, both reassured me, seemingly saying: "Don't worry about anything. Our folks love you." I want to believe that, because I loved them, for who they were as much as for what they were doing for me.

Before KB and I settled into the routines and rhythm of this special summer, which I owed to him, I knew I had to address the Ginger and Janie questions. I was not sure how to solve this dilemma. Ginger referred in letters and in her inscription in my yearbook to "our differences" she hoped had been "straightened out." It had to have been difficult for her when her boyfriend was driven away to California and out of her life. She wanted a normal teenage experience with a boy she saw daily. So she had found one. I'm sure she didn't have to look too hard. The question was: Whom did she want, given my return for a less-than-endless summer?

If I had been a cunning mastermind of my nascent love life, I would have found out the answer to that question before seeing Janie; I wasn't. And, there was something else. The ideal might have been to date both Ginger and Janie, knowing it was unlikely to last or amount to more. Janie had mentioned she missed the card games we used to play at her house. If only I had known how to play these girl cards. I wasn't even sure what hands I had been dealt. It felt wrong to let Janie believe I would be available for her, if, likely, I couldn't be.

When I drove to Janie's house, she was the only one there. Looking pretty and seemingly happy to see me, we hugged and began to talk.

"Would you like a glass of wine?" she asked.

Surprised by the offer—Janie was fifteen but a mature, going-on twenty-one—I was unsure how to respond to the offer of afternoon, underage consumption. Nyla, her older sister, had a wild side I found intriguing; maybe Janie was more like Nyla than I had thought. Then again, this wasn't tea leaves; maybe I was reading too much into a glass of wine. After hemming and hawing, I must have decided to tell Janie what I suspect she knew: I couldn't see her if I wanted to see Ginger steadily. Ginger knew Janie once had been my girlfriend and, if she learned I had gone *first* to see Janie, she might ask: Are you two still a thing?

It made for a brief conversation and prompt exit. Had I done the right thing? All I know is that I received no more invitations for wine in the afternoon. When I saw Ginger, we wound up in a familiar place—on her front porch swing. Her mother, Ona, tried to keep us under surveillance. She did not entirely succeed. Ginger, with word and deed, made it clear she wanted to be with me. No fight required. I didn't ask how long this might last. Why spoil the summer for an answer I couldn't face?

Thanks to Ginger and KB, the summer lay before me as KB had suggested it could. He had done all the things necessary to make this idyll at least a temporary reality. As on the football field, he called just the right play at the right time. We never tired of each other; at least I didn't tire of him. If we were going to spend as much time together as possible, knowing there was no promise of a tomorrow, it would literally require work. KB had lined up a job helping to clear out the Campbell Hotel, which was no longer profitable and in need of a new life. Among the first steps: removal of furnishings and a deep cleaning. I came to wonder if some of those furnishings and equipment had been there more than 50 years.

The Campbell Hotel was not Nowata's first but seemed destined to be its last, as the turn-of-the-century oil-and-gas economy waned. We may not have appreciated our small, physical roles in bringing down the curtain on the building's life as a hotel that dated to 1910. But I knew enough of history and place to realize that what we were about that summer had a feel of finality to it. This would turn out to apply to more than the old hotel.

I had to talk to someone in charge of the project before I could go to work, but I cannot remember who it was. Working hard and cooperatively at any and all assignments given, I do know I managed not to blow up KB's arrangement. The nicest thing was not whatever small earnings the work produced but the time together it bought us. What added to it is that my friends Charles Dugger and, I think, Bucky Buck also were on the job. What a crew. We had almost half a year to discuss, but I may have been guarded in what I said about my new life in California. It wasn't that I didn't want to share my feelings, but negativity can spoil a moment, and I was unsure how to describe my new high school, the people, and how I felt. These guys knew me too well. They would have seen through the veneer to my unhappiness.

Maybe, in a small way, we contributed to the conversion and refurbishing of what would revert to a Native-American name, Noweta Lodge. From afar and on an occasional visit to Nowata, I have observed the effort put in, again and again, to reclaim the Campbell and Savoy hotels. The original Savoy burned to the ground in 1909, two days before its grand opening. Rebuilt by 1911, it became the epicenter of million-dollar oil deals. There have been multiple owners, a civic "Save the Savoy" campaign, repurposing after repurposing—from county hospital to city offices to flea market—all to no avail. Why did nothing work? Could it have been because Nowata no longer worked? All things change, and some cannot be saved, no matter what. Did this include my relationship with Nowata and football and those I loved so much?

These haunting questions came both in the night and in the heat of day. So we did what Oklahoma teenagers who live near the Kansas state line often did. We drove north for beers. I should say *I* drove; the car and a possible driving-under-the-influence risk were mine. The designated-driver concept that began in Scandinavia in the 1920s and was formalized in the 1980s found its way to Canada in 1986 and from there swept into the United States. The designated driver was unknown to us in 1962, and while a good and sound concept, it probably would have been met with no more than a nod in its direction by us invincible teenagers.

In theory, drinking too much north of the border would have been possible. You could buy 3.2 beer—"weak beer"—in Coffeyville bars, but you were supposed to be eighteen to do so. Until passage of the 26th amendment (1971) prevented federal and state governments from using age to prohibit any citizen at least eighteen years old from voting, Kansas, with its more liberal attitude toward 3.2 beer consumption, was beer years ahead of Oklahoma. And, Oklahoma was sexist. It allowed eighteen-year-old women to drink 3.2 beer but required men to be twenty-one. Kansas, in 1949, decided *all* eighteen-year-olds were responsible enough to quaff a beer with less than 4 percent alcohol. With a wink and tug on the tap, the barkeep at the Coffeyville bar we frequented allowed our table of sixteen-year-olds to unilaterally reduce the drinking age an additional two years. Drink up, boys!

Our usual evenings after a day in the Campbell Hotel may have been less adventurous than beer runs to Coffeyville but no less interesting or entertaining. We cruised Nowata, seeing and being seen. Given the town's 3.1 square miles [revised to 3.35]—with no water—this did not take long. Nowata would not have been the backdrop for *American Graffiti*, the 1973 cruising classic set (but not filmed) in Modesto, California, in 1962. The story, directed and co-written by George Lucas, sprang from Lucas's teenage years that corresponded to ours in Nowata. It captured the tenor of the cruising/rock 'n' roll times of us first baby boomers, born in 1946.

Nowata cruisers, like their Modesto counterparts, needed to establish a beachhead. Theirs was the parking lot at Mel's Drive-In diner. Ours was the Dairy Dell parking lot, where cruisers linked up, and those who hitched rides or hoofed it knew to show up. We acted as if we owned the Dairy Dell. [Charles Dugger's folks did, in fact, own it, for a time, and so did the parents of Phyllis Hendricks, my favorite roller-skating squeeze at the rink they also owned.]

As we cruised to the Dairy Dell and passed other cars filled with teenagers, shouts of inquiry were exchanged as friends sought out friends. This was our means of communication before anyone had heard of cellphones and texting. Everyone knew where to look for KB, Charles, Bucky Buck, and me. And they knew what we would be doing—talking to one another and anyone else who stopped. We weren't so much interested in cars as in one another.

"We could talk for hours and just enjoy the company," Bucky remembered.

He was right. The content of the conversations did not matter as much the closeness they generated. We shared everything, without fear of the judgment typical of teenagers. Nothing was off limits, and during that summer with the Berrys, I found myself falling into a similar pattern with Janice that existed between KB and me. Hearing Janice and Helen refer to KB by his given name—Kenneth—I sometimes would do the same. While outwardly it was a term of affection on my part, and KB accepted it as such, I suspect a psychiatrist might say I was attempting to further insinuate myself into his life and family. As the days passed and my presence in the house began to feel more natural to all of us, Janice talked more and more. I listened with genuine interest to the smallest things going on in her life, things that felt—and were—so large to her. I'm not sure she fully appreciated what she had given me: she became the sister I never had—though there was a time I had thought that might change.

My parents never discussed reproductive issues that might have prevented them having another child. My theory is, I was too much of a good thing—or, a bad one. I do know Mama experienced difficulty becoming pregnant when I was the result. In the early-to-mid 1950s, my parents considered adoption and included me in the process—to a point. We visited the United Methodist Children's Home in Tahlequah, which excited me. It seemed the day went well, but nothing more happened, and adoption talk that included me ceased. I hid the disappointment that I would remain an only child, with the plusses and minuses that entailed.

Those summer weeks with Ginger went by in a blur of enjoyment tempered by the knowledge that another leaving loomed. This one would be worse, with greater finality than the sentimental farewell at the Rainbow Café. Maybe because I blocked out this unavoidable moment and what it would mean, the good times are hazy. It probably is ironic that one I remember involved an outing to a small lake near Bartlesville.

Ginger's parents invited me to accompany them, probably because when I was not with KB, I was at their house. The swimming day-trip included a cabin in which we could eat, drink, and change into our swimsuits. There was no separate room for changing. For privacy,

Ginger and sister Jayna slipped behind either a curtain or a giant beach towel draped over a line. Whatever it was, I was on the other side of this barrier, with one or both of her parents and perhaps other adults. Ginger emerged first, and we found ourselves not blocked by the privacy barrier. There was a large mirror in the room, and, from our vantage point, a person could see reflections in that mirror. Jayna had taken off her clothes but had not yet put on her swimsuit. She was nude, her reflection bold, beautiful, a few feet away. Ginger was looking elsewhere. I wasn't.

Teenage voyeuristic instincts took over. What if I got caught? I didn't know which would be worse—Ginger knowing or her parents. Or, Mama. I thought Jayna was looking directly at me in the mirror. I must have imagined that, because the person whose eyes I really felt on me was Mama's, and she was half a continent away. She would have gotten out Daddy's razor strop herself. Guiltily, I averted my eyes. I never mentioned what had happened, and neither did Jayna—if she knew. It was a flash of flesh, no more lasting than the summer itself.

There had been no time to think this through. Time had become my enemy, the hourglass down to its final grains of summer sand. Could time be fleeting yet also feel as if it were closing in on a person? Isn't that a contradiction? Reveries of a last-minute reprieve that would allow me to remain in Nowata filled my every waking moment and many of my dreams. I felt like an ingrate for what I had had during those Nowata weeks, because I knew it was difficult for KB to watch what I was going through and be unable to offer me an answer, much less a resolution. He had done all he could, more than anyone could expect. I knew this special summer was a one-time moment of joy and, that if I had not gained a better foothold in Sacramento, a better sense of my evolving self, by the following year, I would be in trouble.

Something happened during the final days of my stay with the Berrys that affected everyone and stopped me thinking so much about myself: Marilyn Monroe was found dead on August 4, 1962, in California. More than beautiful and sexy, she had become a cultural icon during the 1950s. Beyond physical assets, she was talented but troubled. She had a drug problem and died from a barbiturate overdose. Ugly, unfounded rumors suggested her death may have been murder. We were 16—20 years younger than Miss Monroe—separated by a generation and different worlds. And yet, like so many others, we felt as if she belonged to us, and our longing became lament. It was a first serious step toward a lasting loss of innocence, a loss that would accelerate faster than we could know.

When I first left for California, letters followed. Friends wrote to tell me what was happening back home. Those letters arriving at 2904 Kerria Way were pen-and-paper life preservers. I welcomed and responded to each. Now, I sensed it would be different. Maybe that recognition caused my great and irreparable mistake. Or maybe, the essayist Tim Kreider has a better explanation: Friendships often have lifespans, with beginnings, middles, and endings.

Considering a particular and special friendship, Kreider makes this case with "Escape from Pony Island," an essay in *We Learn Nothing*, his 2012 collection. He begins, ominously: "I'm forfeiting a friendship by writing this. It's a friendship that is effectively dead already, historical rather than active . . ." He goes on to explain the cause of death.

Like the friendship itself, the end, fueled by geographical and emotional distances, was anything but simple. Kreider and friend Ken had moved on and "fallen out of frequent contact." Kreider not only had "somehow" missed Ken's marriage but also his move from Philadelphia to a small Missouri town. "By the time you've realized that an era has a finite life cycle, an inevitable rise and decline," Kreider wrote, "the peak has already passed."

Ginger made it clear she did not want an occasional California boyfriend, one becoming more a stranger with each passing day.

When she excommunicated me from her life, this included letters. My overarching, overreaching, irrational, unspoken salve to this hurt was to go incommunicado, to cut away from my aching heart all things Nowata—everything and everyone who meant anything to me. I don't think anyone except me noticed. The Ironmen had begun another football pre-season. KB, Bucky, and Charles had no time for letters. And except for thank-you notes to the adults whose kindness had made my summer possible, I had come to the fateful conclusion that the only way I could move ahead was to not look back at what I had left behind in Nowata—lost to me, perhaps, forever. Like a turtle, head pulled in, I hid, protecting myself with a hard shell of ignorance and neglect.

LOST IN MY NEW PERMANENT WORLD

The difference between my arrival in Sacramento and returning from a Nowata summer of false hope was a realization that my new reality, unlike revenge, was a dish best served neither cold nor hot. It was a bitter stew best avoided. It was on my table. This was my life. And it would get worse before it got better. I would *make* it worse. Maybe all teenagers feel this way when they struggle to regain lost footing, only to slide down, down, down.

My trip to Nowata may not have been the best way to prepare for my introduction to Mira Loma High School football. Talk about divided focus. I suspect Mama and Daddy understood the trip could have its negatives when they allowed me to "get it out of my system." They gambled that the risk-reward might, at some point, swing to positive and shove me toward accepting my circumstances and better settling into my large, still-strange school. Instead, I wallowed in my misery, behaving as if I were Mopey, an "eighth" dwarf who had lost his Snow White. You would have thought I might have found another love to awaken with a kiss. During the 1962–63 school year, Mira Loma enrolled almost 1,900 students in four classes, 464 in my junior class. [I counted class photos in the 1963 yearbook]. Nowata, in contrast, had 296 in its three classes the year I would have been a senior, 88 in my class.

When pre-season football practice began, with different coaches, players, and rhythms from those I had known as an Ironman, I may have been physically prepared but was in an emotional quagmire. I was ill-prepared for the mental challenge of competing against more and better athletes. I played fullback in early practices, but head coach Don Brown listed me at left halfback—perhaps because of my size, 5-foot-7 and 143 pounds. It certainly was not because this presented a better opportunity. Senior Jan Hoganson, who began at right halfback but moved to the left side, made all-Capital Valley Conference, and, worse for my prospects, I knew left halfback would belong to Jim Spitzer, a fellow junior who was our fastest and best running back. And fullback? My friend Barry Gildberg was the present and future.

Though the players were not as large as I thought they might be, given the number of Mira Loma students, I was the smallest varsity player—and not in the running for fastest, as I had been at Nowata. The most positive response I received from Coach Brown and his two assistants, one of whom, Bill Freeman, was also head basketball coach, occurred during tackling practice. In something similar to the Oklahoma Drill, but without a blocker leading the running back, I took "advantage" of my lack of height and got under the pads of the runner, helmet hard into his chest. A "whoosh" of air followed. A couple of my new teammates nodded appreciatively, and even the coaches took notice. I had shown I was a hitter. Why wasn't I on the defensive depth chart? Maybe Daddy should have told the coaches about my linebacking.

If I had had my mind on the game the previous spring and had not run back to Oklahoma for the summer, it might have dawned on me to request a meeting with Coach Brown to seek advice as to how to best prepare for an offense different from the single wing and to express an interest to play *anywhere* he thought I might help the team. He no doubt would have seen through my obvious self-interest, but I was sincere.

A meeting also would have presented an opportunity to discuss my eyesight. I was Mr. Magoo in cleats. Bats had better eyesight. I began wearing glasses in the fourth grade. I played basketball and baseball in crude athletic versions, after discovering I was ill-suited to the hard contact lenses of the day. I had never worn glasses playing football. I didn't require them playing center, and when I moved to fullback, I could get away with not using them because I did not have to *follow* the ball as I would have to on defense.

As a linebacker during my two-way Nowata days, I could get by despite problematic 20/200 vision. I worried about sweat dripping onto the lenses and having to constantly clean them, which was impractical. But even if I were a fit as a linebacker at Mira Loma—doubtful, given my size—the game would have come at me faster and required quicker reactions. In the defensive backfield—safety?—I would have to read the quarterback's eyes and sort out his run-game feints. Glasses would be a necessity, and so would a different, larger face mask.

If anyone was wearing sports goggles, as National Football League Hall of Famer Eric Dickerson did in 1984, when he set the single-season NFL rushing record, I didn't know it playing 20 years earlier. Dickerson admitted to Vincent Frank on sportsnaut.com: "I hated wearing those goggles. I tried to go without them a couple of times through practice and put contacts in. They worked—the contacts. I'd get in the game [and] I said, 'Keep my goggles on the sideline.' First hit, contacts pop out." Not good, said Dickerson.

"I'm blind as a bat." At least I had one thing in common with an all-time great running back.

The most famous sports goggles may have been those worn by Kareem Abdul Jabbar, who had been poked in the eye so often he wore them on the basketball court for both cornea and career protection. His goggles became as much a signature of his game as the Sky Hook. By 2019, goggles had become common. Giselle Juarez, All-America pitcher for the Oklahoma Sooners softball team, made a stylish red pair her trademark. She tried pitching without corrective lenses for her nearsightedness. "My depth perception was so off," she told *Oklahoman* columnist Jenni Carlson. She couldn't hit the backstop, much less the corner of the plate. She won't go into the pitching circle without her gogs. "It's kind of become my thing now."

I believe a conversation with my coach about better, updated sports glasses might have demonstrated the thought I had put into playing defense. I never had that conversation. I should have tried anything. Before I got the chance, it was too late. I became ill and missed a practice. My greater failure was not notifying the coaches of my situation. I was unaware of the pre-season procedure to follow. I was in bed, feeling lousy, probably as much affected by depression as by whatever had laid me low. If school had been in session, I would have called the office and requested someone inform the coaches. Why didn't I? I didn't even make the effort to do the right thing. Nowata's most reliable kid had become California unreliable.

When I dragged myself to practice the next day—I really had been sick but not as sick as I was going to be—Coach Brown called me in and questioned why I had not notified him I was ill. I didn't have a doctor's excuse. It looked to the coaches as if I didn't want to practice. They dropped me further down the running-back depth chart. Was this the moment to broach playing defense? I knew what they would say: You'd have to come to practice for that. Everything had fallen apart.

Football was over. What else did I have? If I had ever hoped to reestablish regular communication with KB and the guys in Nowata, now I had made it impossible. I knew the questions: *How are you doing out there, Hawk? How's football? Is the team good? Are you start ing? And the girls—what about the girls?* How could I respond? Even if things had gone better, I was not sure I wanted to hear how things were in Nowata. It hurt. It was the reason I erected a wall between me and the past. This wasn't the Internet age of instantaneous communication. Nowata barely had rotary dial phones. It had not been that long ago that our phones had no dials at all. When we picked up the receiver, an operator would say: "Number, please." It was simple. Like Nowata, a three-digit kind of place.

My girlfriend had given up on me, and I had given up on football. As a consequence, I also lost my chance to play basketball that season. Coach Freeman, the football assistant who was head basketball coach, was—how should I put this?—*less than enthusiastic* about me joining his team. Who could blame him? It turned into a long junior year, the highlight of which was getting to know Leonard Frizzi, my United States History teacher, who also advised the student newspaper—*Matador Capers.* (Mira Loma's nickname was the Matadors.) By recruiting me for the newspaper staff for my senior year, he, more than any teacher, changed my life.

THE IRONMEN PROVED BETTER WITHOUT ME

My wall of silence/self-protection worked all too well. Little or no information came from Nowata in real time, and I ducked and covered a half continent away, attempting to avoid the fallout I feared worse than radiation from a nuclear attack. I could have subscribed to the

Nowata Daily Star in the fall of 1962 and had the paper mailed to me. Instead, I waited until 2017 to hunker down in a Nowata County Public Library new to me and read of two seasons my friends, teammates, and coaches—some new—put together without me.

I knew the Ironmen had improved mightily, as I had been sure they would. The library's *Star* microfilm whirred dizzyingly before my eyes, most readable, but some parts I wanted to print for my research, less so. Otherwise, the librarians were welcoming and helpful in the extreme to a former Nowatan whom none of them knew. The name "Love" no longer tinkled memories, much less rang bells.

When Bucky Buck dropped by with materials he had pulled together for me, he explained to the librarians who my parents had been in the scheme of 1940s-to-early-1960s Nowata. Bucky, of course, knew everyone, and his explanation made me feel a little less the exile I was. This was a working trip home, but I spent time with Bucky and his wife, Sandy, and even took in two football games, one in which the Ironmen played in a manner that reminded me of our struggles in 1961, the other more enjoyable, meaningful, and personal.

Tired from a day of microfilm memories, I drove to Bucky and Sandy's inviting home on the outskirts of Nowata to join them for a trip to Oologah, where several junior high teams were engaged, two by two, in pre-season scrimmages. One of the games matched the Oologah and Collinsville eighth-grade teams. Bucky's grandson, Dempsey, played linebacker for Collinsville—a chip off ol' granddad—and I was anxious to watch him. From Bucky's vivid descriptions, I knew he was a good athlete, maybe even better at baseball than football.

After watching Dempsey and experiencing flashbacks to how his granddad had played linebacker, I had doubts Dempsey could be better on a baseball field. He made play after play, tackle after tackle. He dripped helmet to cleats with Buck football genes. He jarred runners with dead-on hits. Sitting next to Bucky, I elbowed my friend in the ribs.

"You didn't tell me just how good Dempsey is, did you?" I asked.

Bucky grinned, and his grin spread across his face like a tidal wave. Under his nose, a tube fed him oxygen. He suffered from COPD and other lung problems, including cancer. He didn't want sympathy. He wanted to see Dempsey make another tackle.

We watched intently, two old guys leaning forward on their bleacher seats with anticipation, hanging on Dempsey's every aggressive move. Living in the moment—and living in yesterday, too. After the game, I got to meet Dempsey and tell him how impressed I had been with his play, especially his aggressiveness. His face lit up. I had not based my opinion on familial consideration. The young man could play. I know, because, apparently, I couldn't.

I may have been the embodiment of addition by subtraction. If losing me helped the Ironmen win, a greater number of players—60 turned out for pre-season practice—and new ones such as Gary Mezger, junior offensive lineman, bolstered expected improvement. The few seniors from the 1961 season had been replaced by a larger number of sophomores, including talented receiver/defensive back Larry Fishpaw and tough-as-nails Roy Miller.

The progress of the juniors and seniors became immediately apparent, if not so much in the season-opening shutout of Chelsea; they added another at the expense of Cushing, defending Class 2A state champion. Coach Dick Noble and new assistants, Glenn Welsh from Bixby and John Merryman from Spiro, demonstrated in pre-season a more diverse offense, mixing T-formation plays with Nowata's forte, the single wing, which the Ironmen relied on to improve from 1–8–1 to 7–3. Even after dominating Cushing, the Ironmen could not be certain of the season's direction. Chelsea had offered Noble the opportunity to learn at which position each player performed best.

Where might I have fit? It's difficult to know but impossible not to wonder. No longer an inexperienced running back, my home might have been defense, given mistakes that occurred during pre-season and against Chelsea.

Filling in for tailback Richard Nash, who had a broken bone in his foot, David Neely ran wild against Chelsea. Punt returns of 67 and 50 yards resulted in a touchdown and set up another. With Neely, on his way to an All-Verdigris Valley season, and Nash healthier, Noble thought his team could run against big-reputation-and-state-champion Cushing.

The offense was set. Neely, Nash, and my old friend Clarence Smith were unstoppable. The defense, meanwhile, showed it could more than hold up against a better, if injured, foe. So, what did beating Cushing 40–0 mean? It meant that, for two weeks, everything looked rosy. But, as Noble liked to say, "You never know about kids." At Vinita, the bloom fell off the rose. This would become the season's pattern: Much promise interrupted by disheartenment.

Vinita had always presented a challenge to the Ironmen, and the 1962 Hornets were no exception. They were comparatively large, had a quarterback, Mike Fritz, who could throw, and multiple runners, including, I think, Joe Lane, with speed equal to or better than Nowata's. They left Noble muttering about "mental relapse" and the boys "being off" after a 36–8 loss.

Typical of the Ironmen's play and Coach Noble's reaction, Charles Dugger remembered, was a sweep on which he came up hard from cornerback to hit someone big and fast, at the ankles, trying to offset a 60-pound difference. "We didn't see many 200-pound backs, and that dude just rolled me," Dugger said. "He kept going until someone finally rode him down." When Dugger went to the sideline, he tried to disappear, but Noble grabbed him, screaming that hitting a big back at the ankles usually brought him down. Then, he shook his head, perhaps rethinking his overreaction. He shrugged. "But not him," Noble admitted.

So it went. Bad followed good: resounding victories over Purcell, 42–14, in a non-conference game, and Tahlequah, 28–8, to even the Verdigris Valley record at 1–1 and push the overall mark to 4–1 before traveling to Claremore. If the Ironmen were varying their offense with the T-formation, it was not obvious from the passing statistics. Even after falling behind Vinita, they threw only seven times, completing two, did not throw once against Purcell, and were 0-for-3 against a heavier but immobile Tahlequah that could not stop the run.

Undefeated Claremore, which had had no trouble dumping Vinita, could concentrate on the running of Nash, Neely, and Smith, and ignore Nowata's non-existent passing attack.

Someone posted signs in Rogers County urging the Zebras to target the best runners in Nowata's "odd offense"—single wing from an unbalanced line. The signs showed the way. On the strength of two long touchdown plays—75-yard pass and 65-yard run—Claremore shut out the Ironmen, 20–0, offsetting the quickness and toughness of a smaller Nowata defensive line.

If my old teammates understood they had been all but eliminated from contention in the Verdigris Valley, they did not play like it. They blitzed Pawhuska, 44–21, taking advantage of KB's effective blocking, came from behind for a 14–13 victory over Pryor, and, thanks to Nash's 62- and 76-yard punt returns for touchdowns, made short shrift of Broken Arrow, 22–8.

With a 4–2 Valley record, Nowata had the opportunity to prevent Miami's first undefeated season in 13 years. Respected *Tulsa World* sportswriter Ernie Smart, whose high school coverage I had followed growing up, considered the Ironmen to be "lurking offstage with the potential strength to upset the Miamians." Smart was wrong. Nowata generated *no* offense and lost 26–0, disappointment again following the hope of three consecutive victories.

When Verdigris Valley coaches chose all-conference players, they recognized the Ironmen's improvement from 0–6–1 in the Valley to 4–3, and honored guards Bruce Love and Charles Driskell, end Ray Jordan, and running back David Neely. I thought they could have at least mentioned how I had contributed by absenting myself from Nowata.

FINDING A RIGHT PATH

An alarm sounds in my head whenever I hear someone—often parent or teacher—throw down this clichéd gauntlet: *You can be or do anything you want, if only you try hard enough.* Mira Loma teachers and fellow students put the lie to that.

It was ice water in my face, cold and humbling. My failure lay in misunderstanding my limits. It wasn't that I didn't think I had them; it was that my cocooned life in little Nowata allowed me a false self-impression. As significant as discovering my athletic shortcomings, beginning in Nowata, was *that* awakening paled in comparison with the intellectual one in a bigger world. I thought I was smart. I got A's or B's. I scored grades ahead on standardized tests.

I can thank Mama, mostly. Her personal teaching and recognition of the value of formal early-childhood education gave me such a head start on most of my fellow students. I went over what others found to be roadblocks as if they were the low hurdles. In the late 1940s and early '50s, Nowata Public Schools did not offer kindergarten. Most learners began with first grade. Not Mama's little Stevie. She enrolled me in private kindergarten.

As valuable as the early-learning experience was, socialization was more so for an only child. Learning to share (and not bite girls).

Giving others a chance to shine. Knowing when to shut up. (I wasn't good at this.) The list goes on and on, and almost everything gave me the confidence that I could succeed. I must have missed the day overconfidence was addressed. I took from Nowata to Sacramento an overblown impression of my abilities. I got a lesson in humility.

I knew from Day One of my sophomore Spanish II class that I was overmatched. I had found a foreign language challenging even in less-demanding Nowata. Two of my three semester grades in Spanish at Nowata were B's, so it should not have come as a surprise the best I could do at Mira Loma was C+. What scared me is that I knew I had been fortunate to get that and had done so with effort more than mastery. I saw and heard the proficiency of my classmates every day. On the football field, I knew my limitations—I was never going to play in college—but I had been forced to accept I had some in the classroom, too.

Worse, if my judgment outside the classroom had been graded, I would have gotten an F. I had forgotten the lesson learned when caught "stealing" Mama's car for a Nowata joyride. That indiscretion did not result in my apprehension by the police. My understanding of what I could get away with in Nowata contributed to this, even if it did not save me from Mama, super sleuth. I had no such luck in Sacramento.

After attending a catechism class at the Catholic church, I ended up in a drag race with another member of the class. I cannot imagine what the person said to cause me to succumb to the idea of racing him in my 1957 Chevy that didn't even have all that powerful an engine. I wasn't a dragster in Nowata. I knew the backroads in and around my hometown on which even an idiot kid like me could get away with breaking the law. I had no similar knowledge in a new environment rife with dangers. I am ashamed to admit that, given my fresh estrangement from my beloved Nowata, I didn't think of the fatal consequences of a similar situation that had killed Warren Berry, a passenger in a friend's vehicle that raced into an unseen oncoming car.

Side by side—my car, naturally, on the wrong side of the street—we raced headlong at a Sacramento County Sheriff's car that the deputy noted on the citation was "forced off the road." Mama made sure to save the citation in a scrapbook of my "accomplishments," along with a letter informing Daddy that the matter of his wayward son had been referred to the Sacramento County Juvenile Probation Department for a hearing. I had had my California driver's license for a year and wouldn't have it much longer.

As I drove home that night, my mind raced faster than my opponent and I had. I was mortified. I knew what I had done was serious and that no explanation would suffice. Anything I said would sound lame. In the end, I didn't have to decide what to tell Mama and Daddy or how. As I would do later at the hearing, I threw myself on the mercy of the court and did not hide my embarrassment or regret for letting them down. My parents' response should not have surprised me—these were such good, smart people—but it did.

No one yelled. No one threatened. No one had to tell me how foolish I had been and that consequences awaited. They did not spell them out; we would go through the Juvenile Probation Department process. Because I took my offense seriously and they recognized my contrition, they did not pile on. They emphasized how out of character for me this was and that there could be no similar behavior. In other words, my lawless days had better be behind me.

The hearing officer reinforced the seriousness of my offense and the dangers a speed contest—more than 50 miles per hour in a residential neighborhood—created. He, too, seemed to appreciate my distress at being before him. Maybe he was used to more defiance and less-demanding parents. I was not trying to play the guy and could not have if I had wanted. He knew a scared 17-year-old when he saw one. He explained his choices: All included suspending my driver's license. I don't remember the exact period, but it was the lesser of his choices, and I was driving when school resumed in the fall for my senior year. I went straight straightaway.

If my arrest proved an unpleasant equivalent to losing football, two or three constructive experiences made senior year more positive than the year before. None of them involved finding myself a California girl—at least not exactly.

My grades in general and in English and social studies, in particular, began to resemble those I obnoxiously considered in Oklahoma my birthright. Still, no one was presenting me engraved invitations to the National Honor Society. I received almost as many A's (5) as B's (7) during the two semesters, which placed me on the Mira Loma honor roll. This honor roll was restricted to those receiving A's and B's, unlike others based on a numerical system that honors students whose average is 3.0 or higher. In other words, those who received, as I did in my final, senior semester, a C+ would not be eligible. (My only C other than Spanish II, this in analytical geometry, appalled Mama.) The offset was membership in the California Scholastic Federation, another academic-honors organization.

Grades, of course, do not necessarily reflect how much a student has learned or that he or she has performed admirably. I got more out of meager capabilities in Spanish II and analytical geometry—damnable C+'s—than from courses in which I received higher grades. Leonard Frizzi, chairman of history and journalism studies, never graded me less than A, but that is not why I respected him so much and credit him with changing my life. Mr. Frizzi saw something in me that someone else might have missed.

I had received encouragement as a writer from English teachers—Richard Casello, in particular—but they had had more opportunity to gauge my potential than had Mr. Frizzi. Maybe Mr. Frizzi liked me because he, like Mr. Holton, my math teacher in Oklahoma, also wrote in my yearbook that I "thought [I] knew more than [my] teachers." I know Mr. Frizzi enjoyed our interaction, because he recruited me to join the staff of the student newspaper as sports editor. Editors-in-Chief Vicki Marvelli (fall) and Ken Mauzy (spring)—class valedictorian—must have concurred. It was not a straight line from Mr. Frizzi to a more-than-40-year career as a journalist and author, but Mr. Frizzi dropped the first breadcrumbs on that path.

Two validations, one involving writing and the other "broadcasting," helped generate warm feelings I still hold for Mira Loma and those who took me in—something they did not have to do, since Mira Loma was not home, and only home is where, in fairytales, they *have* to take you in. At about the time Mr. Frizzi was broaching the idea of working for the student newspaper, I think I also tried out to be one of a two-person team that would read the Morning Bulletin over the school's public-address system at the dawn of each school day. The bulletin could get everyone off to the right start or launch a long day.

The particulars of that tryout or interview escape me, but reliability and personality seemed essential. "I wonder if Mr. Frizzi had something to do with the selection," said Karolyn Pettingell, my Bulletin partner. Maybe they decided to match an accent-free Californian with an Oklahoman's twang. The administration demonstrated an understanding of its audience by following the first Morning Bulletin broadcast team of Ralph Requa and Gerald Newman with Karolyn and me and gave us, within limits, leeway to intersperse banter with information.

"We actually changed the expectations of the Morning Bulletin," Karolyn said.

Because Mira Loma was a new high school, expectations might have been more malleable than they would have been in some place with ivy growing on the walls and moss on the faculty. We had wiggle room, and we took it. Laughter seemed a good prescription to start the day, so we played it for laughs—with limits. If you had asked our listeners, the smart money would have been on me to step over the line, not Karolyn. She was not only quick-witted but also too smart to let her cleverness trip her up. Something unexpected did it.

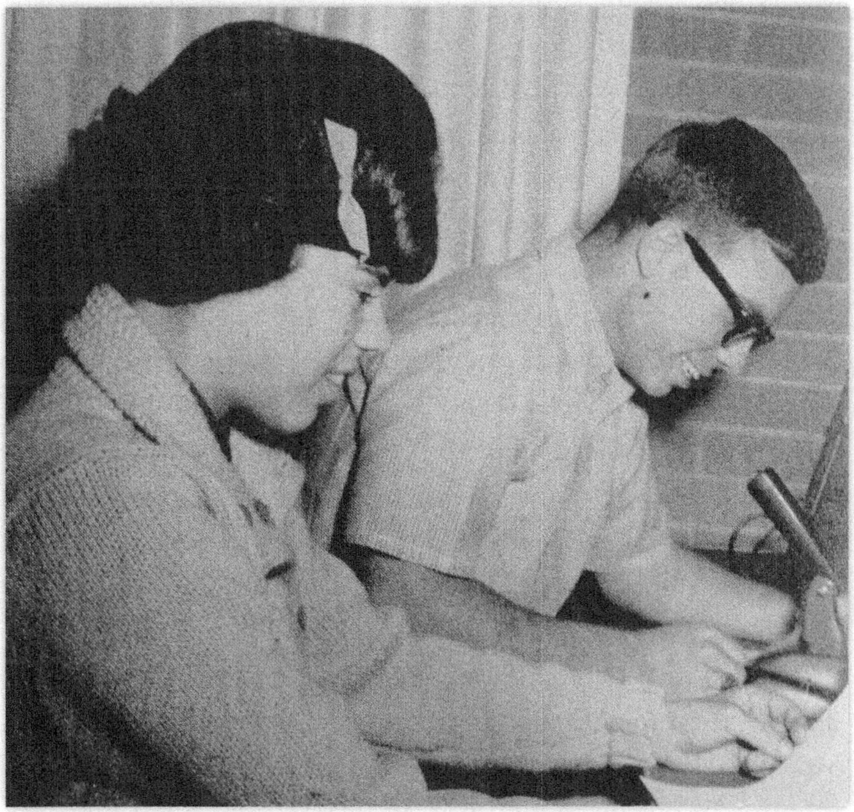

Karolyn Pettingell and Steve Love presenting the Mira Loma Morning Bulletin to the student body, 1963-64. [*Mira Loma yearbook photo*]

Practically running, she slid tardily behind the mic one morning. Her mom had driven her to school, because, she believes, she missed the bus. Our first responsibility, after greeting our unseen audience, was to invite everyone to join us in the Pledge of Allegiance. It was

Karolyn's day to lead the pledge. I should have stepped in to let her catch her breath. "I said the pledge at such breakneck speed that even [famous test pilot] Chuck Yeager would have been impressed," she said, recalling my "confusion and horror." I didn't know how to respond, but that didn't stop me. "Well," I said, "I hope everyone ducked," a reference to duck-and-cover drills we grew up with during the Cold War Fifties. The line—or Karolyn's pledge—got laughs.

Principal James Goodrich wasn't laughing. While I traipsed off to class, Karolyn was invited to Mr. Goodrich's office, where she explained her tardiness and the hurried pledge. "Steve could have done it," Mr. Goodrich replied. (Why didn't I think of that? Oh, yeah—I did but did not follow through as I should have.) After apologizing, Karolyn rose to leave.

"I'm not done yet," Mr. Goodrich said. Oops. He informed Karolyn that he could remove her as my Morning Bulletin partner but that he wanted to give her another chance. Karolyn received a five-day suspension from the Morning Bulletin. Before she returned to the mic, she had to reflect on her actions, compose an apology that she read, and not discuss her absence with anyone. That proved uncomfortable. In class, people stared at her and asked questions, including: Did you and Steve have a fight? "Imagine my awkwardness," she told me.

Karolyn was not alone in her feeling. Her suspension spoiled five days for the audience and forced me to become solo anchor. Mr. Second Fiddle was now the headliner. Without Karolyn, it felt as if I were the one being punished. We were a *team*. Suddenly, I was playing solitaire. Every time I slid all my funny chips to the center of the table, I went bust. No laughs. The laughs mattered. When Karolyn talked to those who attended the Class of '64's fiftieth reunion, people told her that what they remembered all those years later were the laughs.

"I guess we were their brain coffee in the morning," Karolyn said.

Our broadcasting experience may not have provided a direct avenue to a career, but it proved a useful substitute for speech class or debate team. Writers are called upon to respond to questions about their work, sometimes from other media. It helps to be used to a microphone stuck in your face. Typing, on the other hand—a part of the business curriculum, even at an academically challenging school—proved an expedient to writing I appreciated too little before I realized writing would be more than a high school extracurricular activity for me.

Especially during that portion of my journalism career that required writing sports columns hard on deadline from Super Bowls, NCAA basketball tournaments, and the like, the skill developed in typing class allowed me to write quickly, with the clock ticking. I didn't have to think about what my fingers were doing. They did it on their own. It may not have improved my critical thinking or brought to mind the perfect metaphor to describe the moment, but typing became as invaluable to me as a backstop to a catcher, which I had failed to become.

Since I had taken typing as a junior (1962–63), I was able to apply the benefits during my fateful senior year. In mid-October 1963, 13 Mira Loma newspaper and yearbook students attended a Central Valley Scholastic Journalism Association conference in Stockton with our advisors, Mr. Frizzi and Mr. Casello. The conference included writing contests. Sportswriters had to interview a major league baseball scout and write a story, with awards presented before we returned to campuses from Stockton to the Oregon border.

I remember sitting in an auditorium or large lecture hall for the awards ceremony and being so proud of Vicki Marvelli, our fall editor, when her editorial took second-place honors and shocked when my name was called as the sportswriting winner. The small wooden desk set—about three-by-five inches—with a gold plate designating the award, affirmed that I might have a place in sports.

During my career, I won local, state, regional, and national writing awards, including sharing in the Pulitzer Prize for Public Service, the Gold Medal—considered the Pulitzer of Pulitzers—that was awarded to the *Akron Beacon Journal* staff in 1994 for "its broad examination of local racial attitudes and its subsequent effort to promote improved communication in the community." As good as our "Question of Color" series and the consequent "Coming Together" project was, I might never have had the opportunity had it not been for that little pen set. That may sound disingenuous. How could some little high school award be compared with a Pulitzer Prize? It couldn't, if I had won an individual Pulitzer. The Pulitzer for Public Service, won by a newspaper staff, is like all those Lombardi Trophies the New England Patriots took home for winning Super Bowls: *Team victories.*

The staff of the *Matador Capers* became a journalism team—its home court, so to speak, Mr. Frizzi's Room C-1 on the sprawling Mira Loma campus. From that "office," we produced 14 biweekly issues, including special editions. Among my responsibilities as sports editor was writing a column titled "On the Bench." The initial column, on October 25, 1963, included a short roundup of the beginning of the football and cross-country seasons, and noted that the basketball team, with its first game more than a month away, was running a modified cross-country course and practicing individually each evening to prepare for the Capital Valley Conference's La Sierra, El Camino, and San Juan. I should have mentioned Encina, anchored, literally, by 6-foot-11 Jim Eakins, who, after Brigham Young University, played professionally for ten seasons, eight in the American Basketball Association, winning titles with the Oakland Oaks and New York Nets. Eakins was big stuff.

I had a unique perspective on the basketball team—and a potential conflict as sports editor. I played on that team. There were no rules against this. It was not unlike a journalist being embedded with a military unit; neither I nor they got any shots. Because I had not played as a junior, I had to endure a rigorous tryout to win a spot on the team. This was my victory. I played in a handful of games, scored a couple of points, but made no significant contribution to our success except in daily practices. It was like being freshman fodder for the Nowata football team, with an exception. I was a senior. I could literally press our better players as I had been unable to do as a Nowata freshman football player. I had not grown in size, but I had as a player. Coach Freeman had no basis of comparison. He did not feel my presence on the court gave us a better chance to win, but he did, at least, seem to appreciate my effort in practice.

Given my negative football experience as a junior, I should have been happy to make the team, but sometimes I wondered if I really had. When uniforms were distributed, mine looked different from the others. Theirs had the team nickname—Matadors—with their numbers on the front; mine had only a number. I felt like the 13th man on a 12-man team. The good thing about not playing often was my warmup suit prevented anyone from seeing my jersey. It embarrassed me. I would have paid for one that matched the others. The coach never gave a thought to how sensitive a player might be to a uniform that made him look like less than a member of the team. Maybe Coach was trying to tell Mr. "On the Bench" something.

Mira Loma senior point guard Steve Love, 1963-64. [*Mira Loma yearbook photo*]

I still have my 1964 yearbook with its basketball team photo, me kneeling at the end of the front row in my unadorned jersey. [I'm wearing a borrowed jersey in the photo included here.] Someone has drawn a smile in red ink on my face. Another yearbook signatory scrawled above my head and across teammate Hale Mosley's chest: "Bench Warmers Anonymous." Why do people who care enough to sign a yearbook deface what will be one of the few remembrances of that time? We benchwarmers have not forgotten our band of brothers, one more obviously "unlettered" than the others.

I had trouble accepting that making the team was the victory it was. Self-image, once embraced, can be difficult to abandon or alter. I tried. I was grateful to be part of a 16–8 team that finished third in a tough conference and ranked sixth in Northern California. We had at least two players go on to college basketball—All-City junior forward and MVP Gary Foster at Seattle University and Ken Stewart at California State University, Sacramento. It was rewarding to spend countless hours with good guys and friends who could play well. And, I always spelled their names correctly in stories and columns.

In the midst of basketball season, Mira Loma held elections to choose student-body officers for spring semester. Always interested in politics, I ran for boys' vice president and won. Two factors transformed me from unknown Okie transfer student to student-body officer; neither was my handsome bench-warming.

The first factor was that incumbent vice president Tim Foote chose not to run again, giving others an opportunity to experience what he would have been repeating. Had Tim run, he would have won, and the only experience that could have been gained from trying to unseat the "best personality" among the seniors was how to lose gracefully. Every position turned over from fall to spring except student-body president. Dick Azevedo, a strong leader voted most likely to succeed, along with Avril Rovick, continued his presidency.

I suspect the reason I won was the student body's familiarity with me from the Morning Bulletin. Some of the inscriptions in my yearbook indicate as much, including: "Enjoyed hearing your voice in the morning" and "Too bad I could only listen to you one year." Then, there was this: "To our bulletin reader. What's the name of that other one?"

That would be Karolyn. *The* Karolyn Pettingell, now Ainsworth. Karolyn was a verbal whirlwind with tornadic moments, but her intelligence and wit almost always protected her and her trusty sidekick from foot-in-mouth infections. Her Pledge of Allegiance suspension proved the exception for which there was no fail-safe or administration bleep button. If anything, her imagination and cleverness was even larger in print than on the air, and she took risks.

She once wrote a column suggesting how to counteract the mighty winds of March that buffeted the external expanses of our school and turned it into a wind tunnel no coed's hairdo could survive. (Karolyn's hair, it should be noted, could not be moved.) She asked fellow students to "talk to your science teachers, your math teachers, your friends and foes" and collect wind-abatement ideas, the best to be combined in a borrowed thimble from Home Ec.

Her humor was not meant to denigrate young minds, of which Karolyn's served as a fine example. After President John F. Kennedy's assassination during our senior year, she took up the torch for what she believed was his "impact on us, the youth of the nation," so often forgotten and undervalued. "In his many speeches and proposals," she wrote, "President Kennedy made it clear that we did count, and that we had just as much a place in the national government as did our parents. It terrified some people to think that one day we would assume the nation's responsibilities . . . but weren't we, after all, America's future?" Clearly neither JFK nor Karolyn was aware of a Class of '64 member attending a private boarding school, the New

York Military Academy, before his military aspirations were struck down by bone spurs that "prevented" military service but did not keep him from becoming Commander-in-Chief.

Mira Loma students who strived for exceptionalism could work with members of the National Honor Society, Karolyn Pettingell among them. They offered tutoring for 75 cents per hour. Karolyn was worth at least a nickel more. That crack epitomizes our relationship, which may have been misunderstood. On one page of the 1964 yearbook, there is a spring calendar of events and three photos, two—side by side—of identical size. One shows a classroom with two rows of seats and a boy and girl holding hands across the aisle. The other features Karolyn and me, Morning Bulletin microphone between us, and this caption: "In the spring a young man's fancy lightly turns to thoughts of love." The caption under the hand-holders reads: "This day '63-'64, with Karolyn and Steve." The captions/photos had been interchanged. Someone wrote above ours, lines pointing to our heads, "True Love." Given the time we spent together, on air and in the newspaper office, such an assumption was logical. The inscriber must have napped through our squabbles. We could fight like an old married couple. Affection is a funny thing.

I never had any lasting relationships with the girls of Mira Loma. I mostly had to date underclasswomen—*way* under. *Freshmen.* Juniors and seniors didn't find me appealing. I guess they had gotten to know me. I couldn't even make romantic inroads heading a committee, with student-body treasurer Leslie Cooper, to welcome new students who, like me, may not have had a friend, much less girlfriend. It was satisfying to have gone from a lost, unhappy new student to one in a position to help newcomers. Guess none was boyfriend-desperate.

What I did discover, though too late, was that one of the girls I admired most and who had similar interests liked me enough to ask me to walk with her at graduation. Donna Tobin was all-everything—yearbook editor, National Honor Society, majorette, and involved in multiple activities/clubs. I have no idea whether she really was interested in me, but simply to receive *any* attention from her was one of my better Mira Loma moments. Alas, I could not share the graduation procession with her. Responsibility precluded pleasure.

When Mira Loma Class of 1964 graduated, the Okie no one knew two years before joined John Jacoby—class officer as a freshman and junior, football player, jazz-band member, and on and on—in reading the names of our classmates as they came to the stage to receive diplomas. I was scared I would blow a name and practiced long and hard to avoid this. The last thing I wanted to do was spoil the moment for those who had allowed me to become one of them. With my twang twanging, I made it through—as did our accomplished class.

It did not escape me, though, that I shared the stage that day with someone who had done the thing I had wanted to do all my life: Jacoby had played the game I'd frittered away. I keep thinking all these years later about what *The New York Times's* Harvey Araton wrote on the occasion of Chris Mullin's induction in 2011 into the Naismith Basketball Hall of Fame.

Araton set up a scene from the end of Mullins's career, after he had been a St. John's All-American, Warrior star, Dream Teamer, and NBA champion with Indiana. Mullin had done so much, including addressing alcoholism, but had lost his job to the younger Jalen Rose. Instead of minutes and points, he was left with pointed questions. Even his eight-year-old son Sean had one. He wanted to know why his dad had missed a nighttime school event. Chris responded, "You know I have a game." To which Sean responded: "But you don't even play."

Araton fleshed out the vignette: "Mullin didn't know what hurt more, his son's disappointment or the fact that his children would never get to see him draining southpaw jumpers with perfect arc and spin. He shrugged, smiled, and said it was all part of moving forward and avoiding detours into the river of lost dreams."

Though no longer drowning in the river of my own lost dream, neither had I been able to reach the reassurance of shore, which, in my case, was and always would be, Nowata.

HOME AGAIN—IF ONLY IN MY HEART AND MIND

Unlike my dream, the Nowata Ironmen's had not been lost so much as unfulfilled. Charles Dugger gave voice to it years later—to win the Verdigris Valley Conference and advance to the state playoffs. That was the missing piece. Ten seasons had come and gone since Rooster Berry's 1953 Ironmen had reached the playoffs.

Nowata's seniors, my longtime teammates, made their last season together memorable, arguably as good a non-championship season as Nowata ever had. They had help, not least of which was lineman Roger Mezger, who'd arrived after I'd left; Pryor transfer Larry Elkins, a speedster who gave wingback a one-two punch; and a handful of underclassmen.

They validated our junior high successes and the promise we believed in even after our 1–8–1 sophomore season. Quarterback KB Berry and linebacker Bucky Buck became tri-captains with center Karl Middlebusher. Karl had assumed the center role I believed, perhaps mistakenly, I was too small to continue to fulfill. He was 135 pounds of wiry tenacity.

When pre-season practice began, Bucky got the attention of assistant coaches John Merryman and Glenn Welsh. They "could not believe the kind of shape" he was in from "working in the oilfield." "They said I was the best fullback they had ever heard of," Bucky recalled. I could hear him laughing in his email. "They did not know that my uncles made me run seven miles after work every night" to get home. "It was run or be late for supper."

The coaches' opinion of Bucky spoke not only to his ability but also to the strength of the Ironmen, particularly the soon-to-blossom greatness of sophomore fullback Emery Hicks. Hicks, based on his career, prep to pro, was the greatest ever to play *for* Nowata. His only challenger might be Kurt Burris, Oklahoma All-America center and linebacker, and one of only two linemen to finish second in Heisman Trophy voting—the other being Ohio State's John Hicks, who played only offense. Iowa star Alex Karras, who also finished second, played offense but was famously a defensive tackle. Born in Nowata in 1932, Burris never played for the Ironmen. His family moved to Muskogee, where he and five brothers created a family football legend that extended to OU, Buddy Burris becoming a three-time All-American after serving in World War II, the only Sooner besides linebacker Rod Shoate so honored.

Senior Bucky Buck (42) and sophomore Emery Hicks (43), arguably the best tandem of fullbacks/linebackers ever at Nowata High School. [*Nowata High School yearbook photo*]

Drafted by the Cleveland Browns in the first round in 1955, Kurt Burris opted to join the Edmonton Huskies, where he helped win two Grey Cups, the Canadian Football League's Lombardi Trophy. He was inducted posthumously into the College Football Hall of Fame in 2000; he never should have had to wait so long, much less another 15 years, for the Oklahoma Sports Hall of Fame. According to Harold Keith, in the late OU sports information director's book *Forty-Seven Straight*, he and Coach Bud Wilkinson "knew that the sports press had always ignored interior linemen, and Burris, a center, was as interior as one could get. But we decided to try anyhow and strike a blow not only for Burris but for all deserving interior linemen of the future." Burris gave the Heisman campaign much with which to work. Wilkinson said Burris was "probably more deserving of the Heisman than any other man in the nation in any position." Keith and Wilkinson wrote personal notes to every sports editor in the nation, and a hundred students, many of them Burris friends, typed and rushed them into the mail.

Voters must have been impressed, because Kurt Burris, in losing to Wisconsin fullback Alan Ameche, came closer to winning the iconic Heisman than any offensive lineman. He received 838 votes to Ameche's 1,058. In the process, Nowata ended up in Kurt Burris's biographical data, and outsiders may not differentiate between place of birth and hometown.

It took time for Emery Hicks to be fully appreciated, becoming all-everything in Oklahoma high school football by his senior season in 1965. His '65 statewide backfield cohort, selected by legendary *Oklahoman* prep writer Ray Soldan and headlined by future Heisman Trophy winner Steve Owens of Miami, ranked second only to the 1948 backfield class that included future Sooner greats Billy Vessels—the state's first Heisman winner—Eddie Crowder, and Buck McPhail. Joining Owens were Hicks, his Verdigris Valley foe, and these all-decade players: Rick Baldridge of Lawton, Robert Cutburth of Tulsa Webster, Ken Fleming of Lindsay, Mike Harper of Jenks, Doug Matthews of Picher, and Lynn Moore of Ponca City.

Hicks may not have felt on the verge of the greatness that Coach Noble recognized even as he berated him during the 1963 pre-season. Noble's old-school approach worked with some players but could prove debilitating for others. Charles Dugger sensed that, if Emery Hicks did not receive support, it might hurt him and the team.

"I pulled him aside," Dugger remembered, "put my arm around his shoulders, and told him he would get through this, that [Noble] only picked on those he knew were good."

It would have been difficult for Noble or his assistants to envision just how good Emery Hicks would be at the University of Kansas, where he became a two-time All-Big Eight linebacker (1967 and '69) and played in a 1969 Orange Bowl 15–14 loss to Penn State, in which the Jayhawks were penalized for having too many men on the field, giving the Nittany Lions a second chance at the winning two-point conversion. It probably felt to Hicks as if the Ironmen had 12 coaches on the field, all grabbing his face mask and screaming at the young future NFL draft choice who would have a five-year pro career in the CFL and the World Football League.

"Coach was horrible to him," Dugger said. "In practice, he was always on him. It was so sad." Through it all, Hicks endured and added much to the team, but it was the senior Ironmen who were most responsible for an 8–2 season, including Frank Stebbing, 148-pound guard who stepped into the offensive line when the Oklahoma Secondary Schools Activities Association ruled junior Jim Heath ineligible prior to the first game.

Heath was my doppelgänger, a situational likeness whom I never knew yet one who modeled what would have been my dark football future had I tried to wangle a return to Nowata alone. Heath, according to a report in the *Nowata Star*, had attended Nowata High School for "a short time" when his parents lived in Nowata the year before. The family, however, moved on to Texas and then California—sounds familiar—for his father's work. At some point, Heath and a brother returned to Nowata to live with their grandparents. The school asked the OSSAA to grant him eligibility under a hardship rule, explaining the father's transitory construction job and the negative effect on his children, who had to constantly change schools. The OSSAA ruled against Heath, announcing he would have to live a year with the grandparents before he would be eligible. [When his parents returned to Nowata before the fifth game of the season, Heath got to play in, appropriately, a homecoming victory.]

My situation would have been less resolvable. I had no grandparent in Nowata with whom to live, and even if the Berrys had wanted to take me into their home for a longer period, it would have been both an unreasonable burden on them and would not have made me eligible, because we were not related—unless the OSSAA allowed for my love for them. Since I had retreated into my protective, no-Nowata-news cocoon, I did not know about Heath but understand how he must have felt. I would have done anything to again join my teammates.

They got along quite well without me, and though it was Richard Nash (All-State and All-Conference), Clarence Smith (All-Conference), and Gary Mezger (All-Conference) who received the most recognition, I know the leadership of KB Berry, Bucky Buck, and Karl Middlebusher contributed mightily to the success. [The play of KB, Bucky, Karl, and fellow seniors Frank Stebbing, Fred Barrowman, and Ronnie Kincaide merited honorable mention All-Conference.] Though Charles Dugger did not make that list, he was what Ironmen football was all about—effort, teammates, and selflessness.

Years later, talking about that time, Charles shared a story that explains why I missed football and these teammates. As with so many stories from those days, KB was at its heart because of his own generous heart. Charles, playing receiver, had worked his way open on one of Nowata's comparatively rare pass plays, only to have his focus waver. KB threw the ball perfectly, but Charles, moving fast, physically and mentally, made a classic mistake: He took his eye off the ball in order to initiate a move that might generate extra yards.

Instead, he muffed the catch and got nothing. "I felt so bad," Charles said. "I felt like I had let KB down."

KB could have been angry. In the huddle, he could have criticized Charles for the drop. He didn't. "KB wasn't critical," Charles said. He was patient. He was supportive. He was everything a quarterback and team leader should be. "He made you feel as if you can do better." KB made all of us feel that way—especially me, when we were sophomores and I was trying to learn to be a fullback. "He never had a bad word to say about anyone," Charles said.

His captaincy, election as a class officer, and choice as most popular boy in the Class of 1964 did not come out of the clear blue Oklahoma sky. He set out to be a person a proud family could be proud of. If one word describes KB, it is *winner*, a singular characterization based not only on the Ironmen's growth and improved record under KB's guiding hand but also one made more remarkable by the fact he was not as physically gifted as either of his star older brothers.

From a season-opening 20-yard touchdown pass to junior end Doyle Hayes to the last TD pass of his career in the finale against Miami, the player Bucky Buck called "our little leader" stood tall. He inspired others. In that final game, Charles Dugger, like KB, refused to concede and had the satisfaction of putting bullish future Heisman Trophy winner Steve Owens on the ground. "My most shining moment," Charles said. But it was KB who was the beating heart of the Ironmen. He drove them to the Top 10 of Class A with a 5–0 season start that included—*finally*—a 38–8 trouncing of Vinita on the strength of four Richard Nash TD runs.

When the challenges came, KB helped the Ironmen surmount them, sometimes directly, sometimes indirectly, sometimes both. After losing—*yet again*—to Claremore, 34–14, in a battle of unbeatens, KB Berry, team leader, inspiration, and conscience, assured the Ironmen would survive the hangover of a tumble out of the Class A

Top 10. Early in a non-conference game at Sapulpa, another larger school, KB rolled out and surprised the Chieftains by finding Smith alone in the end zone with an 8-yard pass, to which Nash added a 2-point conversion. The defense made that 8–6 lead stand up. Had the Ironmen lost, the season might have withered. KB Berry was having none of that.

After an easy 24–8 victory at Pryor, KB again rescued his team in perhaps the finest moment of his finest season. The Ironmen, with two-way junior lineman Roy Miller playing on an injured knee, trailed the Broken Arrow Tigers 16–14 with 7:40 remaining. The *Nowata Star* reported that KB Berry "coolly called the shots" as he took his team 75 yards in 13 plays on which he, Nash, Smith, and Emery Hicks "methodically overpowered the Tigers." Nash ended the drive from the 6-yard line for a 20–14 victory, the third in three consecutive road games.

With 17 seniors playing their last game—and another far, far away in California—Nowata had a chance to finish second to Claremore in the Verdigris Valley with a victory on Ironman Memorial Field against a Miami without eight players suspended for missing a training film. It didn't matter on this cold, windy November night. After shutting out the Wardogs in the first period, the Ironmen beat themselves with penalties, fumbles, and KB throwing an interception to halt a drive. One of the penalties—clipping—nullified KB's career-long run. Breaking through a mass and then veering to the sideline, he went 87 yards to score, as a Richard Nash block took out two Wardogs at the 50. Post-penalty, the gain was 5 yards.

KB's second-half 9-yard touchdown pass to Larry Fishpaw prevented a shutout but could not erase what must have been an unrelieved feeling of failure against both Claremore and Miami. No championship. No playoff. It was as if nothing had changed during the Class of '64's three varsity seasons. Yet, so much had. The little team from the smallest town had done more than it had a right to do, and my dying lament will be that I could not be a part of it.

KB Berry received a Harmon Grant from the Pearl M. and Julia J. Harmon Foundation, which Nowata oil and gas entrepreneur Claude C. Harmon had established in 1962. The foundation honored his first wife, Pearl McCoy Harmon, who died in 1944, and his second wife, Julia Jasper Harmon, whom he married in 1947. The grant altered KB's life.

He had longed to follow in the footsteps of brother Chuck, who had played at Fort Scott Junior College. In December of 1963, he received a letter from Howard Mahanes, who had coached two-time Greyhound captain Chuck, expressing interest in KB and Nowata's All-State tailback Richard Nash. Mahanes asked KB to arrange for Coach Noble to send him game films, if KB was interested in being one of the 15 out-of-state players the Kansas conference allowed each team. Time was of the essence in Fort Scott's limited out-of-state recruiting, Mahanes wrote, because "we must get them early and the best we can find." KB still wanted to play football.

"I believe that the administrator of the [Harmon] grant," Chuck Berry remembered, "convinced my dad that (KB) needed to go to a four-year school." So it amounted to football or the Harmon Grant. Roy Berry wanted what he believed best for his son, and the Harmon Grant seemed a surer path to a college degree than football, for a 148-pound quarterback who might have to change positions and had no guarantee of a scholarship beyond junior college. The decision must have been excruciating to someone who loved the game so much.

"It was a mistake," Bucky said. "KB was not through with football. He just had a chance with the Harmon Grant to be able to afford college." If in a different way than I had, KB was losing football, and, with the loss came another cost. "I had always been there for him, and [he] for me," Bucky said. KB drew others to him, as he had drawn me. After I left Nowata, KB often went to Bucky's home on game days, and Bucky's mom, Bonnie Lee, would find another steak to cook with taters, even if she had not known KB would be sharing Bucky's pre-game meal. To Bucky, it went without saying: "We had been each other's support for a long time."

Then everything changed. Bucky joined Richard Nash and Clarence Smith to play for Fort Scott, and KB, on his Harmon Grant, attended Northeastern State College in Tahlequah, where brother Rooster once had played so well the game KB loved and no longer had.

It was the beginning of the end.

WHEN FOOTBALL IMITATES REEL LIFE

To understand and appreciate what football can mean to teenagers who play the game in towns that love it, consider it from a different angle: Oblique, the indirect or obtuse, blunt or not sharply focused. Look through a different lens. Filter the familiar through others' eyes. The images may be shocking but also sharper. Sometimes, too sharp.

On the West Texas plains, where those who buy the flat-earth theory probably first bought in, a person can see forever, if sand and grit don't cloud the vision, as in Odessa. When a stranger from the East rode into town in 1988 to live through a football season with phenomenal Permian High School and launch a multimedia *Friday Night Lights* franchise, universal appreciation was not a result for H.G. "Buzz" Bissinger's 1990 book.

Bissinger fell in love with the Permian players, especially the flawed. But, as one might expect of a Pulitzer Prize-winning journalist, he did not ignore the darkest corners of Odessa and its schools—the skewed values that elevated football above education, the racism that had leached in and made black players and others of color equal only if they ran fast, hit hard, and stayed healthy. *Friday Night Lights* shone equally on the good and bad Odessa and its football.

Sports Illustrated celebrated the book in 2002 in "The Top 100 Sports Books of All Time." It ranked No. 4, best of football. In Odessa, they had expected the gridiron equivalent of the feel-good *Hoosiers*, the 1996 film written by Angelo Pizzo and inspired by little Milan High School's 1954 Indiana State Basketball Championship. Odessans thought Bissinger's representation sandbagged them. Though players vouched for the correctness, the truth hurt. Some in the community threatened physical payback if Bissinger returned to sign books. He and his publisher took the threat seriously and cancelled.

It was not until 14 years later, when the movie, co-written and directed by Peter Berg, Bissinger's cousin, debuted, that Odessa got a version of the 1988 season to its liking. The town's history of segregation and its latent racism were whitewashed; football was the sole focus. Based on Bissinger's book, the movie took dramatic liberties. Though the Panthers and their MOJO failed to add to Permian's state championships [four then, with two added in 1989 and 1991], the movie allowed them to lose to Dallas Carter—insult of insults, a virtually all-black school—not in the semifinals at the University of Texas stadium in Austin but in the final that Berg depicted being played in Houston's Astrodome.

By the time the *FNL* franchise morphed into a television series [2006 to 2011], with Bissinger not directly involved, the dramatization had further evolved—and mostly for the better. In 76 episodes, the TV series more fully developed its characters, if fictionally, and tackled issues the movie ignored—racism and football's inherent dangers. Berg, again involved as director and writer, got it right, with substantial contributions from writer-producer-showrunner Jason Katims. The TV series won even greater critical acclaim, if not the large audience it deserved. By turning Odessa into the fictionalized Dillon and filming in Austin, Odessa was more removed from the blowback of this *Friday Night Lights'* hard truths.

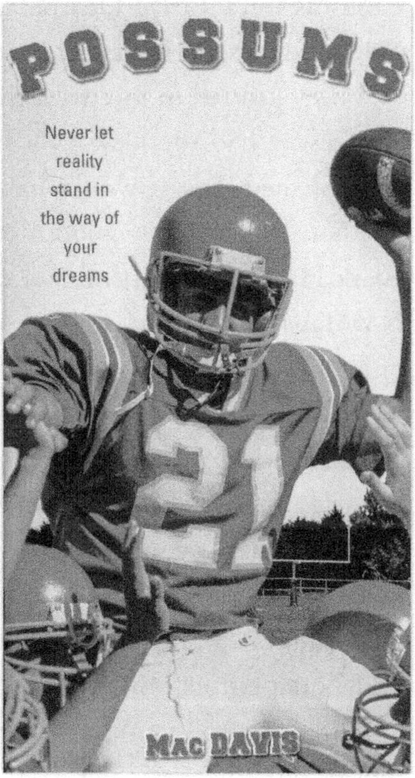

Nowata was the setting for *Possums*, the movie. [*Photo courtesy the author*]

Odessa is not the only town to quarrel with a depiction it refuses to recognize or does not want to see. In 1997, when line producer Bob Roath and writer-director J. Max Burnett scouted sites for a high school football fable set in Burnett's home state of Oklahoma, the logical choice might have been Idabel, where Burnett once lived. The movie's working title was *Idabel Possums* [real town, phony nickname]. Either Idabel rejected the idea or was itself rejected. In any case, *The Oklahoman* newspaper in Oklahoma City reported that communities lined up for the film, despite what could have been construed as a negative storyline: The Possums were losers, the anti-Permian. They had not won in 25 years and had not scored in thirteen. An Odessa welcoming committee would have greeted the filmmakers bearing arms, hearts brimming with resistance. Nowata, on the other hand, embraced them.

Nowata had an open mind and sharp eye for a heartwarming story with positive afterglow. Besides, the money Hollywood throws around, even in a low-budget production like *Possums*, couldn't be ignored. Nowata, like Odessa, had lived through the good times and bad of a boom-or-bust oil economy. Unlike Odessa, with its deeper, richer Permian-basin oil patch, the shallow-well oil fields surrounding Nowata had mostly played out by the time the Oklahoma Film Commission's Tanya Deatherage escorted Roath and Burnett to Nowata on a scouting trip.

"They just fell in love with the town," Deatherage said.

Nowata had the look. Not fancy. Not sophisticated. Certainly not polished. But it would have been easy for the filmmakers to envision two or three good ol' boys sittin' on a bench in front of Clark Hardware whittlin' and chewin' the fat. Equally important, Nowatans have a knack for the soft-sell. Small towns lack the leverage or temperament to be pushy.

Nowata City Manager Nancy Shipley and Chuck Price Jr., who owned the historic Savoy Hotel, laid the groundwork that brought Burnett and Roath to town and, it seems, sold themselves and a feeling of community friendliness after the visitors arrived. Price, who also made commercials and spoke the filmmakers' language, had worked with Shipley to prepare a Nowata promotional package sent to the Oklahoma Film Commission.

The film-production company saw Nowata businesses as ideal movie "sets," in particular, Clark Hardware, whose proprietor Will Clark—Mac Davis starring—also described Possums football games on fictitious radio station KRIG, a set in the Savoy in a no-radio-station town.

"Members of the production team came here quietly and unannounced and talked with the people of Nowata," Price told some seventy-five community leaders, according to *Nowata Star* Managing Editor Bill Foster. "The people of Nowata are the reason why this community was chosen as a shooting location for the movie. [Production team members] were extremely impressed by the courteousness and friendliness of Nowata's citizens."

The response to Hollywood-types, especially in California, could range from ho-hum to hostility because of filming inconveniences. Familiarity can breed contempt. "Movies are one [of] a zillion in California," Roath told the *Star*. A movie set in Nowata, with town and countryside as co-stars, is a once-in-a-lifetime happening. "People here," Roath said, "are treating us nice. It's great to be among friends and family."

Burnett, a Keystone, Oklahoma, native, graduated from the University of Oklahoma. Nowata may not be Norman, OU's home, but when everything was said and done, the two communities shared roles, one the making of *Possums,* the other its launch. Burnett was gratified. "I enjoy," he said, "being able to come back home to shoot a movie."

Burnett's script read as tailor-made for Nowata, if not a depiction of its successful football history. The real Nowata Ironmen were not the losers the Possums were portrayed to be. They had not played dead for years. If fables humanize animals, the writer's choice of Possums was inspired. The team's troubles reflected a deteriorating small town, so desperate for an economic shot in the arm that its fictional mayor Charlie Lawton (Andrew Prine) leads a campaign to abandon football, which would allow a large retailer—Maxi Mart (think Wal-Mart)—to buy the land on which the football stadium stands, tear it down, and build a store.

To Will Clark, broadcasting Possums football is not a second job but his first love. He treasures the team and its players. He grew up sneaking off to the family barn to do pretend-broadcasts. He will let no man put asunder the Possums, especially not his nasty neighbor the mayor. After he loses a fight to save the team, Clark reinvents the Possums, with a gentle push from Jake Malloy (Greg Coolidge), Nowata student and would-be quarterback.

In the pantheon of football movies, especially those about the game as played in high school, *Friday Night Lights* holds an elevated position, won with authenticity, on and off the field. It does so, in part, by focusing tightly on the quarterback and hewing closely to its primary source, Buzz Bissinger's book. Unlike in the National Football League, the quarterback may not *be* the franchise but he plays a critical role in his team's outcomes. This holds true, whether for the real-life Mike Winchell in Odessa or a fictional Matt Saracen in Dillon. Both quarterbacks are afflicted with challenging home lives and self-doubt that manifests itself in a reserve that can slip into shyness. Jake Malloy knows such dysfunction and worse. He doesn't like to be hit.

Will Clark began unearthing this piece of Jake's sketchy back story when, one evening, he found Jake tossing a football on the abandoned field at Ironman Memorial Stadium. Jake had moved to town the previous year, his mother waitressing at Fields, modeled on Bliss Restaurant, iconic Nowata landmark and gathering place. Jake did not play football before the mayor's petition drive set townsfolk against one another and ripped the game away in a town-hall vote. The conflict pitted neighbor against neighbor, including Will and Charlie Lawton, who enjoyed bringing his dog over to poop on Clark's lawn, much as Charlie did on Will's life.

Will Clark had been a professional sportscaster before returning to Nowata to take over his father's hardware store. With the Possums broadcasts, vocation became avocation, one Will used eloquently to explain what a football team can mean to small-town America.

"This whole thing," he said at the town-hall vote, "isn't about me. And it's not about you. It's not about some crummy football team. It's about cool nights and autumn leaves and smoke comin' out of chimneys. It's about those kids going out there every Friday night and playing their guts out." He painted his small town, bright and sharp. He wanted it to send an equivalent message, not one that said, "We're giving up."

That message was not the Nowata I knew, not the one Jake Malloy came to know. He supported the team and the game he feared to play yet loved. When, the next fall, Clark encountered Jake on the field throwing a football, he recognized that love and the promise of Malloy's arm. He saw again what even bad football had given a good town before it had forgotten, worn down by the disappointment of losing.

Clark offered to turn on the stadium lights, which still could light up the night. As Jake threw, Clark learned Jake had attended every game the previous season. That confused Clark. If Jake was into football, why wasn't he on the team? Playing football for Nowata was, I can testify, a rite of passage.

Will Clark tried to draw out Jake, to understand. Jake remained reticent until man and boy fell into a comfortable companionability under the Friday Night Lights, and Jake told Will he had enjoyed listening to his broadcasts: "It made losing almost kind of exciting." This was the "kind of" compliment a Nowata kid might offer an adult—sweet if backhanded.

Inspired, Will Clark has a wild idea and *Possums* a turning point. Will drives to radio station KRIG, Jake in tow, sits down at a microphone and launches into a sports re-creation common in yesteryear. He picks up the season and imagines the fictional Possums scoring a comeback against fictional Marysville, a victory made strikingly real by Will's description.

KRIG owner Earl (Rodney Lay) bursts into his station, sputtering and demanding to know of Will what "the hell" he is doing perpetrating this fantasy. Clark responds by explaining his logic and listener phone calls that supported it: "There are people who want to hear the games. *The town needs a team to support.*" Even if it's imaginary.

The day after the Possums on-air rebirth, Will Clark's *raison d'être*, Jake Malloy reports to Clark Hardware for a job Will offers.

Little by little, boss and employee, man and boy, open up and gain an understanding of each other, a fantasy football team their bond. Jake even risks offering his boss constructive criticism, reminding him he must "get the players' names straight" if he is going to continue his broadcasts. Will gets it. The Possums may be a fiction, but the players are fact. They're Jake's classmates—real boys with proud mamas and daddies.

They are real, if in a different way from people whom Buzz Bissinger encountered in Odessa and at Permian High School, people who cared so deeply about football they transformed it into a grotesque. In each of its subsequent forms—especially the television series—dramatic liberties seep into the *Friday Night Lights* built on a Bissinger foundation.

Will Clark seems to understand it is incumbent upon him to be both accurate *and* imaginative. He blends fact and fiction. Some of Nowata's opponents, like Marysville, do not exist; others do—though they would not be playing Nowata because they are either too distant [Hobart] or too large [6A Enid, 5A Stillwater]. It is, however, *Possums'* characters that elevate the movie from fantasy to enhanced reality. They experience the very problems that beset families in towns, large and small.

Cracks in Will Clark's marriage show when, without consulting his wife, he mortgages their house to pay for airtime to broadcast the imaginary Possums games, popular with the very townsfolk who killed off their real team. Clark is estranged from his son, John, former Possums star now Bartlesville assistant football coach, because he feels guilt for pushing John and the resultant injury that undermined a college scholarship. And then, there is Jake Malloy, whose strong arm looks like a quarterback's, when there are no pass rushers with blood in their eyes and malice in their hearts.

"I just don't like getting hit," Jake reiterates.

But football *is* getting hit.

"I just don't," Jake says. "OK?"

It was not a question but an emphatic nonresponse. Clark's questions remained. Had Jake been physically abused? Where is his father? When Will shows Jake how to take a hit without injury, Jake flinches and flees. In a broadcast, Will inserts Jake into an imaginary scenario of replacing an injured quarterback. That goes better. Jake pulls off a devious fake handoff, spins into "the old quarterback draw," and runs for a touchdown. Classmates who heard the broadcast applaud Jake at school. Even Sarah, whose heart Jake seeks to win, though she can't remember his name, congratulates him. Others are less impressed.

Mayors from towns beaten by a nonexistent team phone Nowata Mayor Charlie Lawton to read him the riot act. Already infuriated with Will and KRIG owner Earl, Lawton demands Will stop pretending Nowata has a football team. Earl tells the mayor to go push a rope, which is how people talk in Nowata, a vernacular for which Burnett had an ear.

"It's a lie," Charlie Lawton argues.

"It's not a lie," Earl explains. "It's like a fantasy, of sorts."

A fantasy, until it wasn't.

Since it is his dime and the townsfolk enjoy winning, fantasy or not, Will Clark imagines the Possums all the way to their first state playoffs. Parents swell with pride as they brag about their sons and the positions they [don't] play. Even Elizabeth, Will's sensible wife, has been won over. When Will, separated from Elizabeth, vice principal at Nowata High, tells her he wants to end the broadcasts and come home, Elizabeth, who has been surreptitiously listening to his broadcasts, objects. She points out he should finish what he started.

And so Will Clark continues to crank up the Possums in his mind, his tales reaching a growing audience. Television sportscasters pick up the story of "a winning season for an imaginary team" and put fascinating little Nowata on the map. For Jake and Sarah, finally dating, Nowata is a place of such familiarity it makes them long for escape after graduation.

As they talk on a bench in front of Clark Hardware, which also sells animal feed, Sarah, eyes twinkling, asks: "Do you always take your dates to feed stores?" Jake, happy as a hog in slop, responds in kind, suggesting it is a perfect ending to a Nowata evening out.

When they turn serious, Sarah asks Jake what he is going to do after graduation. Because he doesn't know, Jake answers her question with the same question.

"I've grown up here most of my life," she says. "And all I know is that I want to do something exciting. Maybe politics. Or writing." Jake's path feels less certain. His response hints at a darkness that prevents him from playing quarterback. "For a long time," he admits, "I thought when I graduate I would just jump on a bus and disappear." *Disappear? From what?* "So what do you think now?" Sarah asks, a blush of affection on the couple.

And now, Jake says he is just happy to be sitting on Clark's bench with her.

"Me, too," Sarah sighs, with a warmth that can change lives.

Though imaginary, the scene is one that has been played out in Nowata and countless small towns since time immemorial, young people discovering perspective, their little worlds shifting suddenly and dramatically when they find themselves with the right person.

The production of *Possums* altered perceptions of those who participated as extras during filming of a climactic scene born from anger of a true state champion overshadowed by a shadow champion. When champion Prattville shows up in Nowata, one of the more recognizable men in Oklahoma climbs off the team bus to call out Will Clark and challenge the Possums to a confrontation out of *Gunfight at the OK Corral*—football teams as weapons.

Prattville's coach is played by Barry Switzer, whose Oklahoma Sooners won three NCAA Championships before he took the Dallas Cowboys to a Super Bowl victory. Only three coaches have ever done such a thing. Despite difficulties to overcome, Switzer tells Will Clark he would bring his team back in two weeks. Even then, if Clark could pull together a team, he might not have a stadium. It was to be demolished to make way for the Maxi Mart, and the mayor refused to delay construction. The real Nowata knew the upheaval a "Wal-Mart" could bring. A real one came to town, prompting closure of businesses, only to pack up a few years later and leave Nowata stunned. The Maxi Mart problem was less intractable, magically disappearing but leaving another: the Possums were imaginary champions, the Prattville Pirates real ones.

"My god, Elizabeth," Will says to his wife, "what have I done? *What have I done?*"

Levelheaded Elizabeth has a solution: Call son John, a real coach. Her logic is offset by a father's bullheadedness and guilt. Meanwhile, Mayor Lawton resorts to fearmongering to pressure Clark to call off the game: "I don't know if Nowata can withstand another disappointment," he says. "If you go ahead with this game, you are going to destroy what's left of the Nowata spirit. You have built this fantasy team that our boys cannot possibly live up to."

Clark understands Nowata is tougher than that and that the game would be about trying and believing in a fantasy. "Show a little faith in your town, for God's sake, Charlie," Clark responds. "For the first time in a long, long time, this town believes it can win."

Whatever hope there is depends on Will swallowing his pride, letting go of his self-blame—the worst kind—and asking for help. John gladly gives it. With John taking charge of the Possums' practices, they begin to look *almost* like a team. "Almost" is one of this movie's strengths, a fantasy that refuses to wallow in fantasy. For all its richly deserved critical acclaim, the football portions of the *Friday Night Lights* television series can be off-putting for the constant miracles quarterback Matt Saracen helps the Dillon Panthers pull off. Saracen, unlike his Odessa Permian model, Mike Winchell, never met a mountain he couldn't conquer. His end-of-big-game Hail Marys, air or ground, appeared blessed by the football gods.

Jake Malloy is not that kind of quarterback. Though he has joined the resurrected Possums—roadkill brought back to life?—he cannot pretend to be something he is not when cheerleader girlfriend Sarah asks him at a practice what position he plays.

"I hold the ball," Jake says sheepishly.

"You're a holder?" Sarah asks.

It is difficult to impress a girl with this football nugget. He adds that he is backup QB.

The knowledgeable Sarah appreciates Jake's honesty, but his position is his position.

"You're a holder," she says, laughing, though not unkindly.

From the look of it, all Nowata turned out for the cinematic showdown—Possums vs. Prattville—planned strategically for when the real Ironmen were playing host to a game. Movie extras bolstered the Ironmen crowd and remained for the Possums filming. It was a long night, by all accounts. It got longer for the Possums after a surprisingly robust first half, during which a Prattville fumble, caused by the hard-hitting Possums, prompted announcer Will Clark to revel in the moment—"these kids are scrapping over the ball like ducks on a junebug"—of holding Prattville to a 6–0 halftime lead over the fantasy-champions-come-to-life. This inspired Switzer to howl like a hyena as he explains to his team: "You stink. They're embarrassing us. I can't go back to Prattville—*we can't go back to Prattville*—if we don't win this game."

Chastised, the Pirates play as if they had suddenly remembered their opponent "ain't played a football game all year long." During a timeout, with Prattville leading 27–0, Will Clark goes to the sideline. He praises his son's coaching in front of the team, compliments the players' heart, and suggests they ignore the scoreboard—perhaps the ultimate fantasy.

Instead, what some offensive linemen ignored was blocking. A Pirate crashed into quarterback Paul Rowlett (Ian Bennett) as he tried to find a receiver. "What a hit!" Clark marvels and reaches into his toolbox of hardware-store metaphors. "He whopped him like a ten-penny finishing nail hit with a greasy ballpeen hammer."

Rowlett, knee injured, struggles to get up. The Possums punt but get the ball back by picking off a Prattville pass. Seventeen seconds remain. When backup quarterback Jake Malloy comes in for Rowlett, Clark tells his listeners it's Jake's "first appearance tonight." It also was Jake's first appearance *ever*—the quarterback averse to being hit. His face mask offered a clue. It looked like a lineman's bird cage.

The beauty and power of Burnett's script, which deserves attention more than 20 years later because *Possums* [I have a VHS copy and saw it on Netflix] made only a blink-of-an-eye appearance in even Oklahoma theaters. Burnett, an artist with words, paints his small-town beautifully but avoids overreaching on the field, as *Friday Night Lights*, movie and TV series, did. In those dying seconds of the "championship" showdown, Prattville delivers Jake a crushing blow. Lying on the ground, no doubt remembering why he did not like to be hit, Jake spots Sarah on the sideline. She is smiling at him. Resurrected, he answers "I'm fine" when quizzed about how he is feeling. With only seven seconds left, he demonstrates his sense of humor has not been knocked out of him. He asks teammates if they can give him "a little more protection." When assured they can, Jake notes, cynically: "I hope it's better than the last time."

With solid protection and a lilting musical score hinting climax, Jake reaches back and flings a perfect pass to a receiver, open deep. It's a short distance to the end zone, where the Possums had not visited for years. As Will Clark blubbers excitedly to his audience—*Touchdown, Possums! Touchdown, Possums!*—Nowata fans and players react as if they *have* won the championship, not lost, 27–6. This befuddles Barry Switzer. He turns to an official:

"Hey, Ref, we won, didn't we?"

Though the official assured Switzer that Prattville had, in this fable, Nowata was the real winner. In the press box, Will Clark is shaking his head in wonder, while down on the field, his wife and son embrace, and a family is put back together not by magic but by a son helping his father craft a believable ending to a season of imagination. The Possums did not have to win; scoring for the first time in 14 years was enough to bring John Clark home to coach his alma mater in the stadium that his father had helped to save from evil Maxi Mart.

There was not even a feel-good ending, much less victory, when Wal-Mart came to town in 1982 only to abandon Nowata a dozen years later in what it euphemistically termed a "consolidation" rather than a "closing." Wal-Mart had recently erected a sign that claimed, "The rumors are false: Wal-Mart will be here always." In 1995 *The New York Times* published a Peter T. Kilborn postmortem on Nowata, which Wal-Mart left for dead after the murder of its Mainstreet businesses. Businesses come and go, but this is the *modus operandi* of the Bentonville, Arkansas, behemoth. Nowata responded with anger not only at Wal-Mart but also itself. It had welcomed the big-box store for its greater choices and lesser prices. But the cost proved too high. *Possums* filmmakers left a much better taste in the mouths of Nowatans than did Oklahoma-born Sam Walton, whose company also ditched Pawhuska and other Northeastern Oklahoma towns.

When *Possums* debuted in 1999, *Variety*, the movie-industry bible, pegged it as a "sweet-tempered sports flick [that] has 'sleeper' written all over it." Nowatans, however, could not stroll downtown to see it at the Rex or Luxor, two theaters on which I grew up in the 1950s. Both had become victims of the economic struggles. Instead of Nowata for its first Oklahoma showing, the movie, which had played the Sundance Film Festival, settled for Norman, where Max Burnett attended college. That's where Bob Colon, longtime sportswriter for *The Oklahoman*, caught it.

Colon claimed to have "seen more high school football games in the past 35 years than most people in Oklahoma." He was dean of Oklahoma high school sportswriting. The theater must not have known. When he arrived for a 7:20 p.m. showing of *Possums*, it was sold out. Not one to throw his weight around, Bob purchased a ticket for 9:40 and caught another flick in the meantime. It was worth the wait. He liked *Possums* so much he returned the next day to see it again. "This is a great movie," Colon wrote, "and would have been worth watching even if the former University of Oklahoma and Dallas Cowboys coach weren't playing a semi-key role."

What won over Colon, even though he recognized some "holes"—Nowata "wouldn't have been playing" the largest schools, "most nicknames are bogus," and "some of the towns or schools don't exist"—was that the movie captured "the spirit of high school football in small towns in Oklahoma." That spirit may have waned, even in Nowata, where, in the second decade of the twenty-first century, it had become difficult to get more than 20 players out for the team, but when I grew up and when *Possums* was made in 1997, the spirit glowed brightly.

"It's about towns that drop their program and wish they still had a team," Colon wrote. "There is nothing like football Friday nights in Oklahoma. From Guymon to Idabel, from Nowata to Mangum. It's about being at an eight-man game in Paoli or Cashion or a traditional powerhouse like Ada or Jenks. Oklahomans look forward to fall, to those Friday nights where you follow the lights to the game." It was *the thing* that brought my family together.

If before *Possums* Mac Davis did not appreciate the deep feeling for high school football that gushes from Oklahoma, he did afterward. That understanding sprang from Nowata. His character, Will Clark, stood in stark contrast to one he played when the singer-songwriter made his film debut in the funny, raunchy *North Dallas Forty* that evolved from a novel by Dallas Cowboy receiver Peter Gent. Gent was a good receiver during his five-year National Football League career, a better basketball player at Michigan State, where he played no football, and tone-sharp writer who mined a vein similar to Jim Bouton's *Ball Four*.

No less an authority on winning football prose than the late, great Dan Jenkins (*Semi-Tough*) described Gent's NFL, populated by drinkers, dopers, sex fiends, and other assorted violent miscreants, as "relentlessly funny and brutally true. Nothing short of brilliant." Of course, one man's brilliant can be another's "good novel and better movie," as Michael Oriard suggested in addressing the lasting effect of *North Dallas Forty* in *Deadspin* following Gent's death in 2011 at the age of 69. "The novel," Oriard concluded, "is darker, a long gaze into the abyss. Hollywood had to humanize it." If Gent's character, Phil Elliott, played by Nick Nolte, is at the heart of this humanizing, sidekick Seth Maxwell (Davis), a fictionalized Don Meredith, quarterback, leader, and occasional contributor of sanity, also plays a role. The Seth Maxwell-Will Clark characters seem a dichotomy but both are trying to hold something together—Maxwell a team, Clark a town and his own life in this small, special place.

Possums never received the attention of either *Friday Night Lights* or *North Dallas Forty,* which can be attributed in part to the fact *Possums* began as a screenplay, not as a controversial book, the acclaim for which made for a bigger splash in Hollywood and deeper-pockets funding. There were those, however, closer to the movie's roots and its fruition, who recognized the difference between *Possums* and depictions of high school football found elsewhere.

"If the raunchy teen hit *Varsity Blues* shows us the darker, cruder devils of high school football, then *Possums* neatly shines a light on its better angels," wrote Dennis King for the *Tulsa World*. "Resolutely upbeat and whimsical and reflecting a can-do attitude that speaks to the unifying power of school sports on small-town populations." *Possums* may be "specific in its locale" but is "universal in its ideals." Hope can light up the most struggling of small towns.

As *Possums* made the rounds, from Seattle Film Festival to Sundance Festival to USA Film Festival in Dallas, it gained a modicum of attention and generally laudatory notices but did not attract the financial backing that would have allowed for broad theatrical release. Instead, it made its way back to Oklahoma, first Norman and then Tulsa. As good as Max Burnett's script was and as—oxymoron alert—believable as his small town turned out, given its fantastical football context, Burnett told the *Tulsa World* writer John Wooley in 1999, "I've learned that it's easy to make a film. What's hard is to market it."

If *Possums* had been a record, it would have had difficulty getting play because it did not fit the strictures of the radio-station playlist. When it comes to creativity, breadth and versatility are often not virtues. Ask Taylor Swift. When she crossed over from country to pop, some people could not wrap their minds around the fact that greatness is greatness. "It's a real audience film," Burnett discovered of *Possums*. "The ending has gotten standing ovations, and people seem to enjoy that kind of setting [theaters' shared experience]. But, you know, it's not a teen film [though it is]. And there's no talking dog, so people out here (in Hollywood) don't consider it a family film [though it does, in fact, showcase Max the Pooping Dog played by Oskie Switzer, Barry Switzer's granddog]. And it's not an adult film that deals with heavy issues [though what are the losses of a small town's economic base and football, if not heavy issues?].

"It's just a feel-good type of film, a general-audience film, and, to Hollywood, that kind of film is hard to market without huge Hollywood names in the cast. It's got some great actors and some good names, but it doesn't have the huge names that they want."

In hindsight, Burnett concluded the film's Oklahoma opening should have been in Tulsa, with proximity to Nowata. "But," he said, "Barry (Switzer) was there in Norman, and I knew it'd be easy to get him to appear at a screening. My family was there. Greg Coolidge [Jake Malloy], one of the stars, went to high school there, and I went to college there. So I knew I could get a strong initial box-office [and reviewers like Bob Colon] in Norman."

Switzer may have been one of the bigger-time coaches in football history, but at heart, he remained son of a bootlegger from Crossett, Arkansas. Small-town guys love their football, their daughters, even their daughter's dog. Switzer gladly reduced himself to portraying a high school coach, with temper approximating his own, to support daughter Kathy, dog trainer. Oskie never fumbled a line. "We had four hours booked [to shoot] Oskie's part," Burnett told the *Tulsa World*, "and he did it in an hour and a half. That's how well-trained he was."

Oskie was as perfect for his role as *Possums* was a name for the reconstituted, losing Ironmen. Burnett told *The Oklahoman* that the unusual nickname came to him while considering what might be the worst imaginable mascot. He even came up with a defining descriptive line: When the going gets tough, the town rolls over and plays dead. "It was a metaphor," Burnett explained, "for what the town was going to do."

The real Nowata did not play dead but instead dove head first into the spirit of Burnett's film. The Possum, contrary to popular belief, cannot, according to mentalfloss.com, choose when to play dead: "The comatose-like state is an involuntary reaction triggered by stress." And what could be more stressful than 25 losing seasons in a row, including the 13 in which the Possums did not score a touchdown? Nowata addressed any stress its new fame-from-football misfortune might have caused by designating September 12, 1997, "Possum Day" and put its best foot forward with a "Possum Day Parade." Parades are a small-town tradition.

"Nowata," Burnett said, "could be any small town anywhere."

The town may possess universality, but don't think it isn't special, even unique. The city commissioners went a long way toward proving as much by honoring the possum as Nowata's "official marsupial." How many towns have one of those—*and* a sense of humor? Still, Ken Murnan, publisher of the weekly *Nowata County People* newspaper, expressed concern that the community would not take well to having its football team branded a loser, even fictionally.

"That's not Nowata," Murnan told *The Oklahoman*. "Nowhere close to it! One of the concerns you have in a small community is [that filmmakers are] going to make you look like a bunch of hicks." Murnan need not have worried. Burnett displayed sensitivity and appreciation for life in the kinds of places he grew up, including Prattville, a place so small I hadn't heard of it. Burnett turned it into a state champion when it did not even have a football team. Prattville students attended Charles Page High School in Sand Springs. In fact, Prattville, located south of Sand Springs, became part of the western Tulsa County city in 1965 when annexed to increase the city's size (19,778 in 2019, approximately five times that of Nowata).

"They didn't make us look like idiots like so many Hollywood productions when they deal with a small town," observed Murnan. He was quick to tell people that Wal-Mart had.

Burnett drew so accurately from his childhood surroundings and people he'd met and observed that he was able to paint a movie small-town with broad, gentle brushstrokes that fit Nowata, even if Idabel or Sand Springs had been the inspirations.

The store where he began work when he was nine years old, Collier's Feed and Seed General in Sand Springs, morphed into Nowata's Clark Hardware. "The movie," Burnett told the *Nowata Star*, "has an amalgamation . . . of different people that I met while working in the store." Former owners Hib and Lib Collier traveled from Hilton Head, South Carolina, for the filming of the movie dedicated to them. Mac Davis's character was originally named Will Collier, to honor Burnett's "second father . . . a strong person based on Hib's influence in my life."

Burnett also drew from college days in Norman, its people, sites, and sights. In *Possums*, Calvin (Nathan Brooks Burgess) delivers newspapers on a moped. Though developmentally challenged, he is a thoughtful young man who seems always perfectly present. When he offers Will Clark hot chocolate from his thermos, only to find he has drunk it all, Calvin volunteers to ride off for more. "I wanted a character," Burnett said, "that was always around this small town, that was the truer heart of everyone here."

The writer-director might have done well with Buster Lunsford, truest of Nowata true hearts. Buster was my classmate during our first years of elementary school but found it difficult to keep pace. He disappeared from the classroom but not from our lives or hearts. Ol' Buss *was* genuine Nowata. Rather than deliver newspapers on a moped, he worked with animals at the South Coffeyville Stock Yards, area rodeos, and events at the Nowata County Fairgrounds. What Buster did most, though, was work the town. He would walk it from end to end, delivering a smile to everyone and an endless banter with whoever had time to listen—and some who didn't. His regular stops included City Drug Store, where he visited with owner Wayne Clark; Star Video, where he chatted up the women who worked there, and

Arvest Bank. When I was young, our banks were Victory National and First National. They had welcoming and nice women who helped me open my first savings account.

Though I unhappily moved from Nowata when I was 16, Buster never left and never changed. He followed the Ironmen faithfully and raised the flag before the home football games. In 2010 another Ironman supporter, Tom Senters, who worked for the Nowata County Assessor, hit on the idea of buying Buster a letterman's jacket to recognize how much he had given to Nowata athletics. "He loves the Ironmen," Senters told the *Nowata Star*. "It doesn't matter if they are up or down. Every time I see him, [it's] always: 'Let's go to the game.'"

When Senters broached the idea, Bron Williams, high school principal and athletic director, embraced and facilitated it. When he arrived in Nowata in 2007, Williams had found a letterman's jacket in his office inscribed "Athletic Director." What could be more perfect for Buster? His friends presented him the coveted jacket during a ceremony at a fairgrounds livestock show, combining Buster's two loves.

Buss was such an institution in Nowata that, when the town learned, in 2013, that he was suffering from brain cancer and had had to move into the Osage Nursing Home, the townsfolk showed up by the hundreds for a special birthday celebration at the fairgrounds. If Buss no longer could come to them, they would go to him, which his family encouraged. Though Buster's birthday was not until May, the celebration was held a couple of months early, with Buster arriving at his beloved fairgrounds in a special van escorted, front and back, by Nowata fire engines. There were presents, including an official Nowata Fire Department shirt that went well with his letterman's jacket. Four hundred fifty-two people signed the guest book at this sendoff for William G. "Buster" Lunsford, 67, who died April 15,

2013, three weeks shy of his 68th birthday. This is the Nowata that had so impressed director Max Burnett and *Possums* co-producer Leanna Creel, who was from Los Angeles.

"As a producer," Creel told the *Tulsa World*, "I couldn't have asked for a better setting than this. People have been so helpful. We had extras come out and sit in the stadium for eight hours and then ask if they could come back the next night. People have offered us props. They've enabled me, as a producer, to save money and put it up on the screen instead."

When shown a little love, Nowata could return it tenfold. When Buster Lunsford died, the town launched a fundraising campaign to erect a remembrance of Buss. The monument, with its life-size image of Buster and his favorite sayings, was placed near the flagpole in Spike's Railroad Park downtown to honor Buster's love for raising the flag. When high winds felled the monument, shattering it, the board that had raised funds for the project did it all over again—ever faithful, always there for Buss, as he had been for them. Buster gave his life *to* his town, showing Nowata how much a person whose life is different from most has to teach others. This is the Nowata that made a lasting impression on *Possums* star Mac Davis.

Two years after the filming of *Possums*, Davis found himself back in Oklahoma to work on a remake of Wilson Rawls' best-selling children's book that was first turned into a family film classic in 1974. Layman D. Dayton produced the first version of *Where the Red Fern Grows* that reveals how a farm boy who hardly has two dog bones to rub together could turn his coon dogs into champion hunting hounds. He returned to direct a remake released in 2000. Dayton teamed with Ned Beatty and Dabney Coleman, and with Davis and rock musician Dave Matthews, who was making his acting debut. Because members of the Cherokee Nation played a big role in Rawls' story, Dayton wanted to film around Tahlequah, capital of the Cherokee Nation. He extended the authenticity to creating a family that would "actually depict (Cherokee lineage)."

Davis, who had relatives in Oklahoma and Texas, was happy to be back north of the Red River. "I spent a wonderful month here in Nowata doing a little movie called *Possums*," he told *The Oklahoman's* Gene Triplett, "and had a great time."

He found making a movie in Oklahoma, specifically Nowata, nothing like Hollywood. "Out in California," he said, "a lot of times people there get mad at you for even being around. They're so blasé about it." Not Nowata or Tahlequah.

"So as far as I'm concerned," Davis said, "Oklahoma is about as good a place as you can find to (make movies). People are nice and tolerant. . . . It may not be the most sophisticated place in the world, but it's where I want to be if I'm gonna have a flat without a spare."

It also is where Davis thought he might again find some companionable ol' boys like those he grew up with in Lubbock, Texas. He knew right where to look—Nowata. "In fact," he said, "I'm gonna sneak down there next week and surprise those old boys at the Nowata Country Club . . ." Maybe hit a ball or two.

Nowata *is* that kind of place, one that even when the director shouts "wrap," it stays with a person. It stayed with Max Burnett after he had finished *Possums* and had taken it to Sundance. "I was really nervous," Burnett told the *Tulsa World*. "I mean, these were film people from New York and Los Angeles, sophisticated people from urban centers, and this was a sweet film that I really thought spoke to the people of the Midwest and the South." Burnett found it went beyond that. "I had several of those same people come up to me and tell me that it spoke to them, too."

That's when he knew that *Friday Night Lights* may have owned the franchise, but he had a little piece of it. "That's when I realized that what the picture's about—the importance of belonging to something greater than yourself, the sense of community—speaks to everybody . . ."

REAL NOWATA FOOTBALL WAS A STAR-CROSSED WINNER

If Hollywood's spotlight elevated Nowata's self-esteem, the reality of high school championship competition has proved more a zero-sum game. Nowata's mostly community-spirited, warm-hearted partisans could take satisfaction in a mere touchdown. In *Possums*, not only did a single touchdown serve as a better marker of realism than beating a true champion, but it also *was* a victory after 13 interminable scoreless seasons and one lost one.

Unlike the Possums, Nowata's Ironmen have climbed high on the football mountain on five occasions only to be stopped short of the summit four times. Not a good percentage, even if the Ironmen were whiffing in rarefied air. A pithy phrase concocted by Peter Berg and popularized by Coach Eric Taylor (Kyle Chandler) in the *Friday Night Lights* TV series—"clear eyes, full hearts, can't lose"—sounded good. But Nowata could and did lose. Were it not for the 1970 Ironmen's stunning turnaround, Nowata might have become more closely associated with a different phrase—the bittersweet "always a bridesmaid, never a bride."

In football's loftiest region, the Buffalo Bills epitomized the bridesmaid. Even with multiple Hall of Famers—Coach Marv Levy, General Manager Bill Polian, quarterback Jim Kelly, running back Thurman Thomas, defensive end Bruce Smith, and receivers Andre Reed and James Lofton—the Bills lost four consecutive Super Bowls, beginning in 1991. It was as if they were star-crossed after losing their first to the New York Giants 20–19 when Scott Norwood missed a 47-yard field goal that would have won on the last play. (The Minnesota Vikings, if it is any comfort, also went 0–4 but spread their losses over the first 11 Super Bowls.)

Nowata has seemed similarly star-crossed since its singular 1970 championship, losing title games in 1988, 1995, 1999, and 2014. The latter two teams built perfect 10–0 regular seasons and 4–0 playoff runs before dropping the Gold Ball, symbol of Oklahoma's best. Reaching the championship game should not be categorized negatively, but what prevented the 1988 Ironmen from making Nowata a multiple state champion is inexplicable.

The Oklahoman's Mike Baldwin ranked the 12–1 Ironmen middle-of-the-32-team playoff field but allowed as how Nowata appeared "capable of reaching the finals" from the weaker side of the bracket. Defending state champion Wynnewood, however, fired a shot across Nowata's bow when it defeated Hobart, No. 1 and playoff-favorite. Wynnewood had begun its season like paupers, not princes. With three weeks to play, it was 1–6 and headed nowhere. Then, *shazam*! It reeled off eight victories to earn the dubious distinction as only state champion to have lost six games. And, Nowata contributed mightily.

With two fumbles and an intercepted pass, the Ironmen couldn't seem to stop turning the ball over to Wynnewood's wishbone. Fullback Rodney Wright scored twice on the way to a 21–0 lead that made the Ironmen a nonfactor similar to Wynnewood in the first five games that Wright missed due to grade problems. "When we got our fullback back," halfback Jack Turner told Baldwin, "the offense really started clicking." If it had legs and carried a football, the Ironmen couldn't tackle it. With fourth-quarter runs of 30, 31, and 47 yards, Turner easily offset Nowata's one moment—a 70-yard touchdown pass from Ty Hewitt to Ron Hubbard—in a 35–7 loss.

In their third trip to a championship game, the 1995 Ironmen again had the misfortune of encountering a wishbone team. They could no more snap Davis's 'bone than they had Wynnewood's. In a reversal of fortunes, Nowata played the Wynnewood role of slow-starter made good. The 11–3 Ironmen's losses had come early on as they learned a new offense and played up in class, losing three of their first five games—to Dewey, Vinita, and Tulsa Cascia Hall—though never by more than nine points. No. 1 Davis was a perfect 14–0.

Since its obliteration by Wynnewood in the 1988 championship game, the Ironmen had not put together a winning season until Coach Scott Briggs arrived from an assistant's job at Oologah. With his guidance, the Ironmen, unranked in pre-season, dominated its district but for a 36–35 close call against Chouteau. By the time the Ironmen had reeled off nine straight victories and climbed to No. 13, Davis Coach Joe Weber was marveling to the *Tulsa World*: "They're so explosive on offense."

Mixing run and pass, the Ironmen could strike with multiple playmakers: receivers, a passer in Jason Pierce, and a running back, Brian Warwick, whom Weber considered "some kind of football player." In the end, though, it was not enough. On the 25th anniversary of Nowata's lone state championship, Davis added a third 2A title to one from Class B, shutting out the Ironmen, 28–0. Weber had believed Davis's offensive line was "the real strength of our team." Quarterback Darren Kapella could testify to that.

Kapella threw only six passes, completing three, but two were for touchdowns, which, given the nature of the wishbone, he supplemented with touchdown runs of 34 and 12 yards. His line cleared the way for 239 yards on the ground and protected Kapella as he threw for 135, almost twice that of Nowata's supposedly more diversified offense. "This line is excellent," Kapella said in victory. "They worked so hard all year, and they won the game for us tonight."

The Ironmen filled another title game with turnovers. They fumbled twice, threw three interceptions, and did not make a first down until late in the first half. Briggs would never have another chance to win a championship. When, four years later, the Ironmen reached the final again, it was with another first-year coach, Greg Werner.

Werner succeeded Briggs, who had been diagnosed with leukemia shortly before the 1998 season and died October 1. Not only had many of the 1999 Ironmen played for Briggs and were dealing with that loss, but two weeks before meeting Fairview for the championship, the community lost three students in a car-train collision that left a fourth student with critical head injuries the night after their team had beaten Wewoka 31–20 to advance to the semifinals.

"The community went from an exciting emotional high to an extreme emotional low in a period of less than 24 hours," principal Cary Conway told *The Oklahoman.* Can a community glory in football when it has suffered wrenching loss? Conflicting emotions filled counselor Sandy Andrison: "I'm really glad we've been winning because it . . . gives the kids something else to think about . . . But, trust me, it's been a very long two weeks."

It is impossible to know how the star-crossed Ironmen might have fared had tragedy not enveloped them. They were 14–0 and ranked No. 3, playing two-loss, 11th-ranked Fairview. Even in their grief, the Ironmen had finally stopped the vaunted wishbone of perennial champion Davis for a 19–18 ticket to the championship game. They had nothing left for Fairview.

Senior quarterback Jeremy Kliewer required only seven completions for four touchdowns—one a 92-yarder on the game's second play. Add a TD run, and his five touchdowns tied a state record in Fairview's 39–14 championship. Nowata? Bridesmaid.

The best of the bridesmaids may have been the 2014 Ironmen, the only state finalist I saw play. The 50th reunion of the Class of 1964—the class I did not graduate with but still feel a part of—was drawn to the Friday Night Lights to be recognized, briefly, at Nowata's game with Vinita. What a treat to watch arguably the best team to reach the state final, a risen-from-the-ashes journey. The senior Ironmen of

2014, most of whom played significant minutes as freshmen, took a big second step toward turning their 0–10 first season on its head when they trounced Vinita. On an evening too chilly for early September, Nowata's 44–16 victory should have had a similarly chilling effect on Class 2A; Vinita was a 4A team the Ironmen never before had beaten three years in a row in what is believed to be the second-oldest high school series in Oklahoma—96 years then, now beyond 100. By halftime, it was a 35–0 laugher.

No matter how large the school, no regular-season opponent was in the Ironmen's class. They pranced through a pre-district schedule of 3A Dewey and 4A Vinita and Miami, outscoring the larger schools 109 to 36. District 2A-8 teams found themselves overmatched. Only non-district, perennial state-contender Vian offered a challenge. The Ironmen met it and then did so again in the playoffs. That first victory, 38–15, allowed everyone to think the unthinkable.

Bryce Bell, an athletic tight end/defensive lineman who would play his way onto an Oklahoma All-State team, recognized Vian's history of playoff success. When the Ironmen were gaining solid footing in 2012 (9–3) and 2013 (10–2), Vian was going a step beyond, to the state semifinals before twice losing to Davis, the 2013 champion. In the seventh game of the '14 season, Nowata not only beat the Wolverines but did so at Vian. "I thought then," Bell told the *Tulsa World's* Barry Lewis, *We can do it. We could win the state championship.* "That gave us a lot of confidence, and so did beating them again (33–27) in the playoffs." Bell caught touchdown passes of 64 and 53 yards, the entirety of his 117 yards.

The playoff victory in the second round reinforced Nowata's belief in itself, as it had to hold off a Wolverine team that refused to stay beaten. Vian scored twice in the final 4:48, and, if Bell had not recovered its onside kick following the second TD, well . . . . "In big situations," Coach Matt Hagebusch said, "big players make big plays."

Hagebusch, who had been an assistant coach at Vinita, inherited Bell and what was left of the winless 2011 team. He made an immediate impact. "When I first saw him," Bell said, "my . . . impression was that he knew what he was doing, and that gave us all confidence." From there, it grew exponentially, until quarterback Wyatt Steigerwald, another All-Stater, believed it could finally be a "bridal" season in Nowata: "I know it's a big deal for the whole town."

The size of the deal grew bigger and bigger. The playoff victory lifted these players, who first had known no success and then could not seem to get beyond second-round roadblocks. Now, they had gone through a formidable one in Vian, whose quarterback had not been at full strength for the regular-season game. The success came thanks in no small part to Nowata's quarterback, whom his coach called the best he had ever been around, "a special field general." "After going 0–10," Hagebusch said, "these guys know how difficult it is to win."

Steigerwald refused to let the opportunity slip by the Ironmen, though the degree of difficulty grew greater each round. A quarterfinal matchup at Washington High School, near Norman, resulted in a tenuous Nowata advantage through much of the game, one that disappeared late in the fourth quarter. Trailing 35–34 with 5:58 to play, Steigerwald took the Ironmen 81 yards, scrambling the final nine to score after a pass-play fell apart.

"Young quarterbacks often give up on a pass play and run too quickly," Hagebusch said. "It was the opposite with Wyatt before this year. He all but refused to run. We focused on that in the off-season, for him to look for the opportunity to scramble when the play breaks down. It has taken his game to another level." And with it, Nowata's.

No team had scored on Nowata as Vian and Washington had. It was enough to make a person wonder if three shutouts and limiting two other opponents to seven points was a mirage. It wasn't. The Ironmen, in their most impressive defensive performance, blanked semifinalist Oklahoma Christian School (OCS), which had averaged 41.3 points in compiling its 13–0 record. The Saints managed only 162 yards. Bryce Bell had considered Nowata's defense soft against Washington; so he and his teammates "practiced hard, and it showed."

The defense was so good it overshadowed Bell's 136 receiving yards, including two of three catches producing touchdowns, with the third setting up another. Even quarterback Steigerwald got in on the big defensive plays, intercepting OCS. The only negative from the 20–0 victory: Davis's wishbone loomed in the final.

If it were not enough that Davis again stood between Nowata and a second state championship, the Wolves had gotten there not only by handling Hennessey, 48–31, in the semifinals but also by doing something these very same Ironmen had been unable to do in previous years—beat Adair, before redistricting separated the teams. If Davis could beat Adair, if only 24–21, it spoke to the Wolves' usual excellence.

Faced with Blake Summers, the quarterback/defensive back who took Davis to the 2013 championship and had it riding a 29-game winning streak, longest in the state, Hagebusch knew what to expect from the team Nowata lost to 28–0 in the 1995 championship game and defeated—for the only time—19–18, in the 1999 semifinals. "Davis runs the same (wishbone) as it did back then or 30 years ago," said Hagebusch, who could have added . . . *only now it runs it even better.*

Summers was equally effective in the championship game. He carried on 30 of Davis's 61 runs, gaining 193 of its 319 yards. He also hit a 2-yard touchdown pass to JT Maynard, as the Nowata defense forced Davis to throw more (just 5) than in any of its previous 14 games.

As he had all season, Steigerwald, once the freshman quarterback who never won, met the challenge head on. First, he gave Ironmen the lead with a 37-yard run and kicked the extra point; then, he found Scott Pruett in the fourth quarter with a 46-yard touchdown pass.

Trailing 20–13 with 4:10 to play, Nowata had one last chance. Steigerwald completed four consecutive passes to move the Ironmen to the Davis 24-yard line. When he dropped back for his 21st and final pass—he completed 14—Steigerwald sent the ball spiraling toward a receiver between the hash marks. "I was a little late getting it over the middle," Steigerwald admitted. Davis safety Trever Merrell made Steigerwald pay. "Their guy made a great play."

Of the best bridesmaids' many excellent players, including senior running back/linebacker Michael Richey, who moved to Nowata from Locust Grove for his senior season, Steigerwald was the one who made a mark collegiately, first at Northeastern Oklahoma A&M College and then in his final season at Missouri Western State University. During his redshirt sophomore season at Northeastern, he took the Golden Norsemen to their fifth Southwest Junior College Championship, along the way being honored as National Junior College Athletic Association Offensive Player of the Week; he completed 26 of 33 passes for 325 yards and a school-record-tying six touchdowns without an interception in beating Arkansas Baptist. As a Missouri Western senior, Steigerwald led his team to a 9–3 record, including a 35–14 victory over Henderson State in a bowl game in which he threw for two touchdowns. Steigerwald's coach also used his Nowata success as a springboard.

Matt Hagebusch left the Ironmen with a 40–10 record after a 7–4 season and playoff berth in 2015. Following two playoff seasons at Claremore Sequoyah, he came full circle, returning to his hometown of Chelsea, where he still lived. He became high school principal, a long-term position with greater security than coaching, but also, in 2019, Chelsea coach, after serving as an over-qualified Green Dragons assistant in 2018—when they were winless. It was reminiscent of how it had all begun for Hagebusch at Nowata, now his competitor.

Hagebusch was not the only Nowata coach to reach the state championship game and take advantage of his and the Ironmen's work to advance his career. Jerry Bailey did so after steering Nowata's 1970 Cinderella team to the school's only state title. The glass slipper fit on the first try, but after that fairytale came the ultimate in horror stories.

Nowata's first and lone state championship blossomed from nowhere, which is where the Ironmen had gone at the start of the 1970 season. It appeared impartial and knowledgeable prep sportswriters at the *Tulsa Tribune* and the *Tulsa World* had been correct when they predicted an Ironman rebuilding year: They would be middling at best and possibly tail end of District 2A-6, ghost of the Verdigris Valley Conference, only Nowata and Vinita remaining in the district.

The first three games offered little evidence that a great dawn was on the horizon. The Ironmen, in order, lost at home to Dewey, 32–12, tied at Collinsville, 6–6, and were shut out at former Verdigris Valley foe Pawhuska, 15–0. An auspicious start, it was not. It resembled the previous 3–6–1 season, Jerry Bailey's first. Bailey had only 30 players, less than two-thirds the usual number in the early 1960s, when I played. Nowata-born Kirk McCracken, former managing editor of the *Sand Springs Leader*, saluted those 1970 Ironmen in a book about Bailey. McCracken's cousin, Dee Paige, had been the team's senior quarterback, one whom Bailey trusted to call plays.

During those first three games, Paige did little to reward such trust. Pawhuska's shutout included key interceptions. Discouraged, according to McCracken, Paige suggested to Bailey that he change quarterbacks. Bailey rejected the idea—and Nowata began to win. First, it trounced Tulsa Union, which was not then the large-school powerhouse it has become. Then, against Stillwell, Nowata's first district opponent, though Paige could generate only 15 yards passing, the running game he, Tom Dennis, and Rick Reid led came alive—256 yards to Stillwell's 37—and the defense was strong in a 20–12 victory. The Ironmen were on their way.

Shutout routs of Locust Grove (52–0) and Jay (42–0), 2A-6's weakest teams, accelerated the turnaround and improved the record to 4–2–1 overall and 3–0 in the district, from which only one team could earn a playoff berth. With Week 8's 27–15 victory at previously unbeaten Wagoner, Nowata positioned itself for a final showdown at Catoosa. Against Wagoner, the running game continued to excel, and not a Paige pass touched the ground. Wagoner intercepted two, and he completed his other five, including a 26-yard touchdown to Bruce Campbell.

Paige remained on the mark in a 32–6 victory over Vinita, but it only looked easy in the final period. Paige's 30-yard touchdown pass to Reid in the fourth quarter provided separation, and his interception set up another TD. When the coaches had voted on district favorite before the season, Bailey had identified Catoosa and was proved correct. The larger Catoosans, tied at 4–1 with Stillwell, trailed only 5–0 Nowata. The winner would get the 2A-6 title and opportunity to face 2A-5 Dewey in the first round of the playoffs.

So much for what Coach Bailey knew. Nowata took the opening kickoff on a cold, rainy night and drove 60 yards to score, Tom Dennis going the final 11. On that muddy Catoosa field, the 170-pound Dennis, largest of the Nowata backs, gained 101 yards on 17 carries, matching Catoosa's total offense. With Ivan Walker getting 42 yards on 10 carries, Paige 35 on 12, and Reid 20 on 10, all that was needed was for 250-pound Mike Jones, Nowata's largest player, and his fellow all-conference defensive linemen Justin Pugh, Ken Griffin, and Dan Covey to make the opening touchdown stand up. They did.

Riding a seven-game win streak, the 7–2–1, No. 10-ranked Ironmen played host to No. 4 Dewey, the team that had beaten them 32–13 in the season-opener. In that pass-happy game—Nowata threw 20 times, Dewey 38—both defenses were ball-hawks, and the Ironmen began to learn to rely more on their running. Still, Dewey was 9–1, losing only to larger and powerful Claremore in its final game. Could there be such a thing as reverse momentum?

With all Nowata festooned to celebrate its playoff team's success, the Ironmen won a back-and-forth showdown, 27–20, by limiting Dewey's passing game after the Bulldoggers' initial success. Rick Reid intercepted four Dewey passes, and Dee Paige actually gave Nowata a 79–76 passing-yardage advantage, completing 3 of 5. The Ironmen defense was again stellar, especially when Dewey had tied the game at 20–20. Reid's 18-yard TD run, followed by his fourth interception, at the Nowata 25-yard line with 1:54 to play, proved the *coup de grace*.

Ahead No. 2 Sallisaw awaited in the semifinals with a quarterback talented enough that the University of Oklahoma gave him a scholarship—even if it was begrudging and its last available—and beyond that loomed No. 1 Lindsay. It looked like a super-sized order for the No. 10 team that once had been 0–2–1 and unranked until the playoffs.

Sallisaw's Steve Davis, a Swiss-army-knife quarterback, could run, throw, punt, and placekick. And yet, if OU assistant coach Leon Cross had not seen something special in him, Davis would not have played football at OU. Offensive coordinator Barry Switzer would have put the bum's rush on Davis if he had had his way. But Cross championed him, persisting in selling Davis to skeptical boss Chuck Fairbanks, disinclined Switzer, and Sooner assistants.

Davis engineered a Black Diamonds lead in the semifinal showdown in Sallisaw between tough-minded running teams, ostensibly because the Ironmen fumbled on their 25-yard line. From then on, however, it was more the Dee Paige-and-Rick Reid show than Steve Davis's. Davis scored a touchdown on a 1-yard run, but he did not get much help. When his passes were perfect, his receivers were not. A Black Diamond tight end, in particular, got behind the Ironman secondary but could not hold onto the ball. Reid had no such problem. He caught what Paige threw to him—and what Davis did, too.

After Tom Dennis, who produced 117 yards on 22 carries, scored Nowata's only touchdown of the first half on a 2-yard run, Reid, in the second half, went 42 yards to score and reduce the deficit to 13–12. For good measure, he added 62 yards in the final period with a pass from Paige for the 18–13 victory—after his interception of Davis had given the Ironmen the possession that made this possible. All-district defensive lineman Ken Griffin's harassment of the future NCAA champion quarterback had affected his throwing.

Nowata had run the playoff table—No. 3 Dewey, No. 2 Sallisaw—and *all* that remained was No. 1 Lindsay. Author Kirk McCracken's spot-on analogy: "If this was the fictitious movie *Possums*, Lindsay would be Prattville, and Nowata would be, well, [it would] still be Nowata."

Lindsay was bigger and, by the size of its accomplishments, better than Nowata. The Leopards not only were unbeaten but also nearly unscored upon, having run up a 204–6 advantage on twelve vanquished foes. That was how the championship game at Edmond's Wantland Stadium began and led to Lindsay's expected statistical dominance—204 yards rushing to 96, 15 first downs to 9. The prohibitive favorite looked the part—early on.

The Leopards put up quick and easy points, taking advantage of fumbles by quarterback Paige and a kick returner. Lindsay's Mike Terry, who became a defensive back at Oklahoma State, was in contention for state player of the year because of his running and showed why with two first-quarter touchdowns. The Leopards failed only at kicking extra points.

This became decisive and an oddity, since the *Nowata Star* described Ironman sophomore Ivan Walker as effective during the regular season but no record-setter. He proved a perfect two-for-two. In contrast,

Lindsay's Bud McGuire, who at one juncture of the season had made 35 extra-point kicks in a row, also missed two field goals. Nowata's hard-charging defense did little to soothe the placekicker's nerves.

As far as Coach Jerry Bailey was concerned, his team's fumblin'-bumblin' start was more asset than cause for nervous breakdown. He had seen this before. "Seriously, I wasn't worried," he told the *Tulsa Tribune*. "I don't know what it is, but we don't start playing until we lose the ball a few times. It looks like we coach that stuff."

If so, Bailey and staff also instilled the confidence to overcome its coaching. Nowata began the third quarter with Justin Pugh's recovery of a Lindsay fumble on its 34-yard line. After the run-game stuttered, Paige connected with Bruce Campbell on a 9-yard touchdown pass. When Nowata forced a short punt on Lindsay's subsequent series, Paige replicated his touchdown, only this time, a 40-yarder to Rick Reid.

Lindsay never recovered. Its 40-points-per-game offense could move but not score. The Leopards' résumé, shiny with current accomplishments and four state championships, meant nothing in the moment. The moment, for the first and, as it has turned out, only time, belonged to the Ironmen. The Possums may have broken the fever with a touchdown after seasons of futility, but these Ironmen found gold, as in the state champion's Gold Football.

Even before that moment arrived, *Nowata Star* publisher R. Marsden Bellatti envisioned it. Perhaps that's a reason Bellatti was inducted posthumously into the Oklahoma Journalism Hall of Fame in 1993. After watching the Ironmen, he concluded that their coaches had instilled in them desire and discipline to hone skills they didn't know they had. "I imagine the 1970 Ironmen football team," Bellatti wrote, "will be an inspiration to those who have yet to play football for Nowata." I can tell you, it has been to those of us who once did.

The *Nowata Star*'s championship story ended on an ominous note, though one hardly unique: "The only thing that marred the happiness of the Nowata crowd was speculation on the size of the salary some of the larger schools are probably mentioning with head coach Jerry Bailey." Bailey, expressing reservations because of what he had found and done in Nowata, nevertheless accepted an offer to become Sapulpa's football coach.

"I have the feeling," he told the *Star*, "that any decision I make may be wrong, however, my ambitions in my profession are such that I cannot do otherwise."

It is hindsight to conclude Bailey did indeed make the wrong decision. What is clear is that, five years later, everything went horribly wrong for him and those who loved him, including Nowatans. Bailey did not achieve the success at Sapulpa, a Class 4A school, that he had at Nowata. He resigned as coach following a losing (4–6) season, not his first, in 1975.

Bailey continued to teach while he considered his possibilities. Then, on a morning in January 1976, he left school with Paul Reagor, Jr., a vice principal whom Bailey had brought from Okmulgee to be his assistant in charge of the offensive line. When he resigned, Bailey recommended several of his assistants as potential successors, but the school chose an outsider, and Reagor, apparently, was outraged enough to kill Bailey, his benefactor.

Kirk McCracken, with dogged reporting and a storyteller's touch, fleshes out in *Because of the Hate* the story of how and why a resentful Reagor murdered Jerry Bailey. I cannot imagine the mixed memories Bailey's murder left with his championship Ironmen. Together, they accomplished the wonderfully impossible—not least of which was beating Steve Davis—only to have the impossibly horrible befall their coach. That has to have scrambled golden memories with an everlasting dark one.

STEVE DAVIS AND HIS HEAVENLY OPTION

By the time Steve Davis, Sallisaw quarterback and preacher, stumbled into the last University of Oklahoma 1971 football scholarship, wishbone operator Jack Mildren was in his ascendancy. The West Texas comet was leaving the brightest of tails across the collegiate galaxy. Mildren broke coaches' hearts when he chose Oklahoma, especially those in Texas, where he had been a schoolboy phenomenon. Davis? He was the runt of the quarterback litter.

Barry Switzer, OU offensive coordinator in those days, so coveted Mildren that he pitched a tent at his Abilene home in 1968. Switzer could have been mistaken for a lawn ornament. He even helped Mildren's mother, Mary Glen, do dishes, to the dismay of other recruiters.

If that were not enough, Merrill Green, Mildren's Cooper High School coach, had played at Oklahoma for legendary Bud Wilkinson, seemingly giving the Sooners an edge, even if Wilkinson were no longer coach. But, Green had other ties: He had coached at Arkansas under Frank Broyles, and Green's college roommate, Eddie Crowder, coached Colorado.

Mildren's father, Larry, once a high school coach and a dutiful dad, gave his son a tour of campus options, of which there were many in Texas, north of the Red River, and beyond. Oklahoma might have had an edge, given Jack Mildren's desire to be a starting quarterback as a sophomore—college freshmen were not eligible—and one day to win a national championship.

Jack Mildren
[*University of Oklahoma Athletics photo*]

Oklahoma's greatest advantage, however, might have been the Southwest Conference, to which many Texas schools belonged. It limited members to visiting a prospect just twice, once at his home. Oklahoma, then a member of the Big Eight Conference, faced no such restriction. With new coach Chuck Fairbanks's blessing, Switzer spent at least three days a week in Abilene courting not only Jack but also the Mildren family. In a *Sports Illustrated* story that became a chapter in *Saturday's America*, Dan Jenkins dissected Oklahoma's advantages, which Switzer corroborated in *Bootlegger's Boy*, written with Bud Shrake, a Jenkins buddy. Switzer would drive Mildren around Abilene, talking quarterbacking. Every now and then, they'd hop out of the car for a few snaps. Switzer demonstrated proper techniques. It was a bonding exercise even if neither then recognized OU's wishbone future and the exalted role Mildren would play in it.

Steve Davis experienced no such moments and little attention. He didn't have his own quarterback coach from the university he had dreamt of playing for since he'd been a squirt. In fact, he had not played quarterback through much of high school. He was a sophomore defensive back, then a junior tailback, because of a player's injury. That made him the decisive, tough runner he became. He scored so many touchdowns that he finished among Oklahoma prep leaders. He got noticed but not recruited.

Finally, as a high school senior, Davis found his way back to quarterback, his junior-high position. Not even demonstrating option-offense skills drew recruiters. Davis did everything for Sallisaw—run, punt, placekick, return kicks and punts. His accurate arm helped turn the Black Diamonds into Class 2A's No. 2-ranked team. He could not, however, penetrate Nowata's team-of-destiny in a playoff semifinal. Davis's future looked bleak.

The service academies showed interest, because he demonstrated leadership ability off the field as well as on it. He served as governor of Oklahoma Boys State and attended Boys Nation. He visited Baylor because he was "a Baptist kid" who was a licensed minister but also because he played quarterback. Arkansas battled Oklahoma for Jack Mildren but showed no more than "soft" interest in Davis despite Sallisaw's proximity to Fayetteville. And Oklahoma? "Coach (Chuck) Fairbanks, I don't think, wanted to offer me a scholarship," Davis recalled years later with stinging accuracy. He did not have to worry about tripping over offensive coordinator Switzer at his home. Leon Cross, assistant coach, showed interest but in no small part because of Sallisaw's location in east central

Steve Davis
[*University of Oklahoma Athletics photo*]

Oklahoma, which, along with southeast Oklahoma, was Cross's recruiting territory and a hotbed of exceptional small-school talent, including the three Selmon brothers at Eufaula, Rod Shoate at Spiro, and Terry Webb at larger Muskogee.

Cross saw something in Davis not obvious to others: "All he did was win," Cross liked to say. Davis looked angelic but played as if the devil himself were after him. Where others focused on Davis's lack of blazing speed, Cross noticed he often ended up in the end zone. And when others poo-pooed his passing arm, Cross observed that it got the ball to his receivers. Steve Davis "did things right," and, in the end, Oklahoma did the right thing.

"Leon Cross called," Davis remembered, "and said: Clyde Crutchmer from Okmulgee is going to Colorado. We got one." Cross meant "one" scholarship left. "Do you want it?"

Davis never forgot his reply. He shared it on a 2003 OU Football Legends DVD: "Hell, yeah, I want it!" he said to a burst of laughter. Davis mostly used "hell" in another context.

Had Davis been a senior a year later, he would not have received a scholarship, not even the last one, claimed by default. The National Collegiate Athletic Association made a draconian 45-to-30 reduction in the number of football scholarships allowed by year. Davis once asked OU assistant Don Jimerson, who made his reputation as a championship coach of Lawton High School, "Coach, if this new scholarship limit had been in effect when I was a high school senior, I wouldn't have received a scholarship, would I?" Jimerson answered bluntly: "NO."

Jimerson elaborated to the *Lawton Constitution*'s Don Luke: "He's right. He was a question mark when we took him. We knew he had possibilities, but he was a long way from being a sure thing." Oklahoma, with a third fewer scholarships, took only sure things. That could have changed football history, and I might never have known the quarterback who proved better than anyone imagined and received too little credit, because he wasn't Mildren.

"I dreamed about being an Oklahoma football player forever and ever," Davis told fellow legends. The dream had a downside, though. "I was the eighth quarterback of eight."

Davis turned to QB1, twinkle in his eye, needle in his tone. "They had recruited all these eight guys to replace *you*—Jack Mildren." Of course, no one could replace the quarterback immortalized in 1968 by Jenkins in "Pursuit of a Big Blue Chipper" for *Sports Illustrated*, certainly not a no-chipper. Davis didn't care how his chance had come: "I was glad to be No. 8."

Rather than see impossibility, Davis's characteristic sense of humor peeked out from his abyss. That humor and wit could surprise those who did not know Davis and based conclusions on his budding reputation in the pulpit. On his first day of practice as a freshman, Davis's coaches—Jimerson, Bobby Warmack, a former OU quarterback whom Davis idolized, and Ron Fletcher—warned not to put stock in the depth chart. Fletcher added a twist Davis took to heart. He challenged each wide-eyed freshman quarterback to "prepare for your opportunity." Davis would seize his. Not even being placed behind QB7 Larry McBroom of Ada discouraged him. So what if McBroom had undergone shoulder surgery and couldn't play?

When Davis called father Larry, he shared the bad news of his lack of standing—and then the "good." Davis expected to move up because friend McBroom "couldn't even practice." Davis passed McBroom, by default, and overtook six healthy quarterbacks. He understood the offense quicker and ran it better than anyone. It was as if he had been made for the wishbone, which demanded smart decision-making, the ability to take a hit on almost every option play, and a knack for limiting mistakes that put the ball on the ground.

If Steve Davis had been born for the wishbone, it was Jack Mildren who first made the offense work better than anyone before or since. Switzer called Mildren *the Father of the wishbone—Oklahoma version:* "We couldn't have accomplished what we did, as fast as we did, without Jack Mildren at quarterback."

Mildren not only became Oklahoma's first wishbone wizard but also did so at a crucial juncture. After years of glory and stability during the Wilkinson era (1947–1963), change and uncharacteristic failure had roiled the Sooners. Talented line coach Gomer Jones succeeded his longtime boss but could not replace him (9–11–1 in 1964–1965) and gave way to former Arkansas assistant Jim Mackenzie (6–4 in 1966), who arrived after much hiring intrigue.

First, Darrell Royal rejected his alma mater's plea to come home made by no less than university president Dr. George Lynn Cross. He had coached archrival Texas for eight years. Royal called it the "hardest decision" of his life. Royal, who quarterbacked the Sooners during one of Wilkinson's early seasons, understood that nostalgia does not fatten a bank account. He had a better financial situation at Texas, including tenure, than the one Cross offered.

Before the Sooners turned to Mackenzie, they attempted to hire Vince Dooley, who in 1965 had not yet gotten Georgia football revved up hotter than a bootlegger's car. Dooley might not have interviewed for the job had a second person not followed up a call from President Cross. Bud Wilkinson himself, whom Dooley admired, asked him to consider OU. He couldn't say "No" and found himself greeted upon arrival at the Oklahoma City Airport on December 14, 1965, by reporters to whom he confirmed his interest. He interviewed with OU leaders the next day and later received a job offer. Georgia officials and media thought Dooley as good as gone, but an outpouring of affection—and money—won the day. Oklahoma turned to Mackenzie. He brought with him a defensive coach, Chuck Fairbanks, and Switzer, who, with Mildren, would soon return the Sooners to the glory to which they had become so accustomed.

Mackenzie did not live to see it. He suffered a fatal heart attack in the spring of 1967 following one year with the Sooners. Fairbanks became Oklahoma's third coach in four seasons. Different coaches and changing personnel dictated dissimilar offenses. OU evolved from vestiges of Wilkinson's Split-T during the Gomer Jones transition to the power-I that Fairbanks deployed, with Heisman Trophy winner Steve Owens propelling it, one thundering, smashing, crashing blast after another. His runs led to Big Eight Championships in 1967 and '68.

Following Owens' departure, Fairbanks, in 1970, installed the Houston veer option. The veer demanded a quarterback—Mildren—throw the ball well enough to prevent defenses from doubling-down on the run to which the quarterback was expected to contribute mightily. And Mildren *could* throw. From the power-I, he had thrown 172 times in 1969—but his completion percentage never rose above 49.1 percent, and that came in 1970, when he threw first from the veer and then from the third offense of his career.

The week before playing Texas, which already ran the 'bone and ran it well, Fairbanks agreed at Switzer's urging to convert the veer into the wishbone. His offensive coordinator had a sharp eye for what would work, given OU's improved recruiting. Switzer had watched Royal's wishbone carve up opponents like Thanksgiving turkeys. He equated what the Sooners could do with the 'bone to what Wilkinson's teams did with the Split-T in the glorious 1950s. It produced two national championships and 47 consecutive victories. As he wrote in *Bootlegger's Boy*, Switzer believed that Mildren "was sort of lost in the veer but was born to run the wishbone." [And here *I* thought that it was Davis.] Switzer was right: "Quarterback was the key." Almost as important was speed at halfback—Greg Pruitt and Joe Wylie taking the QB's pitches.

Switzer could be persuasive. He recruited fellow assistant coaches to his side before broaching the subject with Fairbanks. Fairbanks had taken to heart the "Chuck Chuck" bumper stickers popping up in Norman and spreading throughout Sooner Nation. After OU suffered an unanticipated loss to Oregon State, Fairbanks was pilloried. That may have increased his willingness to try Switzer's idea at an unusual moment. Fairbanks recognized what had to happen, even as he ran what sounded like a crazy mid-season switch by others. "When we got into the season," he told *Sports Illustrated*, "we found ourselves too dependent on the passing game. We had to get run-oriented, and the best way to do it was with the wishbone."

The debut bombed. Texas knew how to run the wishbone, and the Sooners were at the baby-steps stage. They lost 41–9. "The newspapers," Switzer wrote, "practically demanded that we commit suicide." The "Chuck Chuck" campaign moved from car bumpers to parties held in Sooner Nation homes, including those built with oil money that supported OU football. Neither Switzer nor his offense gave up. They won at Colorado the following week on the way to a 7–4–1 record that included playing Nebraska to within a touchdown, precursor of the year to come. Mildren had to swallow blame for abandonment of the veer, and it left him with a sour taste. "When we made the change in our attack and things started falling into place, the team began to have success," Fairbanks said. "And when the team started having success, so did Jack. He just wants to win more than the rest of us." Mildren proved as much in 1971.

That memorable season may be as good as any OU has played, even though the Sooners did not go unbeaten or win a championship. Those consequences were the result of what was exaggeratedly billed as "The Game of the Century," only to, remarkably, exceed the hyperbole. Dan Jenkins tried to be prudent in previewing the contest, tempering the deifying adjectives. After witnessing the spectacle, Jenkins threw caution to the wind.

No. 1-ranked Nebraska defeated No. 2 Oklahoma, 35–31, in a game so rich that the *Sports Illustrated* version got spiced up and countryfied as "The Cream Gravy Game" in *Saturday's America.* Jenkins went purple with his prose about pickup trucks and breakfast cream gravy, a down-home favorite in Oklahoma, where the Thanksgiving game was played. He wrote an account as smooth as Mildren, who matched the Cornhuskers' Jerry Tagge pass for pass and then some. Tagge had the passer's reputation, but Mildren, the stunning, running wishbone operator, threw for 188 yards to Tagge's 65, including four passes to old Abilene teammate Jon Harrison, two for touchdowns. What's more, Mildren ran for two TDs.

Jack Mildren proved himself the "father" of Oklahoma's greatest running offense as the Sooners' first wishbone quarterback. [*University of Oklahoma Athletics photo*]

The cream gravy got ladled on early. Johnny Rodgers, who a season later would win the Heisman Trophy, took a punt, following OU's first possession, 72 yards through a maze of Sooners to score. That provided an edge Mildren spent his best afternoon trying to overcome. He did so twice—OU led 31–28 in the fourth quarter—but Tagge, Rodgers, and Jeff Kinney found a way to take back the lead one final time and defend Nebraska's national championship. In a double-barreled shot of irony, however, it was Mildren whom artist Jay O'Meilia immortalized in a

Game-of-the-Century painting. Mildren, back of his No. 11 crimson jersey ripped, rises resolutely on tiptoes in his protected pocket, trying to spin the ball past the hand of a leaping lineman on the best defense in the nation—*this* the man who blamed himself and his passing for forcing his team to give up the veer offense that required it.

A framed lithograph of this indelible Mildren moment, a gift from my football-loving mother and father, still holds an honored place in the loft of my home fifty years later. O'Meilia, an Oklahoman, who loved sports and played tennis in Tulsa into his nineties, never made Steve Davis the focus of such a work, though he did more than one painting that captured the Selmon brothers, Little Joe Washington, and Horace Ivory during the Davis seasons. Davis is in the background. Given the inauspicious beginning of his Oklahoma quarterbacking career and the number of talented players on Davis's 1973 through 1975 teams, it is not surprising.

When Barry Switzer attended a freshman game in 1971 and got a look at the handsome, baby-faced Davis and his mop of brown hair, he was shocked by this quarterback with the fullback legs. "I didn't have any idea," he told *Oklahoman* columnist Berry Tramel years later. He sought out Galen Hall, another assistant, in the coaches' booth of the press box. "Galen," Switzer remembered saying, "this kid's not a bad player. Gets rid of the ball quick. Runs tough, gets upfield, north and south." Despite this impression, Switzer had reservations.

In particular, Davis remembered one he gave Switzer during a difficult redshirt season of 1972, the year senior Dave Robertson served as bridge quarterback between Mildren and his true heir apparent, Kerry Jackson. Jackson was already getting playing time because freshmen were eligible again. Davis, redshirting as the No. 3 quarterback, traveled with the team. While warming up before its Red River Rivalry game against Texas, he heaved the ball "into about the eleventh row" of the Cotton Bowl. On the way to the dressing room, Switzer pulled

Davis aside: "You're gonna have to get a helluva lot better to play here, boy."

Warning taken. That's why what happened in the next game at Colorado paralyzed Davis. Jackson suffered an injury, and then Robertson went down. "Dave Robertson got his bell rung," Davis said, employing a euphemism for concussion, "and [Coach Chuck] Fairbanks looks down at me to warm up. I hadn't even thrown a ball. I was scared to death." Besides embarrassing himself, Davis would have lost a year of eligibility had he been forced to play. "I'll never forget how proud I was of Dave [when] he crawled back up."

Steve Davis, hard-running, slick "pitcher" in the triple-option wishbone, had game-breaking passing ability when needed. [*University of Oklahoma Athletics photo*]

As it was, Davis struggled during 1972. "I got really overweight, frustrated, and wanted to leave," he recalled. Davis again turned to his father, who responded with tough love. "Son," Jim Davis said, "you haven't even tried to play at Oklahoma. Why don't you get your ass in shape and see if you can make something happen?"

First with the *Lawton Constitution* and then the *Tulsa Tribune*, I bore witness as Steve Davis took his father's admonition to heart. Though I was not around the team much during 1972, I recognize the contradictions between Davis's memories of that redshirt season and how others saw him. Sam Muzny, in an email to Tramel in 2013, recalled Davis from the vantage of a reserve lineman on the Termite Squad (scout team) that Davis ran and for which Muzny blocked. Whereas Davis spoke of being the No. 3 quarterback,

Muzny remembered him as No. 6 or 7. "Dave Robertson was our starting QB, and [freshman] Kerry Jackson was amazing." Scott Hill ranked ahead of Davis, and so did Enid's Jeff Mabry, "who could really throw the ball."

"Davis never bitched or whined," Muzny noted. "He just did it, and was solid." Davis did what Switzer demanded if he hoped to play: He got better. By 1973, Davis's circumstances had changed dramatically. Just weeks after OU blanked Penn State, 14–0, in the Sugar Bowl, Chuck Fairbanks resigned to coach the New England Patriots and Switzer, at 35, succeeded him. Fairbanks may not have wanted to give Davis the last scholarship when he was recruited, but Switzer saw hope for him, even if he remained less than fully sold.

That Sugar Bowl was the first major bowl game I covered. The Lawton newspapers did not make a habit of sending writers to post-season bowls. Almost fifty years later, the player I remember most from that game is not Davis—the redshirt did not play—but Tinker Owens, wide receiver younger brother of Steve Owens, Heisman Trophy winner. Davis and Tinker Owens had a similar burden: Some did not believe Tinker deserved a scholarship and had received one only because of his brother's prominence, which was ludicrous. OU scholarships aren't legacies.

Without the contacts and familiarity of an everyday writer with the team, I arrived in New Orleans later than most and had missed scheduled interview sessions. I found myself wandering the massive lobby of the Sooners' hotel. Who could I find who would do a spur-of-the-moment interview with someone they hardly knew? Answer: Tinker Owens. He and fellow underdog Davis related to and treated with kindness those not high in the pecking order.

Tinker and I discussed the game and his expectations, our hometowns, and the old Verdigris Valley Conference. I wrote about him for the next day's paper, which proved serendipitous. In the first bowl game that freshmen were eligible, Owens, legendary schoolboy athlete in track and basketball as well as football, had the last word, with five catches for 132 yards, a 27-yard first-quarter touchdown, and Sugar Bowl Most Valuable Player Award.

If Tinker's future sparkled on the OU horizon, Davis's flickered. Could he be no more than a career backup to the gifted Kerry Jackson, who had proved himself as a freshman? Not long after Switzer was named coach, the Big Eight Conference and the NCAA announced sanctions against OU and declared Jackson ineligible. His high school transcript had been altered, as had that of Mike Phillips, teammate at Ball High School in Galveston, Texas. In his memoir, Switzer explained that it was not uncommon for coaches and administrators at predominantly black high schools to alter black athletes' transcripts to improve their chances of succeeding; they put a thumb on the scale of justice with the belief the young men had been denied opportunity in not fully integrated schools. Phillips's class standing had been raised—he qualified for a scholarship without this and was not ineligible—as had the ineligible Jackson's.

Switzer argued to no avail that Big Eight and NCAA officials didn't comprehend "the situation that existed in the real world out there in those high schools." He did acknowledge, however, that "the NCAA views academic violations of this nature as the most serious of NCAA transgressions. And that's why we got a jail term instead of a speeding ticket." They threw the book at OU: forfeitures of 1972 games in which Jackson played; an assistant coach fired; Jackson ineligible; bowl ban for 1973 and '74, and a television ban in 1974 and '75. A two-season punishment stretched into four. It also raised the question: Who's OU's quarterback?

Muzny had a lineman's-eye view of Steve Davis's rise, his observations cogent and creditable. "Others were faster, more talented, and could throw better," he told Tramel, joining a long line hailing Davis with too faint praise. He also saw what Davis had: He was nearly flawless in what he did with the football and how. He learned as Termite quarterback. "On busted plays," Muzny recalled, "Davis would eat the ball, just fall on it and cut his losses. All the other QBs would force a bad play, causing a turnover. Steve Davis did not (screw) up."

While recognized, this quality was undervalued by those who put into words what Davis meant to the Sooners from 1973 through 1975. He operated the most stunning running offense in college football history. Everyone noticed but credited great players who surrounded Davis and memorable defenders—especially the Selmons—who got ball and field position with relentless efficiency. Jack Mildren made first-team All-American in 1971. Three of Davis's teammates were similarly honored in 1973, two by consensus. Eight first-team All-Americans, three by consensus, in 1974. Eight more, again three by consensus, in 1975. Davis never so much as made All-Big Eight. Even so, guard John Roush, '74 consensus All-American, thought of Davis as a "mentor, confidant, friend" and recognized the "guy that was our leader."

Still, there remains the inescapable truth of how Steve Davis became the quarterback and unforgettable leader of OU's Second Golden Era. Barry Switzer, never one to sugarcoat his reality, professed admiration for Davis off and on the field but bluntly said: "Kerry Jackson was going to be our quarterback. Steve Davis would never have been the damn quarterback if Kerry had been eligible." That may sound harsh, but even Berry Tramel, OU quarterbacks historian and Davis admirer, concurred: "That's an opinion supported by fact." Tramel laid out Jackson's facts convincingly: First freshman quarterback to play. First black quarterback at OU during a time when they were not accepted at most colleges, especially those in the South and on its fringe. Excellent statistics in four non-conference games before suffering an ankle injury that nearly forced Fairbanks and Switzer, who recruited Jackson, to turn to the frightened, redshirting Davis. Jackson impressed other quarterbacks, including Scott Hill, who would find his place at safety. "He was awfully good in '72," Hill said. And then, he was gone.

"It was devastating," Jackson told Tramel years later. No one told him what had happened. Before he returned from suspension, Jackson's sternum was broken in an automobile accident. A long recovery followed a week in intensive care. He did what he said he would do, what his mother wanted. He remained at Oklahoma. He said he was as fast as ever, his arm as strong. But he could not prove it. Davis was QB1.

"Steve was just on top of his game," Jackson told Tramel. "I just couldn't get back into the groove of being the starting quarterback." Davis's dream had always been to emulate Bobby Warmack. He loved everything about Warmack, whose resume—legendary Ada High School, quarterback of the 1967 Big Eight champions, all-conference—resembled Jack Mildren's more than his own.

A Sallisaw player Oklahoma was recruiting when Davis was in the eighth or ninth grade gave Davis a color brochure from his recruiting materials. On the back was a photo of Warmack in the Sooner huddle, lampblack under his eyes, chin strap double-snapped, small white towel spilling over the front of his football pants. It was how Davis saw himself. He removed the back-of-brochure photo, and, before tucking it into the top drawer of his dresser, he wrote on it in a bold, black Magic Marker: "When?"

Davis never told anyone about the photo he hid beneath his underwear. But, Patsy Davis eventually discovered it, because mothers are supposed to know what is going on in their son's life, up to and including what he has stashed among his underwear. Patsy never said anything to Steve. But before her son's dream began coming true with his first 1973 start at Baylor University, Patsy wrote on the Warmack photo a succinct response to Steve's long-ago, never-shared question and ambition. Mother Patsy added a beautiful answer: "TONIGHT."

Though he and the Sooners fell short of satisfying Switzer's desire to "hang half-a-hundred" on every opponent, their 42–14 victory at Baylor included two Davis touchdowns, more than 100 yards rushing, and served as prelude and promise entering a Game-Two showdown in Los Angeles Coliseum against the University of Southern California. Not only had the Sooners lost Mildren but also other members of the first 'bone backfield: Greg Pruitt, Joe Wylie, and Leon Crosswhite. Switzer was a new, unproven, young head coach, the NCAA had just slapped severe sanctions on the team, *and* the Trojans were defending national champion. The officials should have called a piling-on penalty before the first snap.

Though OU did not leave Los Angeles with a victory, it left with something valuable. As the Sooners fought USC to a 7–7 standoff, they did so despite two early fumbles, one of which set up a Southern Cal touchdown pass, and missed field goals that could have won the game. The offense dominated, with Davis keeping on the option for 102 yards and the tying touchdown, while the defense limited the Trojans to 161 total yards despite Lee Roy Selmon, the greatest defensive lineman ever to play at Oklahoma or perhaps anywhere, not available because he was suffering from pericarditis during the first half of the 1973 season.

The Sooners overcame the self-doubt of those who had not done such a thing, including Davis, and they did it against what seemed a cast of stars, not the least of whom were quarterback Pat Haden, receivers Lynn Swann and J.K. McKay, and running back Anthony Davis. USC entered the game with a gaudy 19-game winning streak.

Steve Davis cried after that game, "because," as he told author Jim Fletcher, "I knew we should have won, (and) it hit me just how passionate I needed to be as a player." Davis considered the tie, one of only two blemishes on his three-season record, "a launching pad for us." Davis and teammates began a three-game run during which they came to believe in themselves and one another. They rallied on Owen Field to defeat seventeenth-ranked Miami, 24–20, with Davis scoring on runs of 3 and 27 yards, and connecting with Tinker Owens for a 52-yard touchdown; as a topper, they thrashed Texas, 52–13, one of six half-a-hundreds Davis quarterbacked, and he did it by throwing and throwing some more. The first and most lopsided of his three victories over Texas, pre-season national-championship favorite, saddled Darrell Royal's Longhorns with their worst loss ever.

Davis completed five of six passes for 185 yards, including first-half touchdown passes of 63 and 47 yards to Owens—good guys do finish first—and Billy Brooks. Joe Washington offered up a surprise with his first halfback pass, good to Owens for a 40-yard touchdown. The Sooners completed 6 of 8 passes for 225 yards of a 508 total. With gallows humor, *Daily Oklahoman* columnist Frank Boggs labeled the outcome "more one sided than a hanging." Ol' Frank was dead on. "The game," Davis told Jake Trotter for his book on OU football, "was just the galvanization of a program, a team. The biggest byproduct of winning is confidence. Some call it swagger. The Texas game gave us that." Yet in three of the most successful seasons an Oklahoma quarterback ever had, I do not recall Davis ever obnoxiously manifesting the swagger. His Christian beliefs, pastoral responsibilities, and personality stifled self-flattery.

As Davis morphed from Mr. Irrelevant as a recruit to difference-maker QB, he became one of my go-to sources of information and insight. This was not merely a consequence of being the quarterback. During the many years that locker rooms were my second home, linemen often offered sharper details of the workings of the offense in general and a particular play than more-guarded quarterbacks. Others agree. The late, great pro-football writer Paul Zimmerman coached his *Sports Illustrated* protégé Peter King to seek out smart offensive linemen. "They know everything," he once told King, "and nobody talks to them much because they don't touch the ball. And they love to talk."

In an Oklahoma locker room that could be intimidating to a young writer, I had the good fortune in the mid-1970s to have not only a lineman who loved to talk but also a quarterback who did. Jaime Melendez, starting offensive guard when his line coach Gene Hochevar was not demoting him or throwing him off the team, liked to talk so much that he would sometimes tell opposing linemen where a third-and-one play would be run and then go back to the huddle laughing about the first down the Sooners had made anyway. Jaime, who died from cancer in March 2013 at age 57, played high school football in Lawton, where I had gotten to know him while writing about the Lawton High School Wolverines.

Hochevar told Jay C. Upchurch for *Tales from the Oklahoma Sooners Sideline* that he removed Melendez and fellow guard Terry Webb from the lineup or kicked them off the team "a dozen times each." Never stuck. "They'd go to Barry and talk him into letting them back on the team, which I knew he would." Good thing. Someone had to block for Davis and tell the tale. "The funny thing was," Hochevar said, "as uninspired as they were during practice, they were both fantastic when Saturday rolled around. They just hated to practice."

Unlike Davis, Melendez had not grown up dreaming of playing for the Sooners. One of eight children in a military family that moved regularly to his father's assignments, he played football because his oldest brother, Marcos, had. Jaime discovered he had the kind of ability that made him an Oklahoma All-Stater, even if he doubted he would be big enough to play in college. In the Melendez house, education came first; football provided the ticket. His mother, Leila, demanded her children bring home no grade less than B. She cared less about crushing blocks. His father, also Marcos, watched Jaime play only once in high school, the Oil Bowl, an Oklahoma-Texas schoolboy all-star game. He admitted afterward he had been unable to follow and appreciate Jaime's play but assumed, since his team had won, that he'd done well.

"From that point on," Melendez told the *Tulsa World* years later, when he himself was a high school coach, "I thought maybe it wasn't all that important. It was just a game." So, he stressed education on the field and in the classroom. Practice was a means to an end. He, like his quarterback, had his priorities straight.

Melendez and Davis could compartmentalize football and aspects of their lives they considered more important. If, for Melendez, that was education, for Davis, it was religion and sharing his feelings and knowledge from the pulpit or wherever he found an interested person. Davis was unlike a prominent latter-day quarterback of his ilk, Tim Tebow. The University of Florida's 2007 Heisman Trophy winner made religiosity an on-field spectacle. His kneeling end-zone prayers became so commonplace the media turned them into a verb—"Tebowing." Compared with Davis's restraint, Tebow's showiness was off-putting.

Davis took a different approach. He did not proselytize. I, of course, knew he was a licensed/ordained Baptist minister. He'd accepted Jesus Christ into his life when he was 10 years old, six years before his father became a Christian. His teammates gave him a hard time about walking the straight and narrow, including being a teetotaler. Some of them did not know what to make of this "Holy Joe" but respected the unquestioned leader of a team of All-Americans.

"First preacher I ever had for a quarterback," said Heisman Trophy running back Billy Sims, who was a freshman in 1975, Davis's final season. "You couldn't get him off his beliefs. Amazing. Especially in the '70s, for a guy like that, being true to the Lord."

The person to whom Davis made more option pitches than anyone, Joe Washington, saw the same quality. "He had an unbelievable faith," Washington said, "but he didn't push it on anybody." That's what I remember and may partially explain why I do not remember ever discussing religion with Davis. Professionally, it was negligent that I didn't.

I must have been one of few Oklahomans not to hear Steve Davis preach or at least talk about religion. When you are the Sooners quarterback in God-fearing, football-fanatical Oklahoma, your reach is long. People liked to say he used the university's plane more than the school president, for whom it was intended. There was no place too small or remote for Davis to visit to preach or speak. He learned to fly and leased a plane during the summers. Why didn't I ask if I could go with him to write a column? The only explanation is that perhaps my boss Bob Hartzell, *Tulsa Tribune* sports editor, already had. Bobbie Gene could talk football *or* religion.

I am unsure how I regarded religion during the years I wrote about Steve Davis for two Oklahoma newspapers. I was brought up in the Protestant faith, mostly as a Methodist. My family attended Sunday School and church. I even earned a God and Country award in Boy Scouts. For reasons too complicated to explain, much less understand—there was a girl involved—I converted to Catholicism in my late teens after moving to California. It was a confusing time, one that deepened a division between my father and me. Bottom line: I didn't get that Catholic girl and no longer knew what, if anything, I believed.

Steve Davis might have enlightened me. On the eve of the first game of his senior season in 1975, he had become such a recognized bearer of a religious message people wanted to hear that the Reverend Billy Graham, most famous preacher in America, invited Davis to share it with thousands attending his Lubbock, Texas, Crusade. He had become a rock star of faith, and, on this biggest of stages, Steve

Davis spoke about how important it had been to him that his father finally embraced their shared faith. I have seen video of that Crusade stop in Lubbock, but it focused on headliner Graham. Others told me Davis was as impressive that night as any on a football field.

Don Jimerson, the assistant who coached freshman quarterback Davis and laid bare the reality of his recruitment and scholarship, had to have been among the first to recognize Davis's multidimensional qualities. Jimerson told Chuck Bowman, Oklahoma Fellowship of Christian Athletes director, he had to "meet this kid from Sallisaw. He could be the next Billy Graham."

His teammates recognized this. According to accounts of the Davis message in Lubbock, he acknowledged that, earlier in his life, he could be self-absorbed with gratitude for everything from being saved and made whole by his Lord to being allowed to be "Oklahoma's quarterback of the wishbone-T." He had learned, however, there was "more to prayer than . . . praying for people's needs." Especially his own. A person had to give of himself to others. "If you want to know Steve Davis," fullback Jimmy Littrell said, "watch that testimony. It was very inspirational for a 20-, 21-year-old kid to say the things he said."

All-America guard John Roush, Davis protector and lifelong friend, thought so, too. "[At] the Billy Graham service," Roush remembered years later, "Steve was absolutely awesome." Roush had long recognized Davis's compelling, almost-mesmerizing abilities. When Davis spoke of his belief in the "resurrected, living Christ," Roush, who had grown up Catholic, was seized by evangelicalism. "I ended up giving my testimony," he remembered. "I never thought I'd wind up talking at the Baptist Student Union, but he brought that out."

This could not have surprised Chuck Bowman. "He *was* the FCA before there was an FCA," the Fellowship of Christian Athletes director said. "He was our poster boy." Not to mention, traveling ambassador. The 1975 Oklahoma football media guide shared an account of a typical Davis week in the off-season: He spoke in Wynnewood on a Sunday, and then at events in Chickasha on Monday and Tuesday. He must have rested on the fourth day rather than the seventh, because his itinerary resumed on Thursday in Lincoln, Nebraska—home of the "enemy"—before going to New Orleans on Friday, and, finally, back to Oklahoma to speak in the small town of Coalgate. Why did he do it? Davis told *The Oklahoman*'s Ray Soldan: "I just see the good that results in it for all of the young people."

The Jesus that Davis brought to these engagements, according to what a professor of religion taught me in graduate school, was the Jesus of Faith found in the Gospels of the New Testament rather than the historical Jesus, the Jewish prophet who bore an apocalyptic message of the imminent coming of the Kingdom of God. Those to whom Davis spoke, especially in churches and at events such as the Billy Graham Crusade, yearned to hear what the Jesus of Faith meant to Davis, but, I think, whether he realized it or not, Steve Davis also knew the Historical Jesus, a flesh-and-blood man rather than the mythologized version.

Miracles of the Jesus of Faith are so unnecessarily unbelievable that, in 1820, Founding Father and former president Thomas Jefferson, who knew a thing or two about creating important and lasting documents, took a sharp instrument, paste, and paper and, after excising mythology from the four Gospels, created *The Life and Morals of Jesus of Nazareth*, more commonly known as *The Jefferson Bible*. He retained Jesus's teachings, such as the Beatitudes, and eliminated those things he considered "contrary to reason," in other words, miracles such as feeding the multitudes with nothing more than five loaves of bread and two fish, raising Lazarus from the dead, and even Jesus's own alleged resurrection. In Jefferson's Bible, Jesus is neither born of a virgin nor walks on water. He does good and tries to get those who follow him to do so. This is the Jesus whom Jefferson loved, and he did not care what others thought. He aligned himself with "the most sublime and benevolent code of morals which has ever been offered to man." He said: "I am a sect by myself, as far as I know."

Jefferson was not a sect of one. I and others agree with him. While Steve Davis might have found Jefferson's beliefs more selective than his own, Davis became the embodiment of a code Jefferson was trying to show others. The Davis example cuts across football and religion (in Oklahoma, that dividing line is imprecise), occurred years after Davis's own career, and held out a kind and understanding hand to a successor coping with OU quarterback consequences.

Davis, having quarterbacked the NCAA-sanctioned Sooners to the national championship the season before without benefit of a bowl game and having never lost, felt himself struggling in 1975. Forced to pick their poison against the OU option offense, opponents tried to make Davis hand the ball to his fullback or keep it himself. "They didn't want Joe Washington carrying the ball," Davis said. Who would? Little Joe did not so much run the ball as perform magic with it. "I felt the pressure of trying to get the ball into Joe's hands."

Though the team did indeed struggle during early victories at unranked Miami (20–17) and over No. 19 Colorado (21–20) and only eked past No. 5 Texas (24–17), Davis's trepidation came a cropper in November on Owen Field against Kansas. The Sooners—especially Davis—could do no right. He completed three passes to teammates and put four others in Jayhawk hands, which, along with four OU fumbles, presented Nolan Cromwell, Kansas's own brilliant wishbone quarterback, all the advantage needed for a shocking 23–3 victory.

Tinker Owens dropped the only pass of his career, and Davis committed mistakes he never made. Switzer said his quarterback had "the worst day of his life." It felt this way not only because his mistakes contributed mightily to the loss and could have ended a bid to repeat as national champion but also because some spoiled Sooner fans tolerate failure with little grace and less generosity. They booed the team, and especially its quarterback, who had a 29–0–1 record, and neither Switzer's arm wrapped around Davis nor his supportive words—"These people we hear are really insignificant"—could take the sting out of the merciless reaction.

Anguished, Davis responded uncharacteristically. He did not turn the other cheek. "It was very painful," he would later say, "and I remember shaking my fist at them." He and his teammates determined not to let others define them but instead to "create our own destiny." Davis walked away from his worst performance with "one of the greatest lessons that athletics ever gave me." It was one he passed on to Landry Jones with the kindness and generosity Thomas Jefferson found in the Historical Jesus and that lived in Steve Davis.

Jones, Oklahoma quarterback from 2009 through 2012, became indelibly linked with Davis. As Jones won game after game—though never enough to satisfy the madding throng—he crept ever closer to exceeding Davis's victory total and came under more severe and sustained criticism than Davis experienced. More reserved and lacking Davis's charisma, Jones was also deeply religious and interested in the ministry. Different personalities and different types of quarterbacks from different eras of Oklahoma football—running versus passing, wishbone versus Air Raid, they shared an understanding that quarterbacking OU places the weight of Sooner Nation on a person's shoulders and can crush the weak or immature.

In a two-page letter, not unlike one he wrote to Nate Hybl when Hybl quarterbacked Oklahoma (2000–02) and found himself publicly abused despite renewing OU's national-championship tradition, Davis offered Jones praise, support, and a sense of history and place. He also reminded him of the boos that had rained down from Sooner fans as a result of the one failure in Davis's three seasons. "It broke my heart," Davis told *The Oklahoman*'s Jason Kersey. "It broke my family's hearts, my teammates' hearts, and my coaches' hearts."

Kersey shared from Davis's two-page letter to Jones a paragraph that offered his perspective on Jones's responsibilities as he was about to succeed Davis as the storied university's winningest quarterback, 39–11 in 50 starts over four seasons:

> *"As you understand, the record for becoming OU's winningest quarterback does not really belong to you, as those victories were a collaborative effort of your offensive and defensive teammates, and a long list of others. Hopefully, your . . . record will establish a higher hurdle for some other young man who may be a fourth-grader somewhere just developing his football dreams to realize for the teams he will someday lead. The 32-game win mark (by a quarterback) took 80 years of Oklahoma football to be established, and it has taken 37 seasons for it to be eclipsed by you and your teams. There are many lessons to be learned in appreciating OU football history. So I encourage you to be mindful of the heritage you are a part of and the tradition you will be forever held responsible for continuing."*

Jones understood what Davis was trying to do. Growing up a Sooner fan, Davis would never have considered booing his QB hero, Bobby Warmack. Even if he made a mistake and lost a game, Warmack could do no wrong in Davis's eyes. As a Warmack successor and predecessor of Hybl and Jones, Davis understood that, despite all the success an Oklahoma quarterback might have, there comes a day, as there did for Jones against Kansas State early in his senior season, when his mistakes—in this case, interceptions—lead to a loss. "I connect with those guys that are struggling in that type of position," Davis said. “I tell them my story. You may be getting a little bit of heat . . . but it’s been that way forever.”

Though it may have felt to Davis as if he were struggling before that fateful 1975 loss to Kansas, he and his teammates had had the most remarkable run of success since Bud Wilkinson’s mid-’50s teams looked as if they might never lose again. Jack Mildren may have returned OU to an equivalent level in 1971, but it was Davis’s teams that put the stars back in the eyes of the Sooner faithful, blinding them to the possibility their heroes could be fallible. The misjudgment was *almost* understandable.

Davis, far down the recognition pecking order, given the multitude of All-Big Eight and All-America players who populated his teams, nevertheless played best in the biggest games. This fact sometimes would be overlooked in heaping hosannas on running backs or the defense, as in the 27–0 shutout of Nebraska in the next-to-last game in the Sooners’ first of two seasons without a bowl. On that launching pad for the 1974 season, Davis carried the ball 18 times for 114 yards, 46 for a touchdown coming on a quarterback sneak. Go for a yard, get 46!

I always thought Barry Switzer failed to publicly recognize Davis in the way he did Joe Washington. In *Bootlegger’s Boy*, Switzer affirmed the sense he had given me. When it came to the 1974 team he believed his best of the best, “it all started with Little Joe Washington” despite an acknowledgment that Washington “didn’t have the strength or great speed” but was instead “just a pure runner.” No one who ever saw Washington’s silver cleats flashing across Owen Field would dispute Switzer’s analysis. To me, however, Davis was similar—pure leader and master wishbone conductor, without whom none of his teams would have been as memorable. The best Switzer could say about Davis? He provided quarterback continuity.

This was the equivalent of Switzer’s estimation of my contributions to our team during an annual coaches-media pre-season golf outing. Someone must have decided to punish Barry by assigning me to his foursome. I forget the exact manner of scoring. Best ball, alternate shot, who knows? Whatever the choice, the intent was to reduce the damage a less-skillful player could do. I could hold my own on and around the greens but was no big-hitter (like Scott Hill). On the occasion one of my "longer shots" had to be used, Switzer, probably just coaching me, rubbed my nose in my shortcomings. He was right—about me . . . not Davis.

In 1974 Davis again proved critical in OU's difficult rivalry games against Texas and Nebraska, twice bringing back his team for fourth-quarter victories. Against Baylor, which won its first Southwest Conference title since 1924, he led the Sooners to three fourth-quarter touchdowns and a 28–11 victory, after fumbling and then being shaken up in the second quarter. The reinstated Kerry Jackson played well, but Davis returned in the third quarter to a paltry 7–2 lead that shrunk to 7–5, with more things going wrong before they went right.

Davis ended a more-than-42-minute scoring drought three seconds into the final period. Washington capped a subsequent 63-yard drive that included a 17-yard pass from Davis to Billy Brooks for a 21–7 lead, and Tinker Owens added an end-around 7-yard run to counter Baylor's only touchdown. Despite the stuttering victory dropping the Sooners from No. 1 in the AP pre-season poll to No. 3—coaches refused to include Oklahoma in their UPI poll because of probation—Davis found 438 reasons for optimism. "When we gain that many yards," he said, "I still think we can be a great offensive team." He was right.

Davis played a critical role in making the Sooners the great offense foreshadowed against Baylor. In the Red River Rivalry, he ran for 71 tough yards, added 42 in the air, scored once and would have had another had he not fumbled going into the end zone. Both teams had contracted fumblitis, a side effect of crushing hits.

Undeterred with Texas leading 13–7 in the fourth quarter, Davis set in motion a reverse with wide receiver Billy Brooks. Switzer nearly overrode offensive coordinator Galen Hall's intuitive play as ill-timed and ill-conceived. Good thing, as he said, he kept his mouth shut. Davis took the ball down the line to his left, but this was no option. Instead, he flipped a pitch to Brooks flying past in the opposite direction. With a convoy, he covered 40 yards to score. The conversion kick failed, but after a fourth Texas fumble, Davis methodically drove the Sooners to the Longhorn 20, and Tony DiRienzo booted the 37-yard field goal for a 16–13 victory, the last close call before going to Lincoln, Nebraska. The statistics—OU 392 total yards to Texas's 209—made Davis quarterback of Jake Trotter's All-Time OU Red River Rivalry team.

Because the unbeaten Sooners were on probation, Barry Switzer designated the Big Eight showdown with the Cornhuskers their bowl game. Switzer may have been the best coach in history at motivation. The NCAA might punish OU, but it could not make it lose. It did not hurt that Switzer's on-field leaders—Davis on offense, the Selmons on defense—supported his psychological ploys or that, in the case of No. 6 Nebraska, OU found itself staring at its strongest opponent of the season and only its second ranked one [Texas had been No. 17].

Nebraska played up to its acclaim with the conference championship at stake. No one expected less. Oklahoma and Nebraska proved themselves two of the top-three college-football programs throughout the 1970s, and Coach Tom Osborne, who succeeded Bob Devaney in 1973, could be as innovative as Switzer, if more strait-laced. Whereas Osborne, who one day would serve in Congress, was professorial, the suave, country-boy Switzer, future coach of the champion Dallas Cowboys, proved he could perform feats of derring-do while managing Oklahoma's three-ring circus. Steve Davis loved Switzer's bravado and fearlessness, but he must have believed that, when he grew up, he would be more like Osborne. It might have surprised Osborne and Davis when Osborne called a throw-back pass to quarterback David Humm for a touchdown and a 14–7 lead in the third quarter. It looked like Switzer, a sincere form of flattery.

The penultimate game during which All-Americans John Roush and Kyle Davis would block for their quarterback and friend turned into a three alarm fire when the Sooners fumbled the ensuing kickoff, giving Nebraska the ball at the OU 15. The Pride of Oklahoma might as well have played *Taps*. But the defense became the Great Wall of Oklahoma—thank you, Lee Roy Selmon—and Davis got the ball back at the 20 and did what he did in big games—made the offense purr. Switzer did not scrimp on the superlatives: "Steve Davis took over and directed three long touchdown drives that were as good as you will ever see a quarterback execute the wishbone." You would've thought Switzer was talking about Jack Mildren. But as good as Mildren was, he couldn't beat Nebraska great Jerry Tagge; conversely, David Humm couldn't beat Davis.

Davis kept the ball 27 times for 112 yards and two touchdowns and—this is what mattered most—a 28–14 victory that put his Sooners in position to impossibly win a national championship [AP's] without benefit of a bowl game. With nary a passing yard, the Sooners produced more offense than Nebraska (482 yards to 366), and their defense adjusted to Nebraska's two-tight-ends offense by sending a four-man rush at Humm and taking away his receivers with man-to-man coverage. It was only the second time in history that three Sooners rushed for more than 100 yards in the same game—Davis, fullback Jim Littrell (147), and Washington (112). Osborne knew who mattered most. "The guy who makes it go is Davis," he said. "He's a great competitor, durable, and really knows the offense. I just didn't think he would be able to carry the ball as much as he did against us."

Davis, as usual, clarified what the game meant: "We didn't consider this a bowl game for us. We came here for the Big Eight championship."

They don't play bowl games in Lincoln in late November, but the trip can be rewarding. "Last year was a big win for us," Davis said, "but it doesn't compare to this year. This year keeps us alive for the national championship."

Two circumstances, separated by months, permitted the Sooners to share a national championship, their first since Bud Wilkinson's undefeated 1956 team produced his third during the record 47-game win streak. During Week One of the 1974 season, Arkansas, with a 22–7 upset of Southern Cal, prevented a Trojans perfect season, and in the final week of the season, Randy Hughes, All-America safety from Tulsa, uncharacteristically screamed at his unproductive offensive teammates to respond when they trailed Oklahoma State 13–10 in the third quarter. After Hughes's verbal smelling salts produced a 16–13 lead, Davis directed four scoring drives for a 44–13 victory and an 11–0 record. When Alabama lost to Notre Dame in the Orange Bowl, the Sooners were the only undefeated I-A team and received the media's AP title, while the coaches chose USC.

With his first championship in hand and the possibility that Davis and Sooner seniors could play their way into a bowl game during their final season, their swashbuckling coach made an understandable, if overcautious, uncharacteristic mistake. To avoid injuries, Switzer withheld Davis and Washington from pre-season contact and scrimmages. It may have contributed to Davis's option pitches being off enough to wreck OU's equivalent of passing's long bombs.

Before the boos in Davis's only loss, excessive fits and starts marred the offense's efficiency. It began in a Game One rout of Oregon State. The score—OU 62–7—does not reveal issues, but statistics do. It was raining fumbles (12) and penalties (11) as much as drops from the sky. A second decisive score—OU 46–10—pitting No. 1 Sooners against No. 15 Pittsburgh was not memorable for the faceoff of two of the best backs ever to play the game as for what safety Scott Hill did. Hill had moved from quarterback to defense because, as excellent an athlete as he was, he could not unseat Davis. What Hill did do was "uncleat" Tony Dorsett and sap the Panthers' will. Hill's hit on Dorsett as good as ended the game and was so spectacular that it is written about decades later, even in an era of heightened emphasis on concussion prevention.

Hill flew high and hard over a blocker, smashed Dorsett, and left him woozy in the second quarter. If football were boxing, the officials would have stopped it. Dorsett and Pitt were done. He gained 17 yards on 12 carries, a career low. Hill redefined the best-back-on-the-field consideration: Joe Washington may have gained 166 yards on 23 carries, but, that day, the best back played defense. "That play," Hill said in *Tales from the Sooners Sideline*, "definitely defined my career."

When, a week later, the Sooners went to Miami to play the Hurricane, Davis's season turned unnerving and frustrating and would culminate in the Kansas fiasco. OU crammed 20 points into the second quarter and barely survived Miami's 10-point fourth quarter. The frustration grew from there. Against No. 19 Colorado, Davis was nursing a 14–0 lead near the end of the first half when a Colorado punt rolled dead on the Oklahoma 2-yard line. Trying to kill off the remaining time, Davis fumbled the snap; Colorado recovered and scored on the next play. Suddenly, it was 14–7. Davis was not the only one to stumble. Joe Washington muffed a punt. Colorado scored to tie the game. Elvis Peacock and Tony DiRienzo put the Sooners back in front, 21–14. The Buffaloes, not finished, mounted their best offensive drive—68 yards. Colorado Coach Bill Mallory played for the tie, but the kicker missed, and that saved the Big Eight championship and eventually the national title. Being humbled can energize a team, but it was not the juice needed before Texas.

Davis's third victory over Texas may not have been a personal statistical success, but it was an intellectual one. Remember Nebraska Coach Tom Osborne complimenting Davis's knowledge of his offense? That knowledge and how to read defenses allowed Davis to salvage victory from the final minutes. The Sooners' 24–17 triumph was among eight that defined the Davis era, according to one of Berry Tramel's readers, Mitch Gray. Tramel found Gray's conclusions "more than valid," and I agree. "It is hard to compare eras . . .," Gray suggested, "but the gauntlet Davis ran is unsurpassed by any other wishbone quarterback. This includes Mildren, Lott, and Watts." Just as opponents usually tried to take away the option pitch to Washington and force Davis to keep the ball, they sometimes reversed this strategy. Texas limited Davis to 13 carries for negative 22 yards. Only because of two completions for 76 did Davis finish with plus yardage. Davis beat Texas with his mind, not his legs or arm.

With 5:31 remaining on a hundred-degree day and OU stuck in a 17–17 deadlock, Davis, in the 27th start of his career, recognized a flaw in the Texas defense and changed the play at the line of scrimmage. Halfback Horace Ivory turned what Davis envisioned into the reality of a 33-yard touchdown run that handed Darrell Royal his fifth consecutive loss to his alma mater, three of them to the detested, downright-perfect Switzer.

Interestingly, as Gray pointed out, of Davis's eight defining games, all BIG games—USC, three Texas, three Nebraska, and Michigan—only two were played in Norman. When he was at his best, Davis most often did not have the homefield advantage he did against Nebraska in 1975. He gave fans who booed when he intentionally went down with the ball to preserve the 21–20 victory over Colorado and booed even louder during the KU fiasco, something to remember and consider. He scored on 1- and 8-yard runs among 29 carries for

130 yards and assured OU an Orange Bowl berth against Michigan and a possible national championship.

When UCLA upset Ohio State in the Rose Bowl, it set the stage for a bone-rattling, defensive battle Davis refused to lose. In the second quarter, Tinker Owens made another of his circus catches, this one a 40-yard Davis pass, to set up Billy Brooks for a 39-yard end-around TD. After a fumble-free first half in a season in which fumbling had become a near-fatal Sooner disease, OU fumbled three times following halftime. Before the first, Davis had kept on the option, cut the corner, and sliced into the end zone. The 14–0 lead shrunk to 14–6 when OU fumbled at its own 2-yard line. Michigan got no closer, and Davis, in the final game of his career, was finally recognized for what he had often been—the Most Valuable Player. In postgame remarks, Michigan Coach Bo Schembechler said: "Oklahoma is a great team with the best manpower we've ever played against. I will vote them Number One."

The next day, he did that, and so did an overwhelming majority of the media in the AP Poll, despite Arizona State's 12–0 and Alabama and Ohio State matching the 11–1 Sooners. Its fifth national championship made OU the first team to win back-to-back titles (1955–56) twice.

Though Davis did not have a professional football career, he used his knowledge of the game and speaking ability enhanced by his preaching to carve out an 18-year career as a respected college-football analyst. From the beginning, Chris Lincoln, longtime great Tulsa sportscaster who worked Davis's first game as a broadcaster in 1976, called him "a natural communicator." With experience, he got better and better. He entertained but resisted urgings to run for public office, representing whichever party he chose; everyone wanted Davis on their side. He knew what happened when Bud Wilkinson, legend of Sooner legends, attempted to convert football success and popularity into a United States Senate seat. Wilkinson's timing was poor. He ran as a Republican in 1964, before Oklahoma turned so red it made OU's crimson pale, and, even with 95-percent name recognition, lost to lesser-known state senator Fred Harris, who rode home on Lyndon Johnson's landslide victory over Barry Goldwater.

Instead of preaching or entering politics, Davis branched out into business, using knowledge he had gained doing college-football commentary for ABC and CBS. With partners, he formed Challenger Productions Inc. in Tulsa in 1983 to build a $3 million mobile television production vehicle that networks used to travel to events, particularly sports. Davis believed he had his bases covered with a quality product—the largest self-contained, mobile production unit ever built—and a talented crew with whom he had been associated. From sports-broadcasting contacts, Davis built a strong client base. He also had marketing experience as vice president of a Tulsa drilling company, before leaving to start Challenger and expand his broadcasting to include playing host to the Barry Switzer Show during football season.

Davis had a five-year run as Challenger Productions president, resigning when the company he had formed merged with Tulsa-based competitor Mobile Productions Inc. in 1989.

It was a good, if not perfect, life, and perhaps not the one Davis and others had anticipated, especially those who thought he could be the next Billy Graham. Some of his other businesses were not successful, and his interest waned. His first marriage failed. As his son Bo grew into a fine athlete in Jenks in football and in his own game—baseball—Steve Davis left the broadcasting that took him away from home. He limited other travel and public speaking. Even his faith, always so strong that it was held up as exemplary, wavered. Tarnish showed on the golden life he had created. He had done so much for others. Why was this happening?

Older brother George Davis diagnosed Steve's inner turmoil and prescribed a cure in 1993, within months of his own death from Lou Gerhig's disease, amyotrophic lateral sclerosis. In a letter, reported by Jenni Carlson in her *Oklahoman* column, George told Steve: "I will be dead soon. Before that blessed event takes place, I hope you will take some time to look around and recognize what you're doing. It is time for you to consider what has been done for you instead of what you have done for others. My life is almost finished. Your life is unfinished."

This tough-love angered Steve. Wasn't doing for others a good thing? Eventually, he recognized what George was telling him. "Passion can empower you," Steve admitted. "Passion can change your life." As it had in church and on the football field, passion lifted Davis again. He stayed at George's bedside on weekends after ALS robbed his brother of speech. He gave him ice chips. He listened to him breathe and considered what his brother had done for him, not what he was doing for George. "What changed my life was seeing his courage," Steve said.

I like to think that, a decade later, Steve Davis clung to his brother's example in the moments during which he knew he was going to die. He was where he had spent so much time when he traveled to preach or speak—in a plane, this time a private jet. He occupied the right cockpit seat. A licensed pilot, Davis had not trained on a twin-engine business jet. After attending church on March 17, 2013, he had accompanied friend Wesley Caves, who was piloting the plane from Tulsa to South Bend, Indiana, on business. At some point during the flight, according to the National Transportation Safety Board (NTSB), the cockpit voice recorder captured Davis and Caves discussing the plane's flight-management systems. Caves let Davis take the controls as they approached South Bend Regional Airport. More than once, Caves could be heard advising Davis to move the throttle back to slow the plane to its landing speed.

Then Caves said: "Uh-Oh."

"What?" Davis replied.

"You went back behind the stops," Caves said, "and we lost power."

The unthinkable had happened. The former quarterback who made his reputation on not making mistakes had made a fatal one. As Caves informed air-traffic controllers of the emergency—"dead engines, dead stick, no power"—he tried to restart the engines. His first radio transmission to controllers came at 3:15:08 p.m. One minute, 24 seconds, and two transmissions later, the recorder stopped. In the last transmission, Caves said: "You're going to have to tell us which way to fly." They had no navigation, no heading, almost no hope.

Davis's mistake occurred because Caves put the plane in his friend's hands as they descended. Davis believed in himself. And why not? He was the eighth-string quarterback with two national championships. He had been flying for what seemed like forever. He could do this.

Caves's second mistake, the NTSB investigation determined, was "his failure to adhere to procedures" during the engine shutdown. Investigators determined Caves had restarted one of the two engines but had to abort a landing because his main landing gear was not extended. Two steps, either of which would have extended the landing gear fully, one involving a battery and another backup handle, were improperly executed. "Had he fully extended the landing gear," the report said, "a successful single-engine landing could have been accomplished."

Instead, the plane bounced off the runway on a second landing attempt, rose again, and crashed into three nearby houses, injuring one person. The investigation faulted Wes Caves. Two passengers in the plane survived. Pilot Caves, 58, and friend Steve Davis, 60, did not.

In that moment, in the land where Oklahoma football is king and the "wind comes sweepin' down the plain and the wavin' wheat can sure smell sweet," hearts broke. An outpouring of love for Steve Davis and grief at his loss washed over the state. Its embodiment occurred at the Tulsa First Baptist Church during a memorial service attended by more than 1,500 mourners. It has become common for schools with ardent followings to label themselves this nation or that nation; mostly, this is affectation. Not at OU. Sooner Nation exists, and it came together for Steve Davis as for no one else, augmented, as it were, by those whom Davis touched from pulpits, enlightened from stadium broadcast booths, and reached with heartfelt pride-of-place.

The funeral program aptly described his pallbearers as "The Dream Team." The eight former Davis teammates—John Roush, Dewey Selmon, Tinker Owens, Jim Littrell, Randy Hughes, Grant Burget, Scott Hill, and Jimbo Elrod—were but a few of many "who cared about Steve Davis and respected Steve Davis. Just look around," Elrod said, surveying the church. "The pillars of Oklahoma football just keep filing in." The enormity of the response surprised even those who shared Davis's life. "I knew he was popular," said younger brother Joe Davis. "I didn't know he was *that* popular." Sometimes those closest to a person may be too close to see what he meant to others, even strangers. "We didn't realize the significance and impact of what he's done for the state of Oklahoma," admitted brother Todd. "What he's done in life in general."

Roush eulogized his friend, and wife Rhonda played piano during the service, before sharing with the *Tulsa World*'s Bill Haisten one of Steve's last letters to the couple whom he had married. Davis told the Roushes how much they meant to him. "You and John have been joys in my life for so many reasons," he wrote. "I am the blessed one for having been touched by your lives. . . . It has not been easy, but, oh, how it's been fun and full of interesting turns. . . . Life has been my most cherished teacher. I've learned empathy is the gift of a challenged life."

Stories after Steve Davis's death described him as an Oklahoma football legend. Bo Davis's eulogy struck a son's heart-piercing note.

"I agree," he said, "Dad is a 'legend,' but for different reasons. He is a legend because he taught me how to ride a bike. He is a legend because he showed me how to break in a new baseball glove, to hit a curveball, and throw a spiral. He is a legend because he taught me how to be humble in victory and gracious in defeat. Finally, he is a legend to me because even though he won two national championships, spent 18 years on the sidelines and in a booth as a broadcaster, and shared the stage with Billy Graham, all he ever wanted was to be a good dad. And that, to me, is legendary."

It is why Steve Davis, the man, ranks first among Oklahoma quarterbacks with me and why, as painful as his premature death was, I take solace in the fact that it prompted reassessment of his qualities as a quarterback. Berry Tramel observed that few of the stories told before, during, and after the memorial service were about football. "The stories were about Davis's smile and charisma and world-class hair," Tramel wrote. "About his depth of spirit and quality of leadership. About overcoming dark times later in life to find the victory he had found as a younger man." But, without quarterbacking, fewer people would have paid attention. Davis knew this. After a book-signing that included the five men who had quarterbacked OU to national championships, Davis told Tramel: "These events always humble me when I think of the devotion of the Sooner fans. Only today am I beginning to realize the full impact of the success of those teams I was honored to lead as its QB."

After Davis's death, Tramel provided an assessment few could offer. He reevaluated Davis's place in the pantheon of Oklahoma quarterbacks after previously omitting him from his Top 10 list. He did not reconfigure his list in 2017 because Davis appeared better to him after death than he had in the flesh. He rethought the list because opinions evolve, times change, and so do we evaluators. "I've learned more about some quarterbacks of the past, I've learned more about football in certain eras, and I've occasionally changed how I prioritize certain elements of quarterback play," Tramel explained. The latter seems especially relevant in this instance, but one thing gives me pause. It is the matter of consistency. During my years as the chief editorial writer in Akron, my editors, first David Cooper and then Michael Douglas, hammered this home as it applied to editorials—unsigned institutional opinion. A change in the newspaper's opinion required solid evidence be presented to explain and justify it.

The same philosophy should apply to a columnist's personal opinion. To maintain credibility, he must write convincingly and authoritatively about the reasons underlying change. Broad strokes can paint a background, but the foreground must be colored with specifics based on sound research, sharp observation, and insightful thinking. Tramel more than met these standards when he inserted Davis among his Top 10 OU quarterbacks.

Four different names appeared on Tramel's 2017 list compared with one from 2008—Davis, No. 1 Baker Mayfield (2015–17), Sam Bradford (2007–09), and Jamelle Holieway (1985–88). Holieway and Davis, Nos. 10 and 8 in '17, were reconsiderations. Davis, essentially, replaced Jimmy Harris, whose calling card and achievements most mirrored his own. They were consummate leaders and winners, both guiding two national champions. Harris never lost, going 25–0 between 1954 and 1956, his quarterbacking at the heart of the Sooners' record 47-game win streak. He also was the better all-around player, having the opportunity in the single-platoon era to prove himself as a defensive back—a position he played in the NFL—and as a punt returner. So why did Tramel elevate Davis, whose 32–1–1 record was "inferior" to Harris's?

"When you're talking about great quarterbacks," Tramel explained, "you look for any evidence you can find to differentiate between players, pro and con." Because Tramel's is "a quarterback list," Harris's defensive-back pro career did not burnish his résumé as did that of Jack Jacobs, whom Tramel considers "OU's greatest pro quarterback," given his legendary Canadian Football League career. [The list may require additional reconsideration if Mayfield or Kyler Murray succeed in the NFL, Murray being Mayfield's OU and Heisman successor for a single season.] Mayfield replaced Mildren atop the 2017 Top 10 list, though he had not yet finished the final season that brought countless honors, including his Heisman Trophy, a third inclusion on All-American teams, and second College Football Playoffs.

"Not all national titles are created equal," Tramel wrote, differentiating Mayfield and Davis from those quarterbacks with whom they are compared. By the time Mayfield succeeded spectacularly, his team had to negotiate not only a conference championship game but also be chosen by a select panel for the four-team College Football Playoffs. Davis's teams played more demanding schedules than Harris's—not to mention having to cope with NCAA sanctions. In the 1950s, the Associated Press awarded its national title *before* challenging bowl games rather than following, as was the case for Davis's 1975 team.

Though Davis could throw better than most believe, given a low completion percentage, he could not be compared with successful quarterbacks of the Bob Stoops-Lincoln Riley passing explosions that produced Heisman Trophy throwers such as Jason White (2003), Sam Bradford (2008), Mayfield (2017), and Murray (2018); Josh Heupel, who started the run, was 2000 runner-up. Davis did not play for a passing team, but both his and Mildren's offenses could be considered quarterback-centric, another Tramel differentiator. The Split-T triple-option teams of Bud Wilkinson did not require Harris or other good operators such as Gene Calame (15–0) to make the kinds of every-play, cutting-edge decisions that Mildren and Davis had to in the Wishbone triple-option. "The pressure on quarterbacks was small compared to the modern load," Tramel noted.

Davis's performance under this pressure set him apart. When he did it—his biggest games, as OU follower Mitch Gray detailed for Tramel—added another differentiation. "He was at his best against Nebraska and Texas, which in the 1970s went a long way in determining OU's season success," Tramel wrote. I can verify that. I was there. Another way of connoting changes to the Top 10 OU Quarterbacks List is to recognize what Tramel has come to appreciate as he continued to study and assess QBs: Winning matters more than how.

In 2015, when Matt Brown ranked the Top 100 College Teams Ever for the website Sports on Earth, he sought objectivity in the Simple Rating System (SRS), metrics created by Sports-Reference.com. I won't detail SRS, but its objective is to determine "which teams were most dominant," regardless of the era. Brown examined 13,000 teams from 1915 to 2015. He knew the results were imperfect but argued they provide "a statistical snapshot of the best teams that produced the most impressive results against the best opponents."

Davis's 1974 unbeaten, national champion Sooners ranked No. 25, with an SRS of 27.8. [To get a predicted winner among teams from different eras, compare their SRS numbers. For instance, OU would have been a 6.97-point underdog to No. 1—1943 Notre Dame (34.77)]. Oklahoma's dominance resulted from beating Texas 16–13 and Nebraska 28–24, with an offense that led the nation in scoring (43 points per game) and a defense that allowed only 8.4 points. Interestingly, this compilation omits the 1975 national championship team—it was No. 102—but ranks the 10–0–1 1973 team Davis quarterbacked as a sophomore highest of all Sooner teams at No. 4, ahead of Jack Mildren's 1971 national champion runner-up at No. 13.

The SRS system favored 1940s and 1970s teams, as evidenced by Davis-quarterbacked teams at Nos. 4, 25, and 102. Bud Wilkinson's three 1950s national champions are ignored, hurt by weaker schedules. The SRS formula liked the 1949 Sooners, quarterbacked by Darrell

Royal [No. 54 at 11–0] and the 1952 Sooners [No. 56 at 8–1–1] but not Jimmy Harris's unbeaten 1955 and 1956 teams. Brown acknowledged his own subjective list would differ.

Two years after Brown's rankings, KC Joyner, in 2017, chose Oklahoma's all-time best teams for *ESPN Insider*, and he, too, preferred Davis teams [1. 1975; 2. 1974; 6. 1973] to those of Harris [7. 1955; 8. 1956]. He emphasized national championships, ranked opponents, number of All-Americans and how the teams were regarded by SRS and strength-of-schedule metrics. There was one obvious flaw. Because he was ranking OU's 46 conference-championship teams, there were no 1971 Sooners and Jack Mildren. That might not have bothered former *Tulsa World* sports columnist Dave Sittler as much as slighting Harris probably did.

Sittler was assigned to write a column for a 2008 series titled "U Decide." It offered college-football addicts a fix during the summer pre-season. They would vote on topics of interest, including the greatest Tulsa, Oklahoma, and Oklahoma State players. Sittler, using his rules, primed the pump by choosing the best quarterback. He listed two rules, but there was actually only one. *Winning*. Forget statistics and honors. With this criterion, "the selection was easy," Sittler wrote. As good as Tulsa's Jerry Rhome and Oklahoma State's Mike Gundy were, they did not approach Jimmy Harris. He was perfect: 25–0 as starter and 31–0 during three varsity seasons. Davis matched Harris's back-to-back national championships, but he had a tie with Southern Cal and a loss to Kansas. Not good enough—though Sittler did allow as how U-Decide voters in a state with "some of the nation's most knowledgeable fans" might want to consider Davis and Sooner quarterbacks who set records, won Heisman Trophies, and the like. Among 12,000 votes, 40 percent chose Mildren, and Harris finished third (14 percent) of five quarterbacks, none of them Davis.

Opinion and sentiment can change. Tramel's did. His 2008 Top 10, done on the occasion of Mildren's death from cancer, placed Mildren first and Harris eighth, Davis's ranking nine years later when Baker Mayfield took No. 1. A year after his 2013 death, in another *Tulsa World* poll, Davis received 58.6 percent of the vote to Mildren's 41.4, though the choice was limited to wishbone quarterbacks. Some opinions, including mine, are influenced by an appreciation of the person as much as the player. Football was important, but there was more to Steve Davis. Another Tulsa columnist, John Hoover, who worked for the *World* long after I left the *Tribune* and before he moved to sports talk radio, thought so. When Davis died, Hoover recalled Steve's response when Hoover was new to opinion writing and the anger it can generate. Hoover was taking flak for columns he had written critical of OU, the team Davis became famous quarterbacking. When Davis saw the reaction, Hoover noted, "He was concerned that I was now the one being booed by Sooner Nation, and he wanted to make sure I was holding up OK."

Davis emailed Hoover encouragement, reaching back to when he was OU quarterback and the man who hired Hoover at the *World*, the late Bill Connors, was writing the column Hoover now wrote. Davis recalled Connors being "a great friend" to him during his Sallisaw days and OU career. "Keep doing what you're doing," Davis told Hoover. "And keep writing with conviction. Bill Connors would be proud of you."

"Steve Davis knew people," Hoover concluded. "He knew what people cared about, and he knew what motivated them." Davis knew what all great leader/quarterbacks know. Safety Randy Hughes, who went on to a distinguished Dallas Cowboys career, compared Davis's leadership favorably with that of Roger Staubach, Pro Football Hall of Fame quarterback. Eufaula's J.C. Watts, who followed in Davis's wishbone footsteps at Oklahoma and made his mark as a Congressman, thought he owed a debt to Steve Davis.

"In terms of how to be a quarterback," Watts told the *Tulsa World*'s John Klein, "Steve Davis was it. Steve Davis defined what it meant to be a quarterback. Steve Davis gave us a picture of what quarterback is supposed to look like. People may not always remember Thomas Lott or J.C. Watts, but they are always going to remember Steve Davis . . . not just because he played at OU. It was the way he played and the kind of person he was."

That picture is indelible.

THE HARDEST GOODBYES

The morning sun, bright and warm, bathed Northern California in hope, making January feel like June. It was one of the better days of my life—until it wasn't. Mama and Daddy had driven north 90 miles from Sacramento to be with me, their only child, as I graduated from what is now California State University at Chico but will always be Chico State to me.

Following my college-selection madness, I had transferred to Chico, which would accept my semester at Virginia Military Institute only upon the condition of academic probation [VMI's grading system did not translate well to other institutions]. Because I managed to graduate *cum laude* in three-and-a-half years, I felt intellectually redeemed. Sigrid Bathen and I won honors as the outstanding graduates among Chico's first journalism class. To others, our program of two professors, Kenneth Gompertz and Richard Eck, might have appeared mom-and-popish (without the mom). But the education we received proved as sound a foundation for real-world work as that laid at such renowned schools of journalism as Missouri or Northwestern.

Catty-corner to a repair shop where my parents had brought me to retrieve my car stood the modest offices of the *Chico Enterprise-Record*, part of that real world of journalism to which I already had been introduced. Sports Editor Ted Blofsky had given me hands-on experience while I completed the academic side of my education. It was an easy choice to join Ted and sportswriter Stu Norenberg rather than devote more time to the Chico State student newspaper. Ted and Stu were excellent teachers in their own right—patient, precise, and persevering, ideal role models for a young journalist on training wheels.

I was thinking about what I owed them and how much I would miss *our team* as I moved on to Barstow, California, in the Mojave Desert, for my first post-graduation job as a news reporter. Mama and Daddy, unusually solemn, interrupted my reverie of past and future. They must have dreaded this moment, even as they had put on happy commencement faces. They had known what loomed. How could they give me the news they had withheld?

I cannot remember the exact words. I don't want to remember. I do know they said their decision to wait until I had completed my final exams and graduated to share what they realized would be the most devastating news of my life had not been made alone. They had discussed it with Roy and Jewel Berry. They had meant well, but their choice was so wrong.

The words—probably Daddy's—broke my heart. He would have thought it a man's job to deliver them. Afterward, I wondered if he had bullied the Berrys into going along with the delay in telling me. He was capable of that. He knew I would have been on the next plane home to Oklahoma as soon as his blow landed—"Steve, KB is dead. He was killed in Vietnam."

I stared into the hard, blue sky at the pitiless sun. I must have wondered why, if the sun is blindingly bright, my world had gone dark. I don't know how I responded. I was numb, and, suddenly, Mama was wrapping me in her arms as I wept uncontrollably.

This couldn't be happening, but, of course, it was. Thousands of service personnel—58,212 men and eight women—died in that feckless, reckless war, each life as important to those who loved the lost ones as KB's was to me. He was part of me, part of our friends and teammates Bucky Buck and Charles Dugger and so many others who filled the Nowata High School gymnasium to pay their last respects to Sergeant Kenneth Beryl Berry, 21.

But not me. I wasn't there.

I didn't know about the service.

I didn't even know KB had been serving in Vietnam.

This fell on me, not on my parents and certainly not on the Berrys, on whom grief had been visited once again in the loss of another son. I had squandered access to any knowledge of KB's life, especially the intimate kind friends share. In service of self-preservation, my unhappy estrangement from Nowata had left me both in the dark and in a dark place.

On Monday, January 8, 1968, when the *Daily Star* landed on hundreds of porches, Nowata knew about KB. A three-paragraph story revealed the Berrys had received a telegram informing them KB was missing in action and had been since Saturday, January 6. The news, as it does, trailed a dark reality made darker by the military's unwillingness to be forthcoming even with families. It follows procedures and protocol, which created misconceptions that KB's family could not sort out for 50 years.

The first newspaper story, for instance, indicated KB had been a helicopter gunner. He had not. He was an infantryman whose leadership abilities had placed him in charge of a squad with Troop B, 3rd Squadron, 17th Air Cavalry. In a letter to the Berrys dated 10 days later, Major Henry W. Shehorn offered praise, some clarity, and more confusion.

"Kenneth," Shehorn wrote, "proved himself to be one of the finest soldiers I have known and an outstanding noncommissioned officer. He was held in high esteem by both officers and enlisted men alike." KB had never been part of a team that felt different. Shehorn explained KB's unit "was conducting a helicopter assault in support of other ground operations" and "approaching the landing zone . . . received heavy ground fire and crash-landed."

While Shehorn added comforting words that KB "did not suffer any pain, as he died instantly," the details were incomplete and misleading. A person could infer KB died as a result of the helicopter crash. A second story in the *Nowata Daily Star*, citing a telegram from Major General Kenneth G. Wickham, clarified that KB had died "as the result of a gunshot wound" not the crash—but again he was incorrectly referred to as a gunner aboard the aircraft. Shehorn, in reply to Roy Berry's inquiry, explained KB had been the squad leader of an eight-man Aero-Rifle team transported to their ground mission by UN-1H (Huey) helicopter.

Nowata's immediate sense of loss eclipsed the desire to more fully understand what defied understanding. None of KB's teammates was closer to him than Bucky Buck. The 1964 *Ironman* yearbook had it right when, among a series of personalizing tag lines with KB's senior photo, the answer to the question of "Usually Seen" was "At Bucky's." For years—until 2017, when he was aiding my research—Bucky could not bring himself to find and confront the facts surrounding KB's death "and hear the details." He clung to the vague "freak accident" explanation of the inexplicable. I understood Bucky's reaction. Though I have had many opportunities to visit the Vietnam Veterans Memorial—The Wall—in Washington, DC, or to view a mobile version that travels the country, I have not been able to bring myself to gaze upon the too-familiar name on the cold, black stone of Panel 33E, Row 56.

Mayor A.E. Richardson issued a proclamation requesting Nowata businesses close during the afternoon of KB's funeral on January 18, 1968, "to show honor for and respect to a Nowata boy who gave his life for his country." KB was the first of three Nowatans who would die in Vietnam, one of 16,899 to perish during the deadliest year of the conflict that author Philip D. Chinney labeled "The Helicopter War," given its heavy reliance on Air Calvary units.

KB's death came just weeks before the North Vietnamese and Viet Cong launched the infamous 1968 Tet Offensive that served as a turning point in the war. Though both sides claimed victory, the offensive proved so costly that it eroded what support there was for a war Americans didn't understand. What was its purpose? Was the U.S. winning or losing? KB's family and friends could relate to the war's cloud of confusion. KB's squadron arrived in South Vietnam between October 14 and November 2, 1967. KB, according to his U.S. Army record of assignments, was in country beginning October 28. By the fatal day, January 6, 1968, the 3rd Squadron was stationed at and flying support missions out of Di An, northeast of Saigon.

Bucky Buck remembered being in the Nowata High School gym "packed to the hilt" with 1,100 people from a town of 4,500. Four years before, the same people had come to see KB play basketball. It was the largest funeral Nowata had ever known. When I wrote about this for the *Tulsa Tribune* ten years later, memory of the response to her son's death remained close to the surface for Jewel Berry. "I felt," she said, "that it showed his life had been worth something."

When Bill Shahan, former Nowata basketball coach, eulogized his player and a person he admired, he left no doubt of the worth of KB's too-short life. Shahan called KB "the all-American boy" and "a young man every parent would be proud to have as a son. . . . I recall small boys, including my own," Shahan said, "expressing their desire to 'be like KB.'" As his son and his friends played, they would argue over who would "be" the idolized KB.

It was difficult, if not impossible, for Jewel Berry not to feel KB's example and promise had been "wasted." She couldn't hide her bitterness, even when KB's father tried to comfort his wife and soften her words. "I wouldn't want to put it quite that way," Roy Berry said.

"I just don't care," Jewel said. "I know how I feel. This is a mother talking." She recalled a book of poems KB had written in high school and how he could talk to anyone and make them feel good about themselves. "If there was anyone who didn't like him," Jewel said, "I don't know who he was. KB had such promise."

That promise was reduced to two quarters, two nickels, a dime, and a battered, strapless wristwatch on which the one remaining hand had stopped just before 11 o'clock on the day Kenneth Beryl Berry died.

"That was all that was left," Jewel said.

On the bleak day KB was buried in Nowata Memorial Park Cemetery, a procession of vehicles to that hallowed ground seemed as if it would never end. "The stark facts reared up" for Bucky Buck beneath a darkened sky and unrelenting rain. "Oh, how it rained that day," Jewel Berry said. It was as if the sodden sky were crying, and its tears would not stop.

As heartbreaking as the day was for the Berry family, it could hardly have been less so for KB's closest friends, Bucky and Charles Dugger. With the Vietnam War raging, the three of them had known they would be drafted when their college deferments expired. Home in Nowata, they found themselves, as always, at the Dairy Dell, the conversation serious as they discussed options to the draft, which no one considered evading. Oklahoma boys did not do such a thing, even if their mamas searched for a way to save them, as Jewel Berry had.

"Unbeknownst to KB," Jewel said, "I went and talked to the clerk of the draft board and told her that we already had given up one son

(Warren, killed in an auto accident). (The clerk) said there wasn't anything she could do. Later, she apologized deeply. But it was too late. I don't think she realized the depth of our feelings about the possibility of losing another son."

Jewel Berry tried to convince her son to apply for conscientious-objector status: "But he told me he didn't think he would be much of a man if he did that and someone else had to go fight. He had resigned himself to it." What KB was feeling, based on his conversations with his best friends, surely included resignation to doing his duty and serving his country, but both Bucky and Charles detected a fatalism that frightened them.

After Advanced Individual Training (AIT) as an infantryman at Fort Polk, Louisiana, KB visited Bucky and Barbara Edmundson at Northeastern State in Tahlequah, where they were attending college. (Barb, a Nowata graduate—Bucky's pet name for her was "Big Barb"—became his first wife in 1967, and they had a daughter, Melissa Dawn Buck.) The visit was more than a reunion for KB and his best friend. Despite the fact he had signed an athletic-scholarship agreement dated February 21, 1964, to play football at Fort Scott Junior College, KB had instead used a Harmon Grant to attend Northeastern State in the fall of 1964.

"KB had wanted to follow me to Fort Scott JuCo," Chuck Berry said in an email. Had he done so, he would have been reunited with Bucky and Nowata teammates Clarence Smith and Richard Nash. He apparently made the final decision with his head rather than his heart and followed the Harmon Grant administrator's advice to Roy Berry that KB attend a four-year school, which meant not playing football. The decision left KB rudderless.

"I had the impression," Chuck said, "that he was not ready emotionally for college, and, without sports for an identity, he was not doing well." KB did not meet the academic requirements to retain the Harmon Grant, and, according to Chuck, became "disillusioned." He left Northeastern State to find the military draft staring him hard in the face.

Back in Nowata and, like old times, parked in one of their cars at the Dairy Dell, KB, Bucky, and Charles got into another conversation about the biggest decision in their young lives. "We all knew we would be drafted," Charles Dugger said. "The Nowata Draft Board was preparing to draft us. We didn't have any influence. We were just country boys." It was a question of when, not if. Decisions had to be made, KB's sooner than those of his friends.

No one would run from their duty. As Bucky put it: "No questions. Man up and serve." To my friends, "Canada" was another word for "coward." Bucky and Charles suggested the better course of action would be to enlist in the Navy or the Air Force for four years. They told KB that all of them "would stand a better chance of not going to Vietnam" by doing so. Had I been there, I might have proposed the alternative I found in Barstow, California, after I reported for my first job. I joined the National Guard and served six years of part-time duty after four-to-six-month basic and advanced training. The problem was: Openings in National Guard and Army Reserve units were few. Charles discovered this when he took a job teaching in Tucumcari, New Mexico. He joined the Air Force, and Bucky went into the Navy, serving a tour off Vietnam.

KB listened to the alternatives, which he already understood. He had made up his mind. No Air Force. No Navy. "Not me," KB told Charles and Bucky. "I'm only going to give them two years, not four." He gave so much more. He gave everything. "We told him," Charles said, "that if he did that, it was about 100 percent sure he was going to Vietnam."

In early September 1966, KB Berry was a new Army recruit on his way to Fort Bliss at El Paso, Texas, for basic training. Two years later, in August, I followed the leader of the Ironmen to Fort Bliss for my own basic training. Though in different training companies of different battalions, I'm sure I went through what KB had, with the exception that, when the last shot had been fired on the rifle range at White Sands, New Mexico, and the screams of drill sergeants had faded, our paths diverged. KB went to Vietnam and died. I returned to my life.

That life was nomadic during the six years I served in National Guard and Army Reserve units as I moved from newspaper to newspaper, unit to unit. Unless you were a journalist at the top of the pecking order, chances were you worked in a one-newspaper town. If you wanted a better job or newspaper, you moved. So the Okie who was lost when forced to move from Nowata became an habitual mover. I served in six units in six years, beginning as a supply clerk and becoming whatever my next unit needed—personnel specialist, armored-unit loader, scout driver, company clerk, and, finally, information specialist, the closest fit with my work. The job furthest removed? Military policeman, 186th Military Police Company, Des Moines, Iowa.

Officially, I was a senior security guard. My unit's primary function—one performed during active duty each summer—was to construct prisoner-of-war compounds, which, we then, theoretically, would run. In reality, we were an all-purpose military-police unit, none of it for which I had been trained. I learned on the fly. My MP moment, while brief, coincided with some of the worst civil and racial unrest in the country. Violence flared on campuses and in inner cities, and my unit was caught up in it in 1970. After someone bombed a Drake University building, our summer became endless night shifts guarding the Iowa Highway Patrol radio tower, state law-enforcement communications hub. We patrolled a perimeter around the tower armed with shotguns. Like the legendary Barney Fife of *The Andy*

Griffith Show, we were even issued ammunition. Unlike Sheriff Andy, our superiors allowed us more than one shell.

Because local law enforcement was able to bring a downtown Des Moines disturbance under control before they had to call us from standby at the armory, I never felt in the danger KB must have known from the moment he arrived in Vietnam. Likewise, in the Air Force, Charles Dugger's worst injury, for which he still draws a disability payment, stemmed from action on a racquetball court while off duty at Lackland Air Force Base in San Antonio. Charles, who had a degree in education, became part of a new program to prepare recruits for technical school. He spent his four-year enlistment at Lackland and came away acknowledging that, while his group had contributed valuable instruction, he was "the luckiest SOB in the world." None of us, not even Storekeeper Second Class Bucky Buck during his days off Vietnam, found ourselves in danger doing what we believed our duty.

Bucky had been privy to a preview of what could go wrong. After basic training and as he was on his way from Fort Bliss to Fort Polk for AIT, KB stopped in Nowata to see the love of his life, Sharon Weaver, and visit Bucky. He and Sharon, Bucky, and Barb were at Bucky's house preparing to go to a dance, as Bucky remembered it, and there was a 30–30 rifle belonging to Bucky's stepfather leaning against the wall of a small bedroom. When KB spotted the rifle, he picked it up, pointed it at a wall, cocked back the hammer and pulled off a round. It was loaded.

The explosion was deafening. Shocked, Bucky grabbed the gun, eyes wide. "Wow," he said. "I hope they don't give you a gun in the Army!" It was *almost* funny.

There was nothing funny, however, about what KB told Bucky after completing AIT without becoming a danger to others. The incident with the loaded rifle was an anomaly. He had proved himself, when he joined his Air Calvary Unit at Fort Knox in February 1967, to be the KB he had been on the football field: A true leader. He may have saved the life of medic Harry Schropp during a training exercise that went wrong.

As Schropp's platoon practiced an assault, dry grass ignited, and the fire was soon out of control. As Schropp helped to fight the blaze, his fatigues caught fire. KB and others got him to the ground—a tackle?—and rolled the medic everyone called "Doc" in the dirt until they had extinguished his clothing. Afterward, KB stayed beside Doc until medics arrived and evacuated him to a hospital. Schropp never forgot. Out of respect, he later named a son Berry Schropp.

The incident and its aftermath suggest KB's leadership and ability to win people's trust remained as strong as on the football field. The stakes, however, were higher. Football sometimes felt to us as if it were life and death. It wasn't. Vietnam would be. For KB, the soldiers of B Troop, 3rd Squadron, 17th Cavalry, 1st Aviation Brigade became his team. One of them was Leon Turman, a Texan born in Abilene and reared in Fort Worth. That gave him something in common with the little quarterback from a small Oklahoma town. "We threw jokes back and forth," Turman said, Red River Rivals becoming comrades. "We were all tight," Turman said of the unit. "If someone needed something, everybody stepped up." Turman was even closer to Schropp, which is how he came to share the fire story and KB's role. Turman and Schropp were prime enemy targets, Schropp as medic and Turman as radio-telephone operator (RTO), literally right-hand man of the officer-in-charge. If the Viet Cong and the North Vietnamese regulars could take out those three, they reduced their enemy's effectiveness.

Turman and KB had something in common besides geography. Both were engaged. Before they shipped out for Vietnam from Oakland, California, on September 15, Leon married his fiancée. KB and Sharon Weaver decided to wait. If anyone had a sense of why, it was Bucky Buck. Among many conversations that filled the days and nights of KB's visit to Tahlequah following AIT, one haunted Bucky. "One disturbing reality," Bucky called it. KB doubted he would survive Vietnam. "I don't know if it was a premonition or what," Bucky told me. Leon Turman also knew KB had shared with Bucky "a notion he would not return [from Nam]."

Could KB have been protecting Sharon from the pain of a losing a husband? No matter what the status of their relationship—fiancée or wife—if you love someone as much as Sharon loved KB, the pain must have been unbearable. When I wrote about KB ten years after his death, Jewel Berry told me the family still heard from Sharon, whom Roy Berry had seen to it received the Harmon Grant that had been KB's. She finished college alone and had not married, "because," Jewel said, "she still looks for the same qualities she had found in KB."

Unlike Sharon, who knew KB loved her, I live with gnawing uncertainty concerning his feelings about me or whether he thought of me at all after he had lost football and cast his fate, against the advice of his friends, with fulfilling his military obligation in the shortest, and, he believed, best way possible. My feelings aren't important, yet I can't rid myself of the question: Why would he feel the same about me or think well of me? I left KB long before he left me, even if only as an unintended consequence of a move that physically separated us.

In reviewing and comparing what he had written in my sophomore yearbook with the words he left me in the 1964 *Ironman* two years later, the change brought a realization: KB no longer knew what to say to me. The fault was unforgivably mine, the result of the injurious relocation to California I lacked the maturity to handle. KB died without me reiterating and showing him how much I loved him.

Fighting a war that grew more and more inexplicable, expended priceless human treasure, and generated lies to cover up Vietnam failures, KB found himself on a fatal mission that went wrong from the get-go. He could have been saved by mission decision-makers the day he died, but they, like those higher in the hierarchy (President Johnson, General Westmoreland, et al), had lost their bearings and sense of right.

When I attended, in 1974, the 10-year reunion of the Nowata High School class of '64, of which I am not a part, yet included through the kindness of old friends, my classmates spoke guardedly of their brightest star, to whom they had dedicated the event. I wonder now how they would respond if they heard, as I have, the story of January 6, 1968, the day Kenneth Beryl Berry died. I finally know the truth, because Leon Turman shared it with me. He was there. He witnessed it, and eventually, in 2017, he sought out the remaining Berrys—Margie Pierce, Erville Orndorff, and Chuck—and told them what the Army never had.

Turman's takeaway? Kenneth Berry did not have to die that day.

Leon Turman tried for years to erase what he saw and heard on January 6 and the damning conclusion to which it led him. He had done everything he could "to try to forget," he said, not only that day but his entire Vietnam experience. He had his work as an electrician, which led to electrical foreman at the Federal Bureau of Prisons (FBOP) in Fort Worth. Transferred to design and construction, Turman's job took him throughout the country to build federal prisons, including a Super Max. As those responsibilities grew, so did his family, with wife Debora and their two children. He had a good life. But Leon Turman could not forget KB, especially each Memorial Day and Veterans Day.

In 2012, Turman was diagnosed with Post Traumatic Stress Disorder (PTSD) and received "intensive inpatient treatment." His psychiatrist encouraged Turman to do what he long had told his wife he had wanted to do, *had* to do—find where KB is buried. Before the Internet and search apps, this was not as simple as it is today. Turman inserted "Kenneth B. Berry" and "Oklahoma" into findagrave.com. Turman had thought KB's hometown was Stillwater. It wasn't. Nowata popped up. "We're going to go," he told his wife.

On a trip east from Colorado in 2015, Turman and his wife stopped in Nowata and visited Memorial Park Cemetery. There, he found a flat, gray military marker, level with the ground, inscribed with KB's name, unit, dates of birth and death. Standard military issue. The place and the grave presented Turman a new opportunity to renew an old connection. It felt different and good to Turman. In January 1968, he and other members of the 17th Air Cavalry had been flown from their base camp to Di An, where they recognized the loss of one of their own. In military tradition, there were boots on the ground, an M-16 stuck into it, helmet atop the rifle butt. A chaplain led the brief service, but he had not known Kenneth, so something was missing besides KB's remains, already on their way home.

KB Berry gravestone, Nowata Memorial Park Cemetery. [*Photo courtesy the author*]

When he located KB's grave in Nowata, Turman placed a letter, prepared in advance and inserted into a plastic bag, into one of two urns that adorn the gravestone of KB's parents, Roy and Jewel Berry. The letter explained who he was, provided contact information, and shared how he had known KB. He then placed a quarter on KB's marker—a symbol among service members, Turman said, that the remembered person had been a "solid comrade."

A couple of weeks later, Turman received a call from Erville Orndorff, KB's sister, who had been given the unopened letter by sister Jan Wyrick, who discovered it. In 2017, Turman made another trip to Oklahoma from his home in Canon City, Colorado, to meet with KB's family and best friend Bucky Buck. "In my heart," Leon Turman said, "I felt I needed to do this, and they just confirmed it. I'm grateful that I did. I think they were relieved knowing that there are other people who cared for KB as much as they did." As he told me the background to the story, Turman's voice cracked with emotion. It is a difficult story to tell, hear, or write.

After KB's unit arrived at their base camp at Black Virgin (Nui Ba Den) Mountain at the end of October 1968, they dug trenches and foxholes, some with paid help from the friendly South Vietnamese. Most days, they mounted up in their Hueys and flew in support of scout ships, gunships, anything that had gone down and left soldiers in need of help. They secured the area as best they could until personnel from the downed chopper could be airlifted out and then dismantled and/or destroyed any airship that could not be made operable.

On January 6, a group of four Bell Huey UH troop carriers departed base camp on a mission into a heavily jungled area in which a North Vietnamese regiment was suspected to be present. Sgt. Kenneth Berry, armed with his M-16, sat in the open doorway on the left side of the Huey, in the squad leader's seat. The crew chief occupied another seat in the opening. With an M-60 machine gun, he assisted the opposite-side gunner in laying down fire to supplement that of the gunships. Heavy ground fire from North Vietnamese 50-caliber machine guns was supposed to have been eliminated, or at least stanched, by B-52 bombers that had preceded the choppers into the dangerous terrain. It hadn't been. There was a hail of gunfire.

"The mission just failed," said Turman, who, with his radio, was seated next to the troop commander in a doorway of the third helicopter. "It failed the minute the B-52s missed the target." They were to bomb the two landing zones. They missed by three-to-five miles, Turman estimates. Air Cav's Troop B went in, despite the failure. It followed a chopper with a platoon of regular infantry, not Air Cav trained especially for such missions. KB's chopper came next. Truman, from his perch, witnessed it all.

"In my opinion," Turman said, "they made the wrong decision." He did not know who made the decision or "where the orders came from." But, sitting with the troop commander, he heard every word. "The commanders should never have put anyone else on the ground." But they did. "We were going to do this recon mission." Come hell or more hell.

Reconnaissance turned into firestorm. In the military, they use a saltier word that begins with "s" to describe such a storm. When the first chopper landed in the zone the bombers had failed to clear, it and its men fell under heavy fire. As KB's Huey approached the second landing zone, with Turman's behind and slightly to the right, KB and his Troop B squad also drew intense fire. It was the type of moment KB had tried to avoid telling his mother about when she sought to learn the level of danger he faced, day in and day out. "'It'd be hard to explain,' he'd hedged, 'but, Mom, we *are* shooting at each other over here.'"

In Leon Turman's estimation, KB never knew he had been hit, probably with a .50-caliber round. U.S. Army letters the Berrys received, including from Major Henry Shehorn, had assured them their Kenneth "did not suffer any pain" because "he died instantly." Turman's more detailed eyewitness account, which he likes neither to remember nor share, was more graphic. He concurred, though, that KB was dead before he tumbled out of the helicopter and "literally fell into the jungle" 60 feet below as the helicopter went down.

The pilots crashed in the landing zone as other choppers, including Turman's, peeled off and away from the gunfire, rotor blades clipping treetops. The crew chief of Turman's helicopter was shouting: "We've been hit. We're going down." Though a blade had indeed been struck, Turman's pilots kept the chopper aloft and flew to a stand-by location for repairs.

With an armored unit on its way to the site, no other Air Cav troop went in until the infantry platoon first on the ground helped to get KB's squad out of the crashed helicopter. One of the four Hueys that had begun the mission returned to evacuate the injured, though still under heavy fire, despite shelling of the jungle on both sides of the landing zones by U.S. gunships. No one could be immediately sent to locate KB's body.

This troubled Turman and his comrades. They knew the atrocities committed on those the Vietnamese found. "They do devastating things to an American serviceman who has fallen into the jungle," Turman said. "(But) if they saw KB fall, they couldn't locate his body."

When the armored unit arrived two days later, they found KB, dog tags around his neck, rifle and ammunition untouched, remains intact except for his fatal wound. KB was awarded posthumously a Purple Heart, Vietnam Service Medal with four bronze service stars, Vietnam Campaign Medal, and National Defense Service Medal. The Berrys received the American flag that draped KB's coffin and a Gold Star lapel button, symbolic "that no one has given more for the nation than the families of the fallen."

For ten years, these pieces, among others, became part of a virtual shrine to KB's memory in the Berry home. Jewel Berry then moved them to a less-obtrusive space that they shared with photos not only of those gone but also other Berry children, grandchildren, and, at the time, one great-grandchild. "I studied and studied before I took the things down," Jewel said. "I finally decided that was what I needed to do." She could not, however, bring herself to open a trunk with, among KB's other belongings, his Nowata Ironman letterman's jacket.

She knew what the letterman jacket had meant to KB. When he and the rest of us first pulled on those jackets with the black leather sleeves and heavy maroon cloth body, a maroon "N" outlined in white and gold footballs and basketballs with little stripes signifying the number of years we had lettered embedded in it, our chests swelled with pride. In the Berry household older brothers Warren and Chuck had made letterman jackets the proud attire of successful Nowata young men. KB's jacket meant more than mine. He had joined an exclusive club—the family club—and he treasured that jacket for the symbol it was to every Berry.

Fifty years after we received those precious jackets—I think it was just after the 1961 football season—the Berry brothers' status in their hometown was enshrined with their induction into the Nowata High School Athletic Hall of Fame, KB and Warren (Rooster) posthumously. In the gym in which KB's packed memorial service had been held, the remaining siblings—Margie Pierce, Erville Orndorff, and Jan Wyrick—joined Chuck to receive the honor. Erville accepted on behalf of KB, and Margie and Jan did the honors for Warren. "It was one more time we could honor the memory of our brothers," Margie told Mike Tupa, sports editor of the *Bartlesville Examiner-Enterprise*. "We were eight children, and all of us participated by being with them and watching them and their love for the sport."

[Oldest brother Wesley Eugene and sister Helen were deceased. Jan, the youngest, died in 2016.]

"It was very, very meaningful," Chuck Berry told Tupa, "particularly since I got to go in with my deceased brothers." Gene Berry had had to work to help support the family, but he shared the family interest in sports, in part through a leadership role in the Quarterback Club. "I don't have a memory of not shooting a basketball, pitching a baseball, or throwing a football," Chuck said. "It was just assumed you could play ball, some kind of ball."

On Friday nights—and more than a few others, too—the Berrys were either playing for the Ironmen or cheering on those who did. Being a Berry in Nowata came not only with joy but also responsibility to live up to the honored name. Despite being the smallest of the four brothers, the joyful KB jumped on that responsibility as if it were a fumble.

"He never realized he was smaller," Chuck said. "Two of us would throw him balls when he was four years old." They never stopped. That's why, when he lost football, KB lost himself. Football, basketball—all sports, really—*were* KB's identity. "Without sports for an identity," as Chuck had said, KB may have felt he had nowhere to turn. I wish I could have talked with him during this time and reminded him that he had always talked of coaching.

KB knew the life he wanted, that his future would be sharing with young athletes what had been shared with him. Everyone saw it. In a Q&A accompanying his senior yearbook photo, the editors had KB down pat:

"Pet Like": "Sports."

"Noted For": "Interest in sports."

"Probable Occupation": "Coach."

"He was a student of the game," Chuck said.

As the littlest brother, with fewer physical assets than Warren or Chuck, KB adapted. Bucky Buck recognized that, as much as his legs or arm, KB used his brain to play quarterback. It's why Bucky and the rest of us listened to KB. Because he knew his X's and O's, the coaches gave him responsibility and allowed him to adjust on the fly. The most difficult aspect of KB's death was accepting the fact of great promise unfulfilled, his effect on young lives forever lost.

When he reads of an Oklahoma high school coach's induction into their Hall of Fame, Charles Dugger cannot help but think: "That probably would have been him." Charles is right. KB's teammates envisioned him coaching high school football or basketball, perhaps remaining in the profession for the entirety of a long, successful career. When Charles lamented our loss and that of players who would never know KB, an analogous backstory came to mind.

Lincoln Riley had been a good quarterback for a small school in Muleshoe, Texas, a place in the Texas Panhandle much like Nowata. When *Oklahoman* columnist Berry Tramel talked to Muleshoe's longtime football coach David Wood on the occasion of Riley succeeding Bob Stoops as Oklahoma coach, Wood could have been describing KB Berry and Nowata. "Kids just loved him," Wood said. "Everyone's a hero in a small town. Young kids look up to the varsity kids. He had a big following when he was coming through high school. Not only did they know him, he would take the time and just visit with those small kids and the junior high kids. He had a great knack for stuff like that." KB had that knack for kindness.

Riley quarterbacked the Muleshoe Mules to great success, even more than KB's with his Ironmen. When he was an 11-year-old playing backyard football, Riley was drawing up plays in the grass. It's what KB did on the playground of Nowata Elementary School. Riley walked on and tried to play quarterback at Texas Tech, only to discover that, despite a mind for the game, he, too, was about to lose football before he was finished with it. That is when Coach Mike Leach gave Riley an option I wish KB had had. Dana Holgorsen,

Tech inside receivers coach, heard Leach tell Riley, "You know, you're not a very good quarterback, but you're asking a lot of really, really smart questions, so you might ought to try coaching." Leach offered a student assistantship, and the smartest kid from Muleshoe accepted.

After four years of go-fering and learning, Riley moved up to graduate assistant coach, and, when he was 23, to a full-time position coaching receivers. Near the end of Riley's tenure at Tech, the university suspended and then fired Leach, and defensive coordinator Ruffin McNeil took over for the 2009 Alamo Bowl against Michigan State. McNeil needed someone to coordinate the offense and call the plays, jobs Leach had done. McNeil turned to Riley. He still looked like a Muleshoe student but produced 579 total yards and guided the Red Raiders from a 31–27 fourth-quarter deficit to a 41–31 victory. "Professionally," said Riley, who was 26, "the toughest thing I ever had to do." The result registered with Oklahoma Coach Bob Stoops.

When Ruffin was hired as East Carolina coach, he took Riley with him as offensive coordinator. Four years later, Stoops hired Riley away, and after two years of continued success in Norman, Stoops retired, in part, because he wanted Riley to succeed him. Riley was 33—a dozen years older than KB Berry when he died in Vietnam. As I have watched Riley, the quarterback-who-couldn't become the coach-who-could, I have concluded that, as exceptional as Riley's football intellect is, it is not unique, and he is not one of a kind.

Lincoln Riley and KB Berry are two sides of the same shiny coin—Lincoln what is, KB what might have been. While it would be overreaching to believe KB could have been our generation's Lincoln Riley, KB's cerebral, sometimes magical answers to the game's riddles was not unlike Riley's. The athletic acumen in the Berry bloodline did not die with KB. His niece, Joni Lehmann, daughter of Erville Orndorff of Bartlesville and Bill James of Nowata, is a chip off the ol' QB. After her parents took Joni to Nowata games to watch her cousins play, she found her niche in athletic communications at her alma mater, the University of Oklahoma, where she and mom still attend Sooner football games together.

"She is my only child," Erville said, "and we have a very special mother-daughter relationship."

Joni was a little more than six months old when her uncle was killed in Vietnam. But she was born into the right extended family, one in which a love of athletics seems genetically encoded, and hers came alive in Nowata, where she did what so many little girls did. She became a cheerleader at four and bonded with the games she loved. She never forsook them. In April 2019, she received, from the College Sports Information Directors of America (CoSIDA), a 25-year Award for her work. "Throughout her storied career," CoSIDA pointed out in a story announcing the award, "Lehmann has developed into a strategic-communications professional with extensive experience in media relations, event management, and leadership." From student assistant in the Oklahoma media-relations office to University of Kentucky intern to Stephen F. Austin State University women's sports-information director to Southeastern Conference assistant media-relations director and, finally, in more than 20 years with the Big 12 Conference, her work put athletes in a spotlight she helped the media shine on them.

Though our career paths never crossed, Joni Lehmann is the kind of professional I admired while spending half my life in press boxes, locker rooms, and press rooms. I would not have expected less from Kenneth Berry's niece. At the time she was honored by CoSIDA, Joni was Big 12 Director of Media Services, which included coordinating Big 12 football and men's basketball championships, as well as media days, for both sports. Maybe most important, she has taught countless students how to be true professionals and then helped them find jobs after they had learned enough to emulate her.

While it may not rise to the level of her CoSIDA 25-Year Award, Joni's induction in 2017 into the Nowata Athletic Hall of Fame, where she joined her illustrious uncles, offered those of us who still mourn KB the solace of continuity we never thought possible.

DOUGLAS MERLE "BUCKY" BUCK: JANUARY 3, 1946—MAY 8, 2018

When he was alive and helping with this book in his inimitable, valuable way, Bucky Buck and I communicated almost daily via email. He answered endless questions with patience and good humor, filling the gaps in my knowledge and memory, propping me up when doubt bedeviled me. I still talk to Bucky daily as I traipse around the Chapel in Green's parking lot and gravel walking path for four-to-five miles of exercise. My pace is good, not great. Bucky would no doubt accuse me of having lost a step since our fullback days, maybe more than one.

Bucky Buck in Delaware Indian garb, his obituary photo. [*Photo provided by Barbara Jo Kerr*]

I choose the Chapel to engage in unrequited conversations with Bucky that make me look like the old fool I am, not because I'm a believer, but because Bucky was. He had it covered: Christian beliefs (divine afterlife? check); Delaware tribal beliefs (guiding spirits? check). Bucky's was a world familiar yet strange to me, one to which he was born and lovingly, knowledgeably supported. In his regalia, he danced at tribal ceremonies, still a star who could make a glad heart sing. Foremost among Bucky's dual faiths, the one with which he kept sadness at bay was the belief he would soon see best friend KB Berry again.

Life's final great mystery is what comes after death. I do not pretend to know. After KB's death, I concluded what is important is not the hereafter but the here and now. I let KB down. I did not want to do the same with Bucky after he came back into my life. At the 50th reunion of Nowata High School's Class of 1964, Bucky and I resurrected a friendship that might have appeared dead but had only gone dormant, victim of time, separation, and malnourishment.

Since I have proved myself an imperfect friend, it is incumbent that the shared bond on which the friendship is based be strong, lest the moment be lost. Kenneth Berry was the glue that bound us. When I mentioned the idea of this book, Bucky was all in. *Great,* I thought, *I have not only a co-conspirator and confidant but also an interested reader.*

I knew Bucky had survived a stroke and lung cancer, but he looked as healthy as any of us old people who, in the fall of 2014, attended that 50th reunion, which, of course, had to include watching the Ironmen play some football. Could it really have been 50 years since we were the ones out there on Ironmen Memorial Field? Before the game, as he always did, Bucky and other veterans who were members of Nowata's American Legion post raised the flag to the top of the staff behind the north end zone, a ceremony he considered both duty and joy.

It was not until three years later, during a research visit to Nowata, that I realized the state of Bucky's health was not what it had been. He had difficulty breathing (COPD) but again marched out to that end zone to raise the flag. Soon his lung cancer would return with a vengeance, the necessary chemotherapy treatments complicated by new problems. His steadfast optimism concerning his ability to again plow through this roadblock required reading between the lines, which sometimes was difficult. Bucky was, I think, protective of me, as I suspect he was of others not in Nowata and unable to observe closely what was going on.

Fewer than three weeks after my 2017 visit, Bucky wound up in a hospital emergency room after spitting up blood. Tests began—CAT scan, X-rays, with antibiotic chaser, and then a bronchoscopy. Within a week, he had a report: the cancer had returned in his lungs and adenoids. Another CAT scan, accompanied by magnetic resonance imaging (MRI) and blood work, determined a course of chemotherapy.

During this initial phase, Bucky seemed more worried about what Bob Craig, who had inherited the Nowata football team, was going through than his own situation. Bucky had had cancer. He knew the drill. He knew its return was serious, but he was the eternal optimist. "I won't back down," he promised. Nobody who knew Bucky believed he would. Bucky, a Quarterback Club member, had met Craig about the time Bucky had ended up in the emergency room. He immediately liked him. He liked the way he treated the players and talked with them. He relished that he prayed with them. "It was indicative," Bucky said, "of someone I would want my kids to play for." An experienced coach but new to Nowata, Craig had been asked to step up from assistant to head coach after his boss resigned as a result of an incident that occurred with a student supporter of the Ironmen following a disastrous first game. "I hope they keep him," he told me when I asked his opinion of the upheaval and Craig's chances.

This was Bucky—concerned about others before himself. Not that he liked everyone. He had strong opinions. He railed at San Francisco quarterback Colin Kaepernick for Kaepernick's means of protesting social and racial injustice; he knelt on the sideline during the national anthem before NFL games. Bucky thought Kaepernick's concern would be better expressed in the neighborhoods where he saw injustices occurring. Bucky virtually quit watching the NFL. Neither could he countenance his Cleveland Indians succumbing to Major League Baseball's pressure to remove Chief Wahoo, their longstanding logo/mascot no longer deemed acceptable. Political correctness had gone too far in the opinion of one of the proudest Native Americans I ever knew. "Jim Thorpe," Bucky said, "would have scalped Kaepernick." That wasn't all: "My Wahoo ballcap remains on my head in Oklahoma, and, if someone differs, we can settle that." Even in his physical condition, Bucky was a fighter, and he was about to prove it.

Before he could begin chemo, Bucky and wife Sandy visited a beach on the Gulf Coast for what they knew might be the last of their good times for a while. As they were downing all-you-can-eat shrimp, Bucky's oncologist called. More bad news. Tests had revealed two lesions on Bucky's brain that his doctors feared were cancerous. "My reaction," Bucky said, "was *Hallelujah*." Huh? He told doctors it was good that someone believes he *has* a brain and that the two spots provide proof. If there had been any time left in his medical schedule to visit a psychiatrist, the person might have suggested he was cloaking other feelings with humor. So?

This, too, was Bucky. I don't believe he was hiding as much as coping, something he wished the rest of us would do. It pained him to see others suffer with him. Faith and fun at his own expense, he believed, would see him through. I attempted to adopt his approach, though he recognized I lacked faith, in a religious sense. "You either have faith, or you don't," he said, uncritically. Our emails, of course, included much about his condition and treatment, but we gave equal attention to our shared love of the Nowata Ironmen and Oklahoma Sooners. I had no road map but tried to be upbeat, to keep him involved in my research, and not to shy from cheap shots for cheap laughs, in which we sometimes indulged.

When his medical team addressed his "fun" little brain boo-boos, they made a mask with holes that permitted intense radiation from a "cyber knife" to be focused on his cancerous lesions. To Bucky, it amounted to putting an arrow in a bulls-eye. "Since I am a [member of the Delaware Nation]," he joked, "the treatment is called KEMOSABE. All I need now is the Lone Ranger and Silver."

Growing up in Nowata, a town that could feel as rural as the countryside, Bucky had had a big white horse named "Silver." Bucky received a hand-me-down "beautiful black saddle with German silver" from his Aunt Avis, whose parade and show horse, a palomino, had grown too old for eye-catching tricks. The gift had a stipulation: Don't use the gear for everyday riding.

Bucky, a good listener, could be imperfect in his hearing, like all us little boys. He abided by the rule until he "wanted to show off [saddle, bridle, breastplate, *himself*]. "I got old Silver all decked out, put on my best cowboy hat, and headed to show the boys a real stud—me!" Bucky said. He met buddies near the golf course, and they raced out of town on Brick Plant road. Bucky and Silver won with an inspired effort that was a bit much for old Silver. To celebrate and cool off, Silver lay down in a muddy pond—"with my fine saddle and me aboard." Bucky rode his clever but dirty horse home and began cleaning gear. When his dad saw the mess, he was not happy. "I hope you learned a lesson," he told Bucky. Indeed his son had—though not the one HL Buck intended. The lesson? "What fun I had," Bucky said, "growing up a heathen."

Bucky never changed. It is why people loved him. When he was telling me about the mask and the dangers inherent with the cyber-knife procedure, he did not dwell on the fact that "this bump in the road is a little tougher than before," including the danger that his brain could swell and a host of other things that could go wrong. Instead, waiting for the first treatment, he reexamined the mask and came to a typically Bucky conclusion: "I think Hannibal Lecter would like a copy." Thomas Harris's cannibalistic forensic psychiatrist could have worn it while dining on "some fava beans and a nice Chianti" with lovely Clarice Starling in *The Silence of the Lambs.*

In early November, some six weeks after he had gone to the emergency room and learned his cancer was no longer in remission, the doctors inserted a port in his chest, below the collarbone, in order to administer chemo drugs, draw blood, give shots, and perform a myriad of other insults to this man, who, one nurse concluded was "tough as a boot." Her conclusion came after the Bucks had failed to apply properly "a dollop of deadening medicine" an hour before arriving at the hospital where the nurse stuck a needle into the port to draw blood. Bucky's response was so pronounced—"I almost pissed my pants"—the nurse felt compelled to ask, unnecessarily: "Did that hurt?" Bucky responded in kind: "Hell, yeah." So she stuck him again. "This time," Bucky said, "it *really* hurt." He and Sandy applied the deadening medicine properly before his next visit—and many to follow.

When communication between his many doctors broke down and resulted in delaying his chemo, Bucky went on the warpath. From the first, he had been proactive in his treatment. "I will guard my rights as to being jerked around by their lack of communication," he told me. He was supposed to begin chemo—finally—on December 4, but it again was pushed back a week. The strain showed. "I ain't got the patience of a baby with poopy drawers," Bucky declared. His situation stunk. But after the first of 12 chemo treatments, which was "not so terrible," Bucky allowed that the fight joined had given him a "rejuvenated state of mind."

Though encouraged, I lacked Bucky's mindset. I am more akin to essayist Tim Kreider, whose "Sister World," a part of *We Learn Nothing*, suggested he and his newly discovered two half-sisters were the same *type* of person: "smarter than was good for us, prone to gloomy introspection, moody and oversensitive." For myself, the latter three descriptors stand, but I would have to alter the first to "not quite as smart as [I] need to be." Bucky possessed different smarts, ones revealed in a practicality born of respect for education, a quality grandson Dempsey seems to have inherited.

After he received two years of education at Fort Scott (Kansas) Community College in exchange for his linebacking toughness, Bucky could have taken his talents to the University of Miami in Coral Gables, Florida. It tempted him, but he knew himself better than his recruiters did. Miami was a place too far. "Too far away for a poor boy," he said. He stayed close to home and obtained in 1968 a bachelor of science degree in business administration, with minors in economics and history, from Northeastern State University in Tahlequah. After four years in the Navy, he discovered his education had set him up perfectly for a career not far removed from the oilfields where he had spent summers alongside his dad and uncles. "My education," he said, "helped me throughout my life—with job, knowledge, and a can-do attitude."

The can-do attitude blossomed in the fresh air. With Williams Pipeline Service and Magellan Pipeline, Bucky welded on pipelines throughout the United States before shutting down his torch in 2006. That was a dozen years after he had suffered a stroke that threatened both his career and golf game. Bucky may have moved on from football but not from sports. He golfed frequently and became a member at Nowata Country Club, a course on which I'd learned the game so long ago; its sand greens made it a one-putt paradise. Greens of grass were more difficult by the time Bucky contrived a contraption that allowed him to get back on the course, despite lingering effects of the stroke. I don't understand the mechanics, but he and a friend accomplished this by acquiring a golf cart, jury-rigging it with a "bungee cord" that enabled his weakened left hand to maintain a grip on the club. "It actually helped my game," Bucky claimed. "I slowed down [the swing] and was hitting the ball more squarely."

This brainstorm, when he shared it with the doctor overseeing his rehabilitation, prompted him to give Bucky permission to return to the pipeline. "If you can do that," he told Bucky, "you can go back to work." He had been off for a couple of months, and his prescribed rehab had not produced the desired results, so Bucky invented his golf version. *Voilà!* "I jumped back in the ditch," Bucky said, "and started welding."

It looked for a time as if Bucky's faith and perseverance might allow him to overcome the brain lesions and recurrence of lung cancer as he had once rehabbed himself following his stroke. Doctors' reports he shared sounded encouraging. The large brain lesion disappeared, and the smaller one shrunk noticeably. A CAT scan following the earliest rounds of chemotherapy looked promising. A radiologist's review supported his doctors' conclusions. Bucky's self-report was: "Have fared quite well with this treatment. Sleeping good, peeing great, hunger for food moderate, but I eat well." Four chemo treatments down, eight to go.

At his oncology center, Bucky encountered a man, three years older, who warned him that, after seven chemo treatments, he would be sick. Bucky expressed doubt based on prior chemo experience. "I'll bet you a hundred-dollar bill you are," the man said. After Bucky elaborated on his "odyssey through the cancer world" and shared testimony concerning how Jesus Christ and prayer had strengthened and guided him, the man asked to call off their bet. "Sure," Bucky replied, no doubt grinning. "I knew from the start I had already won the bet."

Bucky's positivity seemed to have no bounds. After this incident at the oncology center, he bought grandson Dempsey an old electric

Club Car to tool around grandpa's property, because Dempsey had admired Bucky's. They would each need one, because Bucky was going to live. More and more, though, Bucky leaned on his religious beliefs and humor. "I have not gone over the edge," he promised me, before adding, "but I ain't far [from it]."

The week of February 4, 2018 "started on a high note but finished with a new direction," Bucky told me in an email that arrived on a Friday evening. I don't usually check my email at that time, but when I unplugged my phone from its charger, the screen popped on, and his email popped up. "Bud," he said, "I hate to break this to you like this, but the truth works better all the way around." No soft-pedaling. No euphemisms. Just Bucky.

I had worried when I had not heard from him since Sunday. It was not like Bucky. He had spent Tuesday and Wednesday in the hospital with severe breathing problems. After tests, he had reached "a truthful assessment of what condition my condition was in!" Really, Bucky? You can laugh at yourself in this moment when all I could do was cry? "Bottom line," he said, "between the COPD and cancer, plus the chemo, we were losing ground. The chemo was doing more harm to my immune system than [it] was to the cancer." Though he continued to express optimism that he would be able to "kick some more off the bucket list," he and Sandy and others close to him had "chosen to go with hospice to manage the pain and give a better quality of life to whenever" the end might come. To be eligible for hospice under Medicare, Bucky's health insurance, a physician must conclude life expectancy is six months or less.

Though Bucky had never been a quitter, a finality hung over me like a black cloud. Not even the Bucky bucket list—watch another NCAA Basketball Tournament, become the new John Maynard Keynes or the next POTUS—could lift it. I treaded carefully in the strange land and unpracticed role of standing by a dying friend. As

I explained to Bucky: "There are many downsides to finding ourselves in this moment. The one that matters most to me, however, is that I am here, and you are there, and it feels as if there is nothing I can do." Standing by someone from a distance is oxymoronic. I had questions about his hospice care—at home [what I expected] or in a facility? There was time for answers. What was most important, given neither of us would know when the end might arrive, was to tell Bucky, plainly, how much I loved him. This isn't something men instinctively know how to say to each other.

Even in this moment, I may not have been as straightforward as Bucky. Or maybe it is that I cannot divorce myself from trying to be writerly. In any case, I explained that I had showed my wife, Jackie, whom Bucky was always reminding me to give a hug on his behalf, his email. Since my eyes were full of tears as I handed it to her to read, and she had been following closely Bucky's travails, I didn't have to say much. Good thing. I could not speak for sobbing. As always, the response of the woman who is my rock, was perfect. I shared it with Bucky. "I love Bucky, too," she told me, "but I know my love is *nothing* compared with yours."

It took Bucky time to respond. When word of his condition got out, he had had visits from friends for a week. When he finally had time and energy to write, he reiterated, as he would continually, that he had not given up hope. Of course, by accepting hospice's palliative care, he no longer was receiving treatment that might offer that hope, even if false. Bucky understood. "I just know the chemo was fruitless," he said, "and was accomplishing nothing."

He continued to live what life he had left, including attending Nowata basketball games during a season when, unlike football, the team was strong. He saw it win its district and reach the post-season regionals, but he paid a price. "Mentally, I feel well," Bucky explained, "but, physically, my body does not agree."

He wrote philosophically about the place at which he found himself, including his desire to be remembered "for loving people, pets, kids, and the blessings God gives us daily." He could be eloquent in thought and metaphor. "That lucky old sun got nothing to do but roam around Heaven all day; count me in on that one!" On the few days Bucky's sun deems to grace Northeast Ohio, I think of him happily roaming the sky with it.

He found joy in memories of his class's 50th reunion, the kindness of the church ladies who brought chicken enchiladas with rice to the house—ah, prayers and food, what could be better?—and special phone calls, including one from Bill Shahan, our old basketball coach and the man who had delivered a eulogy at KB's funeral 50 years before.

Bucky even read *The Golden Dream*, my first book, written with and about Gerry Faust, the great Cincinnati Moeller High School football coach who lost his magic when he got his wish to jump directly to head coach at fabled Notre Dame before a comedown career ending at Akron. That is a simplified condensation of one life's bumpy road. What Bucky gleaned from his examination of Faust is that "the faith demonstrated was very uplifting, and the impact we have on people sometimes goes unnoticed, [but] there is a reward for such behavior. His ethics, religion, family, and sense of fair and right pointed him down the wrong path, [given] man's compromised beliefs of what we want. . . . He never was given the credit he deserved." When grandson Dempsey asked to read the book, Bucky bequeathed it to him early.

There would be more important bequests as part of Bucky's legacy to the young man who could hit a ton—as a linebacker or with a bat—and read the good and difficult books, at the behest of his father, that helped to make him an "A" student. Dempsey had the Club Car Bucky had bought him, but what was to come would prove priceless. He wrote Dempsey a letter explaining how he had received a Model 15 Springfield .22 single-shot rifle from his grandmother when he was four years old. With it, he learned to shoot, to hunt, and, finally, to clean and prepare game. "There were no Big Macs back then," he said. Most important, he was also passing on to his grandson gear in which he danced at Delaware pow-wows and other celebrations "in hopes that he will carry on our traditions." There was a good chance, because Bucky had brought "Demp into our Circle at a young age," an adult world of Native traditions and rituals that could have a lifelong impact on a boy.

As March turned to April and May loomed, the grains of sand ran relentlessly out of Bucky's hourglass. I could almost hear them ping from the top globe to the bottom. "Hawk," Bucky wrote in late April, "you cannot imagine how special it was to me to hear you ask for my help" with research for the book. "My faith has been bolstered by people like you and blessed beyond belief." Already filled with guilt that Bucky would never read this, I felt compelled to explain why writing is a slow process and that, as usual, I had underestimated the time it would require. Bucky did not have time. I cried instead of laughed when he told me if he were not around for the 2018 football season, I could email him at Heaven.com to discuss the Ironmen and Sooners. He had said something similar regarding this book. "Don't worry," he told me, "I'll be able to read it." Nonbeliever that I am, I doubted Wi-Fi was powerful enough to transmit an ebook or that Amazon Prime offered two-day free delivery to the pearly gates.

I composed a *mea culpa* that attempted to explain the vagaries of the writing process, at least in my unsure hands. I've been known to fumble. It started out as an idea for a series of linked essays about quarterbacks who have touched my life, from my backyard in Nowata through a writing career that included everything from preps to pros. Research can be time consuming. When Bucky made the decision for hospice, I was visiting daily the Pro Football Hall of Fame, which is only a few miles from where I live, to collect what I could from its archives on Fritz Pollard, who made his mark with the Akron Pros, the team recognized as the first NFL champion in 1920, and Bob Griese, about whom I wrote when I worked in Miami. I was, frankly, putting off the Nowata essays because I knew they would be the most personal and difficult. That decision cheated Bucky. "Had I known what your condition would be, I would have started with the Nowata material upon returning from my visit at the end of August/first of September. But you didn't know, and I didn't know." So I apologized.

This confused Bucky. He explained that, when he encouraged me to keep researching and writing, he had not intended to pressure me to increase my pace or for it to serve as lamentation for what we both knew he would never see. "Disappointment," he said, "should never have been mentioned. I am completely satisfied to enjoy the tidbits of information that you share in our correspondence. I hope my condition has no bearing on your project." My hypersensitivity had created a problem that was real to me but not to Bucky.

Eventually Charles Dugger, our mutual friend and teammate, reassured me that Bucky was not simply letting me off the hook for my shortcomings and reiterated that Bucky had "really enjoyed working with you on your research." Even so, my guilt remains. I am a writer. I have spoken on the page for the silenced many times, but, in this instance, I not only had had opportunity to speak *to* Bucky but also *for* him, as I am doing now. The latter comes with responsibility. Alan Canfora has explained how I feel. Canfora was wounded at Kent State University the day—May 4, 1970—Ohio National Guardsmen turned their weapons on students and innocent campus bystanders during a Vietnam War protest. The guardsmen killed Allison Krause, Jeffrey Miller, Sandra Scheuer, and William Schroeder. Canfora was shot in the wrist. That dark stain turned Canfora into a lifelong activist on the May 4th Task Force. He refused to let the rest of us forget what happened that day. I once asked, in a newspaper column, why Canfora returned incessantly to what happened 50 years ago. Hadn't he said enough about what happened to him, to the others, to America? I will forever remember his reply.

"Because they cannot speak for themselves," Canfora said of Schroeder, Scheuer, Miller, and Krause, "I've never thought that I have said enough."

It is how I have felt about Kenneth Berry for more than 50 years and now have come to feel about Bucky Buck. In the final days before Bucky died, his emails ceased, but I kept writing. I did not expect a reply. It is what I do—I write. So I wrote. The silence said to me what Charles Dugger and Bucky's many friends in close proximity had seen. "I think," Charles said, "all had known for several months or longer that the end was near and were prepared."

Perhaps that explains the enlightened atmosphere Charles found when he attended the Friday-evening visitation and was able to spend time with Bucky's family and many friends. "It was much more jovial than I expected," Charles said. That was perfect. Bucky would have loved it—if I may speak for the silenced—because he always had preferred joviality to sad faces. The next day, Charles and others from the Nowata Class of '64—Susie Southall, Nick Richardson, Carol Foster, Joy Whitson, Charlotte Borneman, Linda Driskill, and Everett Stallcop among them—attended Bucky's funeral at First Baptist Church, where the preacher tried to save a few souls, a holy mission Bucky would have celebrated, even if it was on his time.

Unlike the rainy day long ago when they buried Bucky's best friend, the Oklahoma wind blew strong and warm, and the sun shined brightly as Bucky and KB Berry were reunited in Nowata Memorial Park Cemetery. Bucky had been offered space in a new cemetery across from the old city dump where his plot would have allowed him to face the setting sun. "What a happy thought," he said. He had decided he would leave the final arrangements to "whomever is in charge of planting my old carcass or ashes." Always thinking a world ahead of the rest of us, Bucky said, "I just know I will be some of the best fertilizer that has hit this earth."

Bucky, one of God's greatest ecological gifts to earth, would be pleased to learn that a year later, after his beloved Ironman boys' golf team won a Class 2A regional championship, its members honored him for the "equipment and encouragement" he had given them. Maddox Bullen, Luke Price, Alex Covarrubias, Mark Price, Cole Atkisson, and Coach Terry Rogers had not forgotten Bucky. The team told the *Nowata Star*: "We all miss him greatly and will never forget his encouragement to us all." Bucky had always been there with the right words.

Bucky Buck tombstone, Nowata Memorial Park Cemetery. [*Dennis Wilson photo*]

While I may never hear his encouraging words again, I take solace in the knowledge I will spend eternity with Bucky and KB in the place we loved so much that it felt a part of us. The columbarium that will one day contain Jackie's cremains and mine, not to mention those of our sacred kitties, awaits, next to Mama and Daddy's graves. It may not be as befitting as the arrowhead-shaped stone, with feathers on black façade, that marks Bucky's Nowata grave, but it is in our shared place—one, it turns out, we will forever be as much a part of as it was of us.

FOLLOWING THE BREADCRUMBS OF JOURNALISM

The way forward can sneak up from behind, tap a shoulder, and change a life. So sudden, subtle, unexpected, it's like an electrical jolt. I might have understood this had I not spent so much time at Virginia Military Institute up against barracks walls, bracing as gung-ho third classmen screamed in my face to "instill" discipline and character. Subtle, VMI was not.

New Keydets walk the Rat Line at rigid attention—eyes straight ahead, chin tucked so tight it could pop out the back of the neck, backbone thrust forward to the point of protruding through the chest. The Rat Line follows a prescribed route opposite a straight line. It is the longest distance between two points, actual and psychological. It exposes vulnerability. A Rat can be halted at any point, in any moment, for any reason—or no reason. He can be inspected head to toe and ordered to recite VMI knowledge he must possess. Shortcomings will send him diving into a push-up.

"Success in the Rat Line," VMI's website warns, "requires concentration, attention to detail, a sense of humor, resolve, and self-discipline."

I must not have a sense of humor. Though there were no websites in the fall of 1964, I had been warned.

I attribute my inexplicable interest in a military education not to high school years in Sacramento, California, but to visiting the Air Force Academy for the National Boy Scout Jamboree in Colorado Springs, Colorado, in 1960, when I lived in Nowata, Oklahoma. A positive impression of the Air Force Academy must have fixed itself in my subconscious. I settled for VMI after realizing I would not receive a competitive nomination to a federal military school. I applied to civilian colleges and VMI, which placed me on a wait list. When accepted, Jim Sherrard, fellow Californian and fifth Sherrard to attend VMI, visited to provide a preview.

Jim, who was going to be a first classman the fall of 1964, tried neither to persuade nor dissuade me from coming to Lexington, Virginia. Instead, he assured me that, if I decided on VMI, I would have a friend there, one who would be my dyke. Unless there is an understanding such as this, Rats are assigned to a first classman at the end of their Hell Week introduction [no misnomer] to VMI. Dykes guide and mentor their Rat, and if the Rat is fortunate, as I was, become a friend. In return, the Rat helps his dyke in any way he can, including aiding him in getting his parade gear on correctly, making his bed each morning, cleaning his room on the bottom barracks stoop that first classmen occupy. Dykes come in all shapes, sizes, and degrees of kindness. Jim was the best. He deserved better than me—a rat in the worst sense.

However Rats are assigned roommates—I was keeping my head down, not investigating such questions—fortune again smiled on me. I drew Michael Robert Malone, whose father was a colonel in the U.S. Army stationed at Fort Belvoir, Virginia, close enough for Mike to take me with him on visits during those rare opportunities when even Rats were allowed to escape their confinement. At VMI, we were assigned a smaller corner room on the fourth or top tier of the barracks. Unlike multistory civilian accommodations that put penthouses on the top floor, VMI assigned Rats to the fourth tier to make the Rat Line more taxing.

Since every minute of every day—and much of the night, too—is filled with following orders and assimilating into the lowest rank of the corps of cadets, Brother Rats don't have time to learn what makes their new roommates tick. Mike and I did as well as two strangers could. He was supportive when support can make or break. Though life was a blur those first weeks, I knew I could spend four years in a small room with Mike. When VMI offered the opportunity to choose a roommate, as it would, Mike would have been my choice.

I never got that far. My objection wasn't the harsh treatment that included "sweat parties" in the communal shower rooms . . . or eating in the mess hall while sitting at attention on the front two inches of a chair as upperclassmen screamed . . . or marching penalty tours when demerits piled up . . . or learning VMI arcana to spit back when grilled in the Rat Line . . . or even the incessant brass shining, shoes polishing, and room cleaning to avoid the trouble that found shirkers. My dissatisfaction arose from maddeningly askew priorities.

A few Rats, stripped of individuality to be remade as Keydets, still do well academically. But academics were not Priority One during semester one at VMI. Survival was. Every Rat carried a class load of 18 hours, mostly general education. A history major—VMI did not offer journalism; it may have feared scathing manifestoes—I had one 4-hour, four 3-hour, and two 1-hour classes [physical education and military science]. The Institute recognized its Rats faced a different challenge from freshmen in a typical college environment. Fatigue and fear built into the system distract from academics. No malingerer, I studied but never felt I was doing well. Jim Sherrard reassured me, but I had not had the self-awareness to choose a college that fit me.

Some of my Brother Rats dropped out almost immediately. Others quietly disappeared from the ranks, one by one, through that trying fall. Jim encouraged me not to make a rash decision, and I didn't. I even went home for Christmas and returned to finish the first semester in January. Rats who get that far *don't* leave. More than one upperclassman, VMI officer, and non-military official told me this while reminding me that the worst was over. The Rat Line often ends in February with a Break Out at the conclusion of Resurrection Week, a final onslaught by the cadre that attempts to weed out those who value their sanity more than the corps.

Some who hate VMI nevertheless remain because of all they have invested. I didn't hate it, but I knew it was not where I wanted to spend my college career, knew I did not want to become one of the third classmen—and some others—who take out on the next class what was done to them and claim they are only *maintaining tested traditions.* Even so, I was ambivalent about leaving, about having wasted my parents' money, about letting down Jim and losing Mike, about whether I was reinforcing a belief, because of my football experience, that I was a quitter. I wanted something different but not the feeling of failure that could accompany it.

Had I not thought through carefully the idea of a military education? How can a person know what something will be like—though Jim told me—and how he will respond? My tendency to buff to a high shine the positives and shove the negatives into a dark corner in the back of my mind may have betrayed me. As I left Lexington, I wondered what it would have been like to have come to this beautiful little town to attend Washington & Lee, the elite liberal-arts college whose red brick-white columned buildings stood in stark contrast to VMI's muted beige barracks and academic buildings. I can never know. I can't even remember the details of leaving, by bus and then train, and crossing the continent . . . to what? Not home. Oklahoma was home, but, because of my costly VMI mistake, there was not enough money for me to transfer to the University of Oklahoma or Oklahoma State and again pay out-of-state tuition.

My choices were limited—and not just by money—as I slunk back to Sacramento. I no longer was the shining student who had graduated from Mira Loma High School with an academic and extracurricular background that appealed to colleges. I had extricated myself from my educational mistake with as much dignity as I could muster, but, when I found myself in the Chico State College admissions office, speaking with the dean, Daddy there to support me, no dignity remained. My transcript told a story that could be interpreted multiple ways. It might have helped if those finalizing my admission had known more about VMI, understood the added difficulties a Rat faced in his first semester, and translated VMI's 10-point numeric grading system with such understanding. They had my VMI transcript that included both numeric and letter grades, but I don't recall being asked for input. As former National Football League coach Bill Parcells liked to say: "You are your record." No excuses. If it's a losing record, there may have been extenuating circumstances, but you're still a loser. And I was.

By VMI standards, I had done reasonably well. When it comes to academics, the first semester can be one Hell Week after another. The Institute knows grades often suffer because of the stress of the Rat system. I had two good grades out of seven: one in a three-credit Modern Civilization class in my major, the other in, of all things, Military Science, a one-credit class. I received an 8.5 in Modern Civilization and an 8.4 in Military Science, both letter grades of B. I also had one horrible grade, a 5.0—or what VMI considered an E or "conditional failure"—in Basic Swimming. There had been nothing "basic" about it.

I had earned Boy Scout merit badges for swimming and life-saving. I wasn't a sinking rock, though no one would have mistaken me for

Johnny Weissmueller, the great Olympic swimming champion of the 1920s who went on to a career as an actor—most memorably, to a boy born in Nowata, Oklahoma, in 1946—in the role of Tarzan. Where I sank in the class was in an exercise that required jumping into the pool in fatigues, removing them, and knotting the pant legs to allow underwater inflation. I tended to consume more water than I expelled air into the makeshift life preserver. My outcome was not only judged unacceptable, but there also had been some fear I would drown. On more than a few days, I thought that a preferred fate. Chico State's grading lexicon didn't include E. Swimming transferred as an F and, thus, probation.

I have tried to fathom why this qualified acceptance haunts me. It worked out. I graduated with honors a semester early by attending summer sessions and acing my journalism courses, most of which I loved and was driven to excel in to prove Professor Ken Gompertz had been clairvoyant when, as I alluded to, he tapped me on the shoulder to talk about journalism, a new major at Chico, as I was registering for classes in a mob scene: Gym floor. Hundreds of students. Long lines. Best classes snapped up. I was not thinking about journalism. I was still angry that the dean of admissions could not digest the VMI numeric grading system and see the promise behind the numbers that did not translate well into letter grades.

Consider this class list from my VMI semester—numeric and transferred letter grades:

General Chemistry (4 credit hours)	7.8 on 10-point scale	C (2.0)
English Composition (3 hours)	7.8	C (2.0)
Modern Civilization (3 hours)	8.5	B (3.0)
College Algebra (3 hours)	6.8	D (1.0)
Military Science (1 hour)	8.4	B (3.0)
Basic Swimming (1 hour)	5.0	E (0.0)
Elementary Spanish (3 hours)	7.9	C (2.0)

In four classes—chemistry, English, algebra, and Spanish—I was a cumulative 0.7 points from the higher grade; in other words, three more B's and a C. I believed the letter grades underrepresented the work I had done, as the Rat system nibbled away my brain. I whined silently and took my medicine, though resentfully—an unappealing personality trait.

I enrolled at Chico State in February 1965 as a political science/pre-law major. I was enough of a student politician to win election to student council as sophomore class president, but, by November, I had switched my major to journalism—and with that, changed my life and begun to obsessively follow the journalistic breadcrumbs Leonard Frizzi first dropped in my path at Mira Loma High School. I did not take a journalism class in the fall of 1965, but I received a one-hour credit from working on the college newspaper. That changed spring 1966, and academic success returned. I had found something I loved. I thought the same about a young woman named Linda, whom I'd met in a United States History class.

As it turned out, my love of journalism lasted, and my marriage to Linda did not. My unending moves in an incessant search for the right job contributed to the failure of the marriage. On the other hand, journalism led me to the right place at the right time to meet the perfect partner. We met in a newsroom, and I was smitten the moment I saw her. I still am.

Marriage, any merging of lives, is complicated. While I learned *how* complicated over time, Linda knew this when we met. Perhaps that is why she didn't tell me she was divorced. She was only 21 or 22. Parked in the country, not far from her family's home, to which she had returned after her first marriage ended, she introduced this vital fact that begged for thorough discussion at a time when I was thinking more with a part of a body located below the waist than above the shoulders. Her timing was perfect, not unlike what I believed our future could be if we survived a year during which I was to study at Uppsala University in Sweden. Chosen to participate in an international studies program—*before I met Linda*—I neither wanted to forgo the experience nor forfeit the feeling of accomplishment.

So I journeyed to the land of blondes, midnight in the afternoon, and the oldest university (1477) I could have hoped to attend in Scandinavia. While we could audit elementary Swedish, for-credit courses were taught by both Swedish professors and those from the California State College system. I got five A's and a B, in, of all things, the most compelling course: Scandinavian Drama. We studied two renowned playwrights, Norway's Henrik Ibsen and Sweden's August Strindberg. I could almost feel their presence. What I missed was Linda's.

Rather than spend the entire 1966–67 school year at Uppsala, I returned to Chico for the spring semester. My parents did not object to my decision but disapproved of the reason. Linda and I wanted to get married. They hardly knew her and thought I was being impulsive. I could not argue the point, given my ill-considered decisions. But as Woody Allen famously recast Emily Dickinson: The heart wants what it wants. I would add a caveat: Even if it can be the most dangerous organ in the body. I did not know this then. I was not quite 21.

Because of the marriage, I accelerated my academic pace. We needed money. I had facilitated Linda getting a job at the *Chico Enterprise-Record*, where I worked part-time in the sports department. I think her job, which she later reprised at the *Tulsa Tribune*, was taking classified ads. In any case, it was an office position. She was no writer and had little interest in completing her college degree. My priority was to earn as many credits as possible during two 1967 summer-school sessions to graduate in January 1968, a semester early. I wanted a head start on finding a full-time journalism job.

My plan worked, with limitations. Before the Internet and its plethora of job websites, *Editor & Publisher* was a prime source of journalism opportunities. I began subscribing to the industry bible in college. I scoured it relentlessly. I had job-seeker pluses and minuses—part-time experience with and references from the *Chico Enterprise-Record*; examples of my writing; an honors academic record; and, with no full-time experience, a willingness to start anywhere and do anything. I also was soon to be reclassified 1-A and made subject to the draft.

I got lucky. I did not wander the job desert for forty days and forty nights but found hope—in the Mojave Desert. The *Barstow Desert Dispatch* hired me as a general-assignment reporter for about $95 a week, a humble beginning in a business that feeds egos with bylines.

Most people think of Barstow as a gas stop between Southern California metropolises and Las Vegas. The beauty of the desert, however, and the best Mexican food I've ever eaten made Barstow appealing. Linda and I found a one-bedroom apartment from which I could have walked to the *Desert Dispatch* had I not needed my car for assignments. In that apartment, I experienced my first, but not worst, earthquake. It knocked me off the couch and onto the floor. That got my attention but did no real damage. What shook me was an early assignment.

One of the worst accidents imaginable occurred one evening on the interstate outside Barstow. I knew there were fatalities but no other particulars as I drove to the accident, involving a bus hit by a car traveling the wrong direction. I was the first journalist on the gruesome scene. Sportswriting does not prepare a person for this. Nothing would.

The drunken wrong-way driver had clipped a front corner of the bus, causing it to overturn and catch fire. Multiple charred bodies remained in seats, or were sprawled through the bus. It looked and felt apocalyptic. If the sight did not turn a person's stomach, the smell would. It resembled the scorched aftermath of U.S. warplanes raining napalm on the Vietnam countryside in defoliation attacks that killed more than the foliage. If I confronted mass death that night, I would stare into its everyday face in the weeks and months ahead as the war came home to Barstow and its military neighbors, Fort Irwin and the Marine Corps Supply Depot.

What I did not know but later learned from my parents is that, after I reported on the catastrophic Barstow bus crash, David Illig, my best friend in Sacramento and baseball teammate, also died the victim of a drunken driver that spring of 1968. He was 21 and died trying to help a young woman.

He and other Mira Loma Class of 1964 members were pushing a car in which they had been passengers of a Julie Marie Lane. The vehicle stalled on the Yolo causeway near Woodland, California, northwest of Sacramento. Dave, Barry Gildberg, and Bruce Waltrip climbed out to push the car to the road's shoulder. Dave pushed the left, rear corner, nearest the right vehicular lane, Barry the right fender, with Bruce in between, according to the California Highway Patrol. A driver veered off the roadway and crashed into the car, pinning Dave between the vehicles. Bruce was hurled into the air and clear of the crash. He incurred minor injuries. Barry was unhurt. Ms. Lane and the other driver, Albert Walton, suffered slight injuries.

Dave Illig, Mira Loma High School baseball star, 1964. [*Mira Loma yearbook photo*]

David Illig, a junior at Sacramento State College, where he was an outstanding baseball player, died as a result of head and internal injuries. A story from the *Woodland Daily Democrat* I found years later offered no measure of who Dave had been and how much promise his life held, on and off the baseball field. It made me appreciate my responsibility to the silenced. I had to be their voice. In difficult-to-impossible circumstances, I had not done right by the bus-crash victims. I promised myself I would do better by those whose lives touched mine, and there were many. When the *Desert Dispatch* teletype machine clacked out names of the war dead, I visited homes to obtain photos and learn about them and how their loss was Barstow's loss. I had come from journalism's toy department (sports) to a new reality—the Death Beat.

This was my apocalypse. In a matter of months, I had been touched, personally and professionally, by two of the Four Horsemen of Modernity—war and alcohol. I would come to learn painfully about cold-eyed disease and murder as they rode hard into my life. Before this incomprehensible human wrack and ruin, I did glimpse what might be professionally. The sports editor of the *Desert Dispatch*, learning of my love for football, invited me to accompany him to the Los Angeles Rams pre-season training camp, where I had the opportunity to meet Roman Gabriel, Rams quarterback. I wasn't writing a story, but the accommodating Gabriel made us feel welcome, more like grown-up fanboys than the journalists we were. It made me uneasy.

The awkwardness stemmed from a realization that our likeable sports editor had used his credentials to gain me access I did not merit. While it rekindled a desire to return to sports, I wanted to do so as a responsible journalist, not a starry-eyed sycophant. I knew what I saw and how unprofessional it made me feel, but I had little time to dwell on it.

The publisher of the *Desert Dispatch* wanted me to move to Colton, near San Bernardino, to run his one-person, twice-weekly *Courier*. I can neither imagine nor understand why I agreed. Pressure, I suppose.

The boss said do it. It was an unrewarding job under the thumb of a man for whom I had little regard, the opposite of my feeling and respect for Gay Helen Barnett, my Barstow editor. I almost immediately began trying to rectify my mistake by discussing jobs with two larger newspapers, the *San Bernardino Sun* and the *Riverside Press-Enterprise.* Though I hoped to join the sports staff of the respected *Press-Enterprise*, the *Sun* had an immediate opening for someone to run its bureau in—*wait for it*—Barstow. My limited but local knowledge won the day, and Jack Blue, who supervised the bureaus, hired me as bureau chief. It sounds more important than it was. The only other person in the bureau ran the office and assisted me. My return to Barstow to compete with the *Desert Dispatch's* news coverage did not please my boss, who told me so in the most unflattering words he knew. He was the first boss who told me he "wished he had never met me," but he wouldn't be the last. Spurned editors and publishers can be touchy.

Returning to the desert proved not only aesthetically appealing but also put me in closer proximity to the 123rd Maintenance Company of the California National Guard, the unit with which I began fulfilling six years of part-time military duty. Sitting beside former *Desert Dispatch* colleague Greg Spence at meetings and competing with him for stories felt odd. But Greg, even if I scooped him on a story, responded with equanimity and steady friendship.

The two moments I best remember from my time as the *Sun* bureau chief had nothing to do with stories. One was personal but occurred, in part, in the *Sun* office; the other, both personal and professional, became the breadcrumb that put me back on the sportswriting path in which I invested 60 percent of a 40-year journalism career. When the phone rang in the office in what must have been June 1969, I had been expecting the call. Linda had gone to her doctor for a test. She was calling with the result. She was pregnant. My happiness was tempered by the realization that we would be very young parents, a concern bordering on fear.

The other call should have been equally scary, but I was too excited to realize it. Stu Norenberg, who had moved from the *Chico Enterprise-Record* to become sports editor of the *Salinas Californian*, had tracked me down to inquire if I would be interested in the job he was leaving to work for the *Hayward Daily Review*. Interested? I was drooling on the telephone receiver. Stu, a one-man sports staff who had the help of stringers to cover events, explained the job. That's when I should have begun shaking. The job had many moving parts and responsibilities—coverage of multiple high schools, Hartnell Community College, columns, notes, feature stories and, of course, desk work, which included editing and page layout. If joy could be a killer, it had come calling. I understood why Stu needed a change.

Salinas, the Salinas Valley, and nearby Monterey Peninsula presented strikingly different geography and scenery from Barstow and the desert. Irrigation had turned dry grazing land into a hub of vegetable production, from Salinas lettuce to Watsonville artichokes. Nobel Laureate John Steinbeck made Salinas, his hometown, and Monterey's Cannery Row famous. The *Californian* office stood across the street from the inspiring John Steinbeck Library.

I coveted the chance to hang out in the Steinbeck Library almost as much as I loved to hit the road to write about football. Photographer Clay Peterson and I traveled together to Hartnell games. Kindred spirits in our love of sports, Clay and I relished creating images—photographic and word—that complemented each other and made *Californian* sports a must-read. Clay did not so much take photos as make art as striking as any I saw in my career.

Maybe it was the water, but another of the best of the photographers in my life was one born in Salinas on February 2, 1970—Kenneth David Love, named for two friends—Kenneth Berry and David Illig.

Kenny's birth occurred before it became common for fathers to be in the delivery room. Instead, I held Linda's hand in her hospital room and attempted to assist and encourage her breathing exercises, as the contractions came. When the hospital staff wheeled her away to give birth to our child, I retreated to an expectant-father's room. I sat alone for forever until someone informed me that we had a son; this also was before it was routine to know the sex of the child before birth. The person led me to a window through which I got my first glimpse of Kenny. He seemed to have the right parts in the proper places, reinforcing the news that he was perfect and healthy. There was one thing: he appeared bluish. While that's the "boy color," I thought pinkish preferable. When I inquired, I was told not to worry. Easy for them to say. I have done nothing but worry for more than 50 years.

Linda's mother, Fran, whom I liked and got along with well, came to Salinas to help us following Kenny's birth. Since I had no experience with babies, being an only child and still feeling more child than adult, I probably was more useless than usual. I tried, though. And I kept trying when it appeared Kenny might be the son I deserved—a difficult one. He cried. A lot. And then, kept crying.

It did not help Linda's and my adjustment to parenthood that I received a call from the *Des Moines Register*, Iowa's leading newspaper, its legendary sports section one of the better ones in the Midwest. Printed on peach-colored newsprint, it was uniquely known as The Big Peach. It was big and peachily thorough, informative, and smartly written and edited. I had decided to try to make my way back to the Midwest/Southwest and find a place on a larger, better newspaper. I was willing to trade the authority of a one-man sports department to broaden and improve my professional and personal life.

Linda knew only California. As difficult as her life was as a new mother, she was not eager to add the challenge of moving halfway across the country to satisfy my ambition. This may have been the beginning of the end of our marriage, but I wouldn't realize it for a few years. I listened to her without hearing. I cared more about advancing my career than about Linda's concerns. In the years since, Linda's lucky successor has asked me if I treated Linda as I treat her. The truth? Worse.

When I visited Des Moines to interview with Sports Editor Leighton Housh, I received some unsettling news I would have known had I better investigated the *Register*. It did not *hire* sportswriters; it *made* them. The *Register* hired journalists willing to spend time on the sports desk as a copy editor. Those who wanted to write would have opportunities to prove they could, but deskwork came first.

If I had a blind spot when seeking jobs, it was clinging to preconceptions. This may have been the most blatant example but was hardly the last. I was enamored of the *Register's* reputation. Every job has downsides. The question an interviewee must answer: Is it possible to live with them? I was good at self-deception and allowing new-job euphoria to wash away concerns. Leighton Housh didn't deceive me. I deceived myself and marched into a situation that might have worked for someone else but did not work for me. I failed a tenet of journalism 101: ask tough questions, especially of yourself.

Des Moines looked good to Linda and me, once we had survived a serious automotive breakdown, with a virtual newborn, to get there. Good and knowledgeable people populated the sports desk, top to bottom. The latter included part-timers such as Bill Bryson. His father, Bill Bryson Sr., renowned baseball writer, when baseball attracted the best, also did duty in the slot, assigning stories to edit to those of us on the rim and reading behind us with eagle eyes and fine-toothed combs to see if we knew a noun from a verb and could spot holes in stories in need of backfilling. Bill was six years my junior but with an advantage. His dad—at least *I think* Bill Sr. was his father—offered a live-in example of how to write and edit.

My doubt concerning Bill's parentage is his fault, stemming from *The Life and Times of the Thunderbolt Kid: A Memoir.* Though nonfiction, Bill takes liberties in service of humor. Imagination turns into "facts." Compared with some memoirists, though, Bill makes this obvious, as when, not quite six years old, he discovered in the Bryson basement a fine woolen jersey with a faded golden thunderbolt across the chest. Bill's dad thought it an old college football or ice hockey jersey. Bill didn't: "It was, obviously, the Sacred Jersey of Zap, left to me by King Volton, my late natural father, who had brought me to Earth in a silver spaceship in Earth year 1951 . . . He had placed me with this innocuous family in the middle of America and hypnotized them into believing I was a normal boy, so that I might perpetuate the Electron powers and creed. This jersey then was the foundation garment of my superpowers." [Like most of us boys in the '50s, Bill had a fondness for superpower characters in comic books or on newfangled televisions.] "It transformed me," Bill continued, describing the jersey's powers and the "accoutrements" he added to become The Thunderbolt Kid.

Bill also delineated the "particular specialties" of heroes from Superman, who "fought for truth, justice, and the American way" to the Lone Ranger, who "fought for law and order in the early West." The Thunderbolt Kid behaved more roguishly: "I kill morons. Still do." Had I realized this, I might not have sat so close to Bill on the sports copy desk.

Bill Bryson wouldn't remember me, but I would have remembered him, even if he had not become a world-famous author who has spent much of his life living in Britain after dropping out of Drake University and backpacking across Europe. Guess he became acclimated, given that he has written as well and knowledgeably about his adopted country as his native one. The *Register's* odd way of training writers served at least one of us well.

Bryson and I do have in common the expenditure of shoe leather in service of story. This inclination has taken him throughout Britain [*Notes from a Small Island*] and America [*A Walk in the Woods: Rediscovering America on the Appalachian Trail*]. He cut a bright, wide swath while climbing higher and higher on the literary mountain. Meanwhile, I tiptoed in the shallows, stepping from one wobbly stone to another, often slipping on my journalistic breadcrumb trail.

Bryson's path eventually led back to memories of Des Moines days, as side-splittingly expounded on in the *Thunderbolt Kid*. I don't know what it felt like for Bill to write about his father, but I sometimes feel uncomfortable writing about Daddy. Perhaps this is because I'm less generous than Bill was to his dad. Bill does make clear his father was cheap and eccentric—roaming the house at night without underwear. But he paid him the compliment of concluding his dad "was the best baseball writer of his generation," offering supporting evidence of how Bill Sr. memorialized such great moments as Bill Mazeroski's ninth-inning World Series home run that allowed the Pirates to beat the Yankees. The memory's trickiness can make the writing terrain treacherous. Add familial subjectivity, and one can slip uncomfortably close to hagiography. But volumes of *Best Sports Stories* in the Bryson library, each containing one or more of his father's stories, attest that Bill Sr. was every bit as good as advertised and left Bill "amazed to realize that the bare-assed old fool was capable of . . . flights of verbal scintillation."

If Bill found the courage and means to break free of the desk to exercise his writerly genes, the work's physical confines undermined my own ambition; there might as well have been shackles attached to the horseshoe around which we sat. Though assigned to report on Iowa small-college athletics, my tool was the phone, not shoe leather.

I spent little time on campuses or in press boxes, the exception being Luther College in Decorah, Iowa. I traveled there for the

Iowa Conference football championship and to Capital University in Columbus, Ohio, for the subsequent 1970 Amos Alonzo Stagg Bowl, at which I witnessed Bernie Peeters, Luther's all-time greatest running back, Norse rushing record holder, and All-American. I had been tracking Peeters from afar, but when I finally caught up with him, so did Capital. It deciphered Luther's offense, 34–21. The offense *was* Bernie Peeters, and Bernie had no means of escape from Capital, but I was planning mine. Writing prospects at the *Register* held little promise. People liked the *Register*. Few left. This included Bill's father. Bill recounts in *The Thunderbolt Kid* family pow-wows at which Bill Sr. broached job offers from big-league cities to be a full-time baseball writer. "I was always for it," Bill wrote. The family stayed put, comfortable with Des Moines, because, I think, Bill Sr. knew himself. Had I remained in Des Moines, I might have learned from him and wife Mary how they put together a two-career success story—he sportswriter/editor, she home furnishings editor.

Instead, I jumped down a stopgap escape hatch. It worked out so well I removed it from my résumé—not the most honest thing to do—in a sad attempt to reduce the number of ill-conceived moves making me look more like a migrant worker than a journalist. When I wasn't taking myself so seriously, I could laugh about this aimlessness and suggest I deserved honorary membership in Cesar Chavez's National Farm Workers Association.

The thing that sold me on the *Bluffton News-Banner* in Indiana, south of Fort Wayne: It offered a reporting job *and* rent-free house near the newspaper. Today, few if any newspapers provide both bailout *and* hideaway, in one bad job. Only Gary Books made Bluffton, with its crazed newspaper general manager, briefly survivable.

Gary and I were young men of a certain age, temperament, and interests. In him, I saw my childhood and adolescent friend KB Berry. Like KB, Gary had served in Vietnam. Gary had been severely wounded but not embittered. Whereas Vietnam veterans are often portrayed as dark and silent, Gary was luminescent and joyful. Few had been as badly wounded, but Gary soldiered on, sharing his life in talks and slide shows about the war. His photos and view offered an understanding different from and beyond even the finest Vietnam writers and documentarians. In Gary Books, I could see, hear, and touch an indescribable something that enabled a person to recognize that the goodness of good men could survive the worst war.

Given what Gary had endured, I should have been helping him find the way ahead. Gary, however, saw through me. He had a job he cared about and that suited him. I did not. I was marking time at best, wasting it at worst. So he shared with me a passion that didn't replace writing but did remind me what I might find by looking outward and doing for others; in other words, shift my incessant and reductive inward gaze. He introduced me to girls—a team of girls. I fell in love and joined him coaching girls' baseball. *A League of Their Own* came to life in small-town Indiana. It made me think I might harbor other passions, coaching for one. Not that I turned my team into a juggernaut. But the joy I saw in my players was what I had felt growing up in Nowata, Oklahoma—love for a game. Football for me, baseball for them.

While writing this, I came upon a quote from Matt Campbell, Iowa State University football coach. He began his career as player for and then as coach with Mount Union University, the gold standard of Division III football, about which I often wrote when I was sports columnist for the *Akron Beacon Journal*. I first noticed Campbell when he played for Perry High School in Stark County's football hotbed, including Massillon and Canton McKinley. He has found a secret to recruiting in Iowa, which has more small towns than Football Bowl Subdivision players, a tool to identify prospects from small schools in small places.

"One of the great things about being in [Iowa] . . .," he said at a 2019 press conference, "is watching so many kids who are four-sport athletes. It wasn't that way, being in Ohio." Campbell likes athletes who compete in multiple sports, as we did in small-town Oklahoma.

"When you're competing is when you're winning and losing . . . figuring out a way to win," Campbell said. "You can't compete in the weight room." Strength is one thing. Heart is another. "So to me, that is a huge piece to our recruiting process, because it gives us at least one answer to the intangible that's really important: How do you compete? How do you act when things don't go well? How do you respond to adversity?"

I had not found the right response. Leaving Bluffton, I may have, led to it in an unanticipated way. I ran home to Oklahoma, where my heart was, and Daddy was the impetus. I have been hard on Daddy. Maybe too hard. My reaction stems less from the corporal punishment to which he subjected me than from the emotional damage his move to California inflicted. Daddy had every right to advance his career, but, as collateral damage, I never fully recovered.

The best example of Daddy's contradictory thoughtfulness—and there were others—led me to join the sports staff of the *Lawton Morning Press* and *Constitution*. It felt like a dual homecoming—to Oklahoma and to the type of department, if slightly larger, I had known in Chico attending college. There was camaraderie missing in a one-person, autonomous operation such as the *Salinas Californian*'s. It bordered on affection, and that was what I felt for my new home. I don't know if I knew first of the opening in Lawton or whether Daddy had discovered it while supervising animal-disease eradication in southwestern Oklahoma for the Department of Agriculture after he and Mama returned to the state when things did not work out in California. I do know he hand-carried to the newspaper copies of stories I hoped would catch the eye of Sports Editor Herb Jacobs.

Daddy's help did not end there. He scouted the housing market. We were leaving free housing, and while Linda and I had saved money for a home, we did not have enough to swing the down payment on a new $16,500 house, incentive for Linda to move again. Without being asked, Daddy helped. He never let us repay him, not even when subsequent events demanded we do so. I think his financial aid was as much a gift to Mama as to me and Linda. Mama wanted us and her grandson closer so she could visit regularly. It was a bonus for all concerned.

Herb Jacobs had put together a mostly homegrown staff of Don Luke, Gene Thrasher, Joey Goodman, and part-timer Danny Collier, who later found great success in football—i.e., selling synthetic-turf fields. They liked Lawton and the newspapers; it became more a family than guys drawing a paycheck. In that sense, I was an outlier. Given my work history, and despite the stability of home-ownership, I would not have been a good bet to end my career in Lawton. Jacobs, by giving me freedom to write columns, especially for the afternoon *Constitution*, both scratched an itch of mine and reinforced my work on Lawton's high schools. I would venture that the quality of those learner's columns helped to kill the *Constitution*, if I did not know that, even then, afternoon papers were, in and of themselves, a dying breed.

Herb and I sometimes ran together—when I still ran for exercise rather than walked—and all of us would occasionally take late-night, post-deadline jaunts to a raunchy bar or two haunted by the servicemen from Fort Sill. I did not share this with Linda. She had her hands full with Kenny, our toddler and hellion-in-training, and this would not have struck her as an appropriate after-work choice. Such outings, however, drew the staff closer—Gene, who worked the desk; Don, who knew more about the small high schools that dotted Southwest Oklahoma than anyone, and Joey, who both worked in the office and as a writer. Herb put out the afternoon *Constitution*, and covered Cameron, the Lawton school that grew from junior college to university, where my Nowata basketball coach had ended up.

Given the few medium-sized-to-larger newspapers in Oklahoma in the early 1970s, sportswriters came to know one another covering events together and reading the resulting work. Names got around, which is how Jim Weeks, sports editor of the *Norman Transcript*, came to contact me with a job possibility. I was not looking, but when he told me what it was, I agreed to talk with him. He wanted someone to cover the Oklahoma Sooners, something I had done on occasion at Lawton. Our coverage was limited, mostly to home football games or feature stories about athletes from our area. The Sooners were the most important sports beat at the *Transcript*.

Jim Weeks also covered OU and wrote columns. I liked him and thought I could work well for and with him. What I did not know was how it would feel to be writing about the Sooners for their hometown newspaper. The *Transcript* was a good smaller newspaper, with a profile raised by the university and its closely followed sports. I kept asking myself: Who reads the *Transcript*? Would anyone care about or pay attention to what I wrote? Most serious OU followers made a beeline for Oklahoma City and Tulsa newspapers. I decided playing second string to the "big boys" would bother me, so, for the first time, I turned down a job. As usual, I wondered if I had made the right decision. Second-guessing myself became a lifelong affliction.

After I met Bill Harper from the *Tulsa Tribune*, my job-choice anxiety diminished. We were covering a state high school track meet. We talked. We worked in close proximity, as we gathered material and did interviews for our stories. Bill, I would discover, was a master of many skills—writing, desk work (especially page design), and recognizing others' talents. When he returned to Tulsa, he approached Bob Hartzell, his boss, and suggested Bob talk with me. *The Tribune* was looking for someone to oversee high school coverage as lead prep writer. I would be going home, or close to it, to do the work in which I had found a niche.

Though I knew the challenges afternoon newspapers faced, the *Tribune* seemed a relatively safe harbor, with a joint operating agreement with *The Tulsa World*. It looked perfect for me. Sports Editor Bob Hartzell, Bill Harper, and staff were producing, six days a week, a section that sparkled with character, so compellingly designed and written that even readers who knew an event's outcome from television, radio, or *World* coverage bought the *Tribune* because Hartzell knew how to write for this another-view audience and to find others whom he could mold. This had happened to him when he worked for the *Topeka Capital Journal* before becoming *Tribune* sports editor. Bobbie Gene—his full name and what I liked to call him—proved a great leader and teacher, as well as a generous soul.

If a person tried to judge Bobbie Gene Hartzell from the column sig that accompanied his writing, he might come away with the wrong impression. The artist's caricature of Bobbie Gene—cigar in hand, head swirled in smoke—grabbed attention but couldn't convey the kind, emotive, supportive essence of this good ol' boy from Carmargo, up around Woodward, in Northwest Oklahoma, near the Panhandle. Bobbie Gene saw me through one of the rougher patches in my life and stood by me, literally, as I began a better one.

Though sick of moving and, I think, of me as well, Linda did not object to this relocation. She had not cared for Lawton and arid Southwest Oklahoma. Tulsa, in Green Country, as Northeast Oklahoma is known, held more promise. Accepting the job had downsides: we had to find a buyer for the house my parents had helped us purchase. Luckily, the market was as hot as the climate, and the property sold quickly. We rolled the money into a modest new house in the growing southeast Tulsa suburbs. I had been fortunate, with all the moves, to find spots in National Guard or Army Reserve units, and though we were moving from one corner of Oklahoma to another, both my Army Reserve unit in Lawton and one in Tulsa were part of the 95th Training Division. It would be my final stop on a six-year forced march to an honorable discharge and a commitment fulfilled.

During our second year in Tulsa, Linda resumed her newspaper work in classified advertising sales, a combined operation of the *Tulsa World* and *Tulsa Tribune*. The job brought her into contact with new, and, apparently, interesting people, one of whom she made a part of her life. She told me she was divorcing me not long after we attended my Nowata High School Class of 1964 reunion in July 1974. Relationships with my first classmates lasted far longer than my first marriage.

Linda's bombshell gobsmacked me, though it shouldn't have. I knew she was not happy but was too obtuse to recognize her unhappiness had reached the point she would push me off the cliff that is divorce. When it became clear that there would be no reconsideration, much less a reconciliation, I turned to Bobbie Gene Hartzell. He invited me to his house to talk. He had an open-door policy, office and home. He had supported other staff members during similar personal crises. One of them, Jim Carley, also stepped up, inviting me to move in with him when I had no place to go, too little money to afford an apartment, and payments on a house that suddenly belonged to Linda. His gesture, generous in itself, was made more so by the fact it was Jim whom I displaced from the high school beat, a move Jim felt had been forced on him.

Such responses to stress and needs proved a remarkable characteristic of the *Tribune* sports staff. It came natural to Bobbie Gene to help and guide me, a lost young staffer, but Jim Carley's reaction was much like Bill Harper's when another Hartzell decision benefitted me and brought unsought change to Bill's life. Harper had been writing columns, among other duties, and backing up Hartzell. When Hartzell changed my life by making me a columnist—everyone knew Bobbie Gene was No. 1 and I was, at best, 1A—he also altered Bill's. Bill displayed no animosity, and, ultimately, it contributed to his 2008 induction into the Oklahoma Journalism Hall of Fame. Bill became the *Tribune's* administrative sports editor, and when the *Tulsa World* killed the *Tribune* by not renewing the joint operating agreement, Bill was one of the few invited to join the *World*. He served as operations editor, overseeing production, special-event coverage, computers, and design. Bill's talent was deep, broad, and complemented by fair-mindedness that also led to the Oklahoma (High School) Officials Association Hall of Fame.

Over more than 40 years, I worked on some good and congenial staffs and on others that made me feel as if I had been dropped into a pit of vipers. The *Tribune* sports staff was so good, it was as if Bobbie Gene Hartzell had been blessed with the perfect clay to mold. He spun his magic wheel, poking and prodding, pushing and pulling, and turned out a miracle in the competitive, often hostile, world that can be newsrooms. Even our most senior staff member, Jim Menzies, who covered Tulsa University athletics after helping put out the paper each morning, lost some crustiness when working with Bobbie Gene. In the course of my career, I encountered more than one crusty, irredeemable character, but Menzies had a sweet spot for those who cared deeply about what they were doing and who worked at it as unrelentingly as he did. In that regard, he served as an example to us younger staffers, perhaps even to his boss.

Most of us were in our late twenties-to-mid-thirties, and personalities ran from precise, buttoned-down, brilliant Phil Ford to fastidious, sharpest-pencil-in-the-box John Scott, who reminded me of Lucy, Charlie Brown's foil, in the Charles Schultz *Peanuts* comic strip. That's what I called John Scott "Lucy." By contrast, I resembled

"Pigpen" or "Linus," without his "blankie." Most often, though, I felt like Charlie Brown as Lucy snatched away the football as he was about to kick it. That's what divorce felt like and why I could not believe my good fortune when Jacquelyn Boucher walked into the *Tribune* newsroom in 1974 and turned heads.

I knew she was coming. Reporting begins at home. I had sources in the glass-enclosed room referred to as "the women's department" or, more accurately, "the features department." Editor Jean Simpson hired Jackie after she'd visited Tulsa with a friend and, unplanned, walked into the *Tribune* and applied for a job. She had been living at home in Manchester, Connecticut, with her domineering mother, Edith "Toots" Boucher, and her saintly father, Francis, after graduating Annhurst College, a private Catholic school for women in South Woodstock, Connecticut, sometimes confused with the more prestigious Amherst. Jackie, a bright young woman, never disabused anyone of their Amherst confusion. When later Jean called Jackie and offered her a job, Toots accompanied her to Tulsa to check out this wild-west frontier city, probably fearing her daughter would meet up with one of those Joads—or worse, me.

Panting, I sprinted to her department to introduce myself to the new woman I immediately thought would be a serious upgrade from the former Mrs. Love. I gallantly volunteered to save her from a lonely first weekend in her new city by inviting her to—of all places—an Oklahoma State University football game (not one I was covering). I failed to consider that the lovely Jackie might consider this a tad forward. The only thing that prevented her from turning me down on the spot was that she did not want to embarrass me in front of her new colleagues, who were boring holes into my back with hard, mean eyes. She intended to call me later and privately reject me.

A funny thing happened. She didn't call. We fell in love, in fits and starts, and remain so after more than 45 years, a lasting marriage for which I credit her. After the former Mrs. Love, whom Mama had not cared for even before she put Little Stevie out like the garbage, Mama embraced Jackie despite her bad habits. She smoked like a chimney. To save my new love's life, I soon began tossing her cigarettes. This had not yet broken her of smoking when she met Mama, whom she loved at first sight. The feeling was mutual. Jackie became the daughter Mama always wanted, Mama the loving, caring mother Jackie deserved. It was a match made in heaven—or the newsroom, which is as close to heaven as most journalists will get.

The one thing that concerned Mama was only indirectly related to Jackie. Mama never said so, but she thought I'd remarried hastily. How do I know? Because Mama always thought me heedless of the wrecks my impetuousness invited. Mama came to know Little Stevie was in good hands. Sometimes, when she is angry, Jackie will say: "You just wanted another mother." On this, she is wrong. There was only one Mama. What I *wanted* was someone with Mama's qualities. Jackie has them and more. From a woman who once tried to broil a frozen TV dinner, she even became a good cook. She can prepare Mama's greatest hits as well as Mama.

When Jackie and I married in a chapel on the University of Tulsa campus in July 1975, Bobbie Gene Hartzell stood up as my best man. I cherish his name on the wedding certificate, he and Joy Hart, Jackie's matron of honor, our everlasting witnesses. It was practically an all-*Tribune* affair, what with Joy one of Jackie's colleagues and Mary Hargrove, another *Tribune* reporter who went on to journalistic fame, playing guitar. Dan Osborne could just as well have been my best man but for the fact he had only recently joined the sports department from another position in the *Tribune* newsroom. We became such fast friends that Jackie and I would sleep over at Dan and his wife, Jane's, home when late nights turned into wee-hour mornings. Snuggies became nightie *de rigueur* for Jack and Jane—and maybe Dan, too.

Dan was playful like that. And funny. In the office, though, he meant business. He could do everything when it came to writing and editing, but his true genius was editing and grammar. I thought I knew a lot. He left me in his Oklahoma-red dust. He was a grammarian's grammarian. When I described, in a conversation, the forte of an athlete about whom I was writing, Dan had this look of mock horror, brow furrowed. I had pronounced the word "for-tay," as I had heard others do. Dan explained, patiently, nonjudgmentally, that the proper pronunciation was "fort" if I meant, as he knew I did, a person's strength. I believe he provided the derivation—it's French and in English refers to one's talent or ability—and how it is often confused with the Italian word meaning "loud" when applied to music, as it often is.

Like me, Dan had a mother who schooled him well. She was a librarian in Lawrence, Kansas, and he liked to call her "Big Norma." I think it was because of her personality and the fact that she played such a big role in him becoming the man he was. I got to know Big Norma when she visited Dan, Jane, and grandson Ben. She was not large in stature, but "Big" fit her. She and Dan were as close as mother and son could be.

Dan was not the only fount of writerly knowledge and inspiration at the *Tribune*. Jay Cronley conquered his and our world from an office conveniently adjacent to the sports department. The location suited Jay and rest of us. He and Bobbie Gene Hartzell were buddies, though Jay could be one's buddy one minute and have you backed against the wall the next, at least figuratively. Jay, son of the late famed *Oklahoman* Sports Editor John Cronley, had played baseball at the University of Oklahoma, where he proved talented enough to be named all-conference second baseman. He had the genes and home-training for writing. John Cronley, member of the Oklahoma Journalism Hall of Fame, taught three generations of sportswriters, his son included, to follow his example of accuracy, literacy, and fairness. When it came to talent, Jay proved even better with words than with glove or bat. He was only two or three years older than me but already had established himself as a columnist as well as a budding novelist, whose work would find its way to the big screen (*Funny Farm* with Chevy Chase, *Quick Change* with Bill Murray, and *Let It Ride* with Richard Dreyfuss, whom my wife tells me I resemble, only not as good-looking and with much shallower pockets).

Jay took an interest in me and enjoyed cleaning my clock on the shuffleboard at Arnie's, Jay's favorite haunt and thus the *Tribune*'s unofficial bar. With the Good Writer Seal of Approval, it should have been on the register of great neighborhood/dive bars. For a time after Jackie and I were married—maybe the best time—we lived in Center Plaza, a downtown high-rise apartment building, where Jay and his wife, Connie, also lived, in a larger two-bedroom. To me, the one bedroom—1809—Jackie and I rented was a step up from the studio apartment where I had lived after striking out on my own after Jim Carley provided me time to regain my equilibrium. Jim never forgot how he had felt when his marriage ended. My studio offered solitude, which I coveted, but little else. There was enough space to turn around, if you limited your movements. In a way, that was ideal: My furniture—Linda kept ours—was a couch-by-day, bed-at-night. Just as Jackie was a step up—*way up*—so, too, was the move to Center Plaza.

In a sense, the building, with Connie Cronley there, felt like home. Connie and I grew up 50 miles north of our building in the small town of Nowata. Her name was Connie Condray, and she had a sister a year younger than me, Candy. They were Nowata beauties. I dared not gaze at them lest I turn to stone. Connie was three years older. She didn't know I existed. But when we ended up in what I grandiosely thought of as Tulsa's edifice for fine writers, she graciously pretended she had known who I was. *Right.* Don't I wish. Even before Jay invited me to their apartment to meet a writer friend even more famous than he, the building could lay claim to Jay, Connie (Nowata's best), me, and Jackie. This was living in high literary cotton.

The writer Jay wanted me to meet was one I admired by any name: Ed McBain, Evan Hunter (the person to whom I was introduced), or Salvatore Albert Lombino. Regardless of the *nom de plumes* or birth name (Lombino), I found it remarkable I had the opportunity to sit in Jay's apartment with the man who had legally become Evan Hunter, listen to him discuss writing, and ask questions. I don't remember what I asked, but Evan was kind and treated me as if I belonged in a conversation with real writers discussing their craft. Evan Hunter was Jay Cronley writ large. (Later, at the *Akron Beacon Journal*, I interviewed many famous authors for a books column, but this was a first, and Jay had made it possible with his thoughtful gesture.)

I cannot remember a good reason why Jackie and I moved from Center Plaza and bought a home in Broken Arrow, a Tulsa suburb. We both liked Center Plaza and its convenience. I delighted in living in the same building with Jay and Connie and, perhaps, having the opportunity to build a closer relationship. Both had much to teach and share. Connie, as it turned out, had multiple admirable and marketable skills. The one I have come to realize I underappreciated was her writing. It is so obvious—overwhelming, really—and it shines through collections of her essays: *Sometimes a Wheel Falls Off: Essays from Public Radio* (2000, Hawk Publishing); *Light and Variable: A Year of Celebrations, Holidays, Recipes, and Emily Dickinson* (2006, University of Oklahoma Press); *Poke a Stick at It: Unexpected True Stories* (2016, University of Oklahoma Press). I blame my failure on Jay. He and his writing could *blind* those around him in a way that led a person to mistakenly believe all light emanated from him. It didn't. Read Connie. She's as unique as he was.

Gardener Connie could have turned Broken Arrow into a humorous essay. I did not like yard work as an adult any more than I had as a boy in Nowata. If I mowed the yard, it still resembled a pasture in need of a thrasher. It was embarrassing. Neighborhood property values plummeted. I thought I missed owning a home. I didn't realize I had become an apartment dweller. (For the past 30 years, Jackie and I have lived in what I think of as a halfway house—a condo; it's an owned, attached house, but, for a maintenance fee, others do the work I hate.)

If we had remained at Center Plaza, I would not have become the Peach Street Pariah, and our Tulsa exit would have been cleaner. No house to sell. No property to make presentable. Nothing to cause me to hesitate leaving the place to which I had worked long and hard to return. I was about to discover—*have reinforced* would be more accurate—that the breadcrumbs are not always strewn along the right trail. Ambition made a fool of me, and if I paid for it, Jackie paid much more, so that I could join the sports staff of the *Miami Herald*, where I began a long association with Knight-Ridder, once the best group of newspapers in the country.

Jackie was happy and successful at the *Tulsa Tribune*. She had found her niche after fighting her way into the *Hartford Times* newsroom—Manchester bureau, to be precise—through classified and retail advertising. Newswriting was anathema to her, but feature writing fit her and she it. So what do I do? I move her to Miami and back into an apartment not as nice as Center Place, unless one was fond of Palmetto bugs—cockroaches on steroids. She called me once at the *Herald* screaming that a Palmetto bug had her trapped on a chair she had climbed to escape it. If I didn't come home immediately, I would find her dead from fright. This was lose-lose: Lose my job or lose my wife. Neither calamity occurred, but others did.

When Jackie applied for a job in the *Herald* features department and interviewed with the appropriate editors, the newspaper vacillated over whether to enforce a nepotism policy not exactly set in stone. If it had been, my boss, Ed Storin, whom I liked and admired, would not have told me that Jackie should apply for the job. The *Herald* jerked her around like a yo-yo before deciding against hiring spouses, even if qualified. The newspaper offered to reverse course when, some months later, I announced I was leaving, this long after Jackie had gotten a job with the *Fort Lauderdale News*. She found the drive from our Fontainebleau Park apartment, west of downtown Miami, to Fort Lauderdale longer and more harrowing than the job was rewarding. She chose to become the most overqualified receptionist in South Florida at the downtown Miami headquarters of the Arvida Corporation, one of the state's larger real estate and development corporations. So began an employment odyssey for which I am to blame.

When I joined the *Herald,* it was ostensibly to be considered to replace Bill Braucher. He had left for the No. 1 column job in Fort Lauderdale after being No. 2 to Edwin Pope at the *Herald*. Edwin was a legend, a fixture at the *Herald* from the time he could type. To understudy him would have been a privilege. My competitors, Jonathan Rand and Bob Rubin, were smart, skilled writers and thinkers. We all tried our hands at columns while performing other duties, mine backup Miami Dolphins writer, plus general assignment. If there were a finish line, no electronic photo equipment determined a "winner" of this nose-to-nose-to-nose race.

I had hoped that receiving a regional writing award in a contest for Southeastern newspapers would bolster my prospects. The story laid bare the pain of final Dolphins' roster cuts. The day dripped with drama, as dreams and careers ended up splattered on Coach Don Shula's blood-red carpet. It did not win me the column, but I suspect it contributed to Knight-Ridder Vice President James Batten's belief in me, something I would not realize until, out of patience, I had returned to Tulsa. Batten cared about people in ways above and beyond his job, which was in the executive suite, floors above the *Herald* newsroom. Back in Tulsa, I received a letter from Jim that shared not only positive impressions of my work but also encouraged me to contact him if I ever wanted to rejoin Knight-Ridder. Maybe he believed the caveat in Thomas Wolfe's *You Can't Go Home Again*—home will never be the same as remembered. I learned that to be painfully true in Tulsa.

Though some things remained in place—our relationship with Dan and Jane Osborne—different jobs doomed our return to the *Tulsa Tribune.* Jackie ended up on the news desk, editing copy, and I became a general-assignment writer. At least it felt right with Dan and Jane. They opened their home to us while we searched for one of our own. We became the guests who wouldn't leave, and, true friends, they laughed and wished we'd stay forever.

There were other good things. The house we bought in Owasso was north of Tulsa, closer to Nowata, true home, but still a million miles away. Owasso did have its attractions, chief among them the Branding Iron Restaurant, our go-to place for chicken-fried steak and good-ol'-boy atmosphere that reminded us why we love Oklahoma. It just wasn't enough. Again, my fault. Work was more important than place. Work had become my everything, my identity. Not pretty, perhaps. Not what I was supposed to feel. But there it was. I sought jobs that would permit me to return to writing sports columns. I had two opportunities, one as No. 2 columnist to Bob Hurt at the *Arizona Republic.* I knew Bob, longtime columnist, along with Frank Boggs, at *The Oklahoman*, and former co-worker of Bobbie Gene Hartzell at the *Topeka Capital-Journal.* It would have been a comfortable fit, and Jackie liked Phoenix, to which she had been introduced when she accompanied me to a Fiesta Bowl. One concern: Would there have been enough to satisfy two columnists? This was before the NFL's St. Louis Cardinals became the Arizona Cardinals. The NBA's Phoenix

Suns were the only pro game in town, and the Cactus League had not yet consolidated its Arizona spring-training sites around Phoenix. Moreover, Arizona State football was not OU.

My other offer came from a Knight-Ridder newspaper in Wichita. The afternoon *Beacon*, smaller of the two Ridder newspapers subsumed by Knight, wanted me to become its sports columnist, and, if the grim newspaper reaper came for this afternoon edition, I could move to the *Wichita Eagle*, largest newspaper in Kansas. I had had a better offer—Eagle columnist—from Mal Elliott, former *Tribune* sports editor who ran the *Eagle's* sports department, when Linda announced she was divorcing me. I turned it down because I feared even a veteran migrant worker such as myself would find this too much upheaval without the support Bobbie Gene and *Tribune* editor Jenk Jones Jr. provided. I had to have been reeling to say "No."

Against Jackie's better judgment, I accepted Wichita's new offer, which had been facilitated by Jim Batten. Jackie again paid an unfair price. Wichita had a nepotism policy. While she looked for a position to which she could apply her writing skill, eventually finding work with first Vickers Petroleum and then Beech Aircraft as publications writer and editor, Jackie worked as manager of Snooty Tooty, a Wichita women's apparel store with stock and clientele the antithesis of the name. She did this for one reason: To help us. Saint Jackie had married the devil. Not only did she work long hours on her feet, but she also couldn't be choosy in the help she hired, given high turnover. When she came home from the store—hole-in-the-wall?—she sometimes had to return after a call from police informing her the burglar alarm was going off . . . again. I could not imagine why anyone would want to steal the clothes Snooty Tooty sold. I was surprised they didn't have to give them away.

I liked Wichita not only because, like Oklahoma, it was in the heart of evolving Big Six-Big Eight (and, eventually) Big Twelve country but also for its sphere of interest that included Kansas City's professional sports. A columnist might spend more time driving than writing, but that was little different from Tulsa, and Wichita State had not yet jettisoned football when I arrived. Its basketball and baseball were elite, thanks to the likes of Antoine Carr and Cliff Levingston on the basketball court and Joe Carter on the baseball field. It felt comfortable.

It also became where Jackie's and my life changed. In Tulsa, following my divorce, Linda and I played roles similar to those in the child custodial drama *Kramer vs. Kramer* (1979), winner of five Academy Awards and ranked No. 1 divorce-movie by tasteofcinema.com. When we divorced, I was foundering and worried about money, since two households are not cheaper than one. Instead of hiring my own attorney, I conceded to hers representing both of us, since we had agreed to share custody, with Kenny, four, living with his mother. Even if I had thought I could care for him as an inexperienced single father living with a co-worker, a judge would have disagreed. In that day, if a mother was breathing, she got the child.

When, concerned for Kenny's well-being, I later sought custody, the judge noticed I was still a man and declined to grant it, ignoring my ex-wife's trial omissions (she failed to correct the number of men to whom she had been married), her sketchy picture of when and how she had met the new man in her life, and her rosy exaggerations about the conditions in which she and our son were living. Kenny was too young to testify, or he could have blown the whistle on her.

Kenny blames me for the odyssey his life became—shunted from one set of grandparents to the other—and the help I attempted to get him at Tulsa's Children's Hospital after Jackie and I were married. He felt I had abandoned him to a fate worse than Guantanamo rather than had put him in the hands of trained, caring professionals who attempted to address emotional and other problems. The custodial question resolved itself when, after Jackie and I were in Wichita, Linda called to request Kenny come to live with us. He had become an impediment to Linda's new life. My answer was simple: We would be happy for Kenny to be with us, but it had to be a legal and permanent change that could not be revoked on a whim.

It was not an easy or simple transition from childless couple to family of three, and the greatest burden too often fell on Jackie, given the nature of my job and its travel. We were, however, better able to take on the responsibilities of parenthood than we had been when we left Tulsa for Miami, virtual newlyweds still learning about each other. As challenging as childrearing can be, even under ideal circumstances, having Kenny come unexpectedly into our life proved less traumatic than having someone snatched from it.

Bobbie Gene Hartzell died February 1981 after battling cancer for more than a decade. He was 43. He had undergone many surgeries for throat cancer, one of which damaged his vocal cords and left him with a raspy voice, permanently hoarse. Mike Sowell, my successor as *Tulsa Tribune* sports columnist, who would succeed Bobbie Gene as sports editor, recalled that "sometimes he would cough so hard it seemed he was about to spit up parts of his lungs."

When I drove to Tulsa for Bobbie Gene's funeral, I found, as I knew I would, a service that brought together the best of journalism and sports from Oklahoma and the Midwest. I sat in the midst of this congregation of those who loved Bobbie Gene Hartzell, my heart in my throat, with an affirmation that my "best man" had been that to many. I cried on the drive back to Wichita. Bobbie Gene would have hated that. He had not allowed his plight to diminish him or bring him—or others—down. He sought to make the lives of those around him brighter. But on this dark day, made more so by my choice to have left Bobbie Gene before I had had to, all I could think about was the fact that he had had no choice.

I knew the *Tribune* sports department was in good hands, that Mike Sowell would build on Bobbie Gene's legacy. It was impossible not to wonder what would have happened had I not ridden off on my high horse of ambition to Miami. Would I have become sports editor? Could I have done half the job that Mike had for eleven years?

At the end of September 1992, Sowell wrote one last column for the final edition of the *Tulsa Tribune* and, in it, eloquently recast the sad ending of a newspaper with memories of Bobbie Gene Hartzell, a reason it had been great. He recognized that the end of the *Tribune* allowed him and others to "get on with our lives" and that "there have been worse days around here." For one, the day Bobbie Gene died while getting ready for work.

I might have died one day doing the same in Wichita, where I thought I would have a long career to try to become as good a columnist as Bobbie Gene. Following discontinuation of the afternoon *Beacon*, I was, after some internal machinations, assured I would become *Eagle* sports columnist. But, as in Miami, the column proved illusory. Editor Davis "Buzz" Merritt had a change of heart. He could not bring himself to reassign the *Eagle's* columnist. Instead, he offered to help me explore other Knight-Ridder possibilities. Just another day in journalistic paradise. Another lesson. Another move. What could possibly go wrong?

RUBBER CITY PEAKS AND VALLEYS

Given my lack of staying power along a breadcrumb trail of journalism from California to Akron, this place, once famous as the Rubber Capital of the World, should after 40 years feel like home. I know Akron and rubber. I co-wrote the history. So why doesn't it feel like home?

An unorthodox obituary I prepared to save others from having to put words in my cold, dead mouth suggests an indirect answer: It is less about me than about Nowata, Oklahoma, the *place* that made me who I am—uh, *was*. If I began life wrapped in Nowata's small-town warmth, the final piece of its puzzle takes its shape from the cold *Akron Beacon Journal* newsroom I walked into during a hot summer in 1981.

A cold shoulder would have been swell compared with what cold-cocked me. I should have seen it coming. It had been telegraphed the moment my phone rang at the *Wichita Eagle* and I began talking about Akron with *Beacon Journal* Editor Paul Poorman, Executive Editor Dale Allen, and their trusted henchmen. Before his death in

2019, Allen shared a recollection from his unpublished memoir of identifying and recruiting a local columnist after concluding he had "no prime candidate in house." As Shakespeare once put it in *Hamlet*, "there's the rub."

Identifying a columnist can be difficult for a number of reasons, not the least of which is that, in any newsroom, there are those who think themselves not only prime but also perfect for the job. If not them, who? Certainly not some sports yokel from Wichita whose editor no longer wants him. What would such a person know about writing a local column about Akron?

Even if self-serving, they had a point. Allen had been through a similar experience in Philadelphia, where he had been an *Inquirer* editor involved in choosing a columnist. "We assigned first one, then another, then another reporter to the job of writing columns and found all of them wanting," he wrote. Allen knew such harsh conclusions, whether in Philly or Akron, dashed hopes and dreams. "It's almost axiomatic," he realized, "that young reporters across the country see column writing as their 'dream assignment.'" He believed it had to do with "some inner need for recognition from their peers and readers." While true, what columns offer—and I wrote every type, from sports to local to feature to books to editorial—is the freedom to form an opinion, support it with facts and cogent argument, and write it, mostly, as the writer will.

With freedom and responsibility come consequences. Good columns spring from original ideas supported by reporting, reasoning, and sharp writing. In sports, events offer a foundation; the columnist knows his audience will respond to a good athlete competing in an important situation in which he/she performs feats of derring-do that the clever writer can describe and interpret in ways not considered by his fellow columnists. It all falls on the columnist's shoulders. Editors don't assign columns, though, with high expectations, they may send a columnist to particular places or events. Columnists, as Allen put it, "assume the roles of both assigning editor and reporter. It is an immutable law in newsrooms that columnists are not given assignments." Allen adhered to the law, but his violation may have been worse. It doomed me. He and Poorman had in mind a local column of short items in which the subjects were "doing good" or "doing well" in the community. Poorman wrote a Sunday column after gathering such *bon mots* for days or even weeks, refining them with an *elan* of which not all are capable. People in the community fed him information; the staff, to score brownie points, dropped nuggets on his desk that did not fit news stories, and Poorman worked his magic.

The new local columnist had fewer advantages. He would be expected to produce five columns a week to fit into a "Goldilocks" bit of space on the page—not too long, not too short, but just right. "It is unusual for a workaday reporter," Allen conceded, "to be required to write that many 'major' stories in a given week and to fill an exact amount of space." The new columnist would be introduced to community movers and shakers, including at social gatherings Poorman played host to at his home, and staff members were encouraged to feed appropriate morsels into the column's hungry maw. The plan left something to be desired.

If the staff did not want me to fail, neither was it eager to help me succeed. This was particularly true for those who had coveted the column for themselves or a newsroom ally. As for the community, I remember my introduction to the Diamond Grille, famous Akron steakhouse with the city's best selection of seafood, where everybody who was somebody showed up. The biggest names from national events such as the Professional Golfers Association tournament, played on Firestone Country Club's South Course, made a point of dropping in and adding to the restaurant's star power. When I was introduced to the Diamond Grille's bar and dining-room staff, whom I tried to cultivate as sources, I might as well have been plowing a rocky field protected by a stone wall.

Dale Allen and Tim Smith, my immediate editor, not only tried to help and guide me but also, as much as such a thing is possible between management and employee, befriend me. It created a Catch-22 situation that Allen recognized and I felt daily. I needed friends, but if they came from management in a strong union newsroom, it created a perception problem. I was management's "boy," their Chosen One before anyone in Akron or beyond—*Sports Illustrated*—bestowed the title, more appropriately, upon LeBron James, basketball legend from St. Vincent-St. Mary High School as he put the city on the worldwide sporting map.

It wasn't easy for Allen to find me, my profile being somewhat lower than LeBron's. Allen called editors he knew around the country seeking names of potential columnists. No one had one. Undaunted, Allen came up with an ingenious idea: From the *Editor & Publisher Yearbook*, he culled names of editors in competitive markets [now almost disappeared]. He wrote to a hundred or so "begging for assistance" to find a columnist. He added a twist. If an editor wanted to see a competitor's columnist leave town, Allen would try to "coax them . . . to Akron." Failing that, perhaps the editor had a staffer "who might profit from a change of scenery." He might as well have said . . . *someone you would like to get rid of.* That was me.

Wichita Eagle Editor Davis "Buzz" Merritt, whom Allen knew because both men had worked at the *Charlotte Observer*, another Knight newspaper, called Dale and suggested he had a sports columnist with broader interests who might make a good local columnist. I don't know how much Buzz went into the backstory of his two-sports-columnists-for-one-job dilemma, but that did not matter to me when Allen called to ascertain my interest.

When I visited Akron to discuss the position, Jackie accompanied me, an unusual perk. I believe it came about because I had shared with Dale the grief my moves had caused Jackie and told him that he would have to sell Akron to my wife as much as to me. I'm sure I did not mention that, when Wichita hired me, Jackie and I had driven from Tulsa to Wichita so she could see Wichita; this did not require the newspaper to fork over airline tickets, as did the Akron visit. When Buzz Merritt took Jackie and me to dinner, it nearly ended in gunfire. She and Buzz got into a disagreement. "I'm surprised he hired you after that," she remembered.

Steve and Jackie Love. [*Photo courtesy the author*]

The Akron experience was different. Dale, Paul Poorman, Tim Smith, and other editors and their wives whom Jackie met won her over, as did Akron. She may have been receptive because she did not like her situation in the Beech Aircraft public relations department. As a carrot, I also suggested she choose the house. "We promised him," Dale recalled, "we would do all we could to help make his transition from Kansas to Ohio as easy as possible."

There was a hitch: the notes column Dale and Paul envisioned. I should have pushed back for what I did best, a reporting-based, single-subject column fueled by sharp observations, thoughtful conclusions, and writing that drew in the reader and left the person smiling or seething. Just as an editor does not assign topics, neither should he dictate the type of column. "I'm not sure," Dale admitted of his preordained format, "that's the kind of column Steve would have written, given his own preference, but he indicated a willingness to try it." Editors should hire the columnist and give him his head—right up to the moment they hand it to him.

The best thing about that original column was the column sig and promotion for "Love in the Afternoon." (The *Beacon Journal* was an afternoon newspaper at the time.) Editorial cartoonist Chuck Ayers created an evocative silhouette with a hand and arm reaching up to pull down a window shade. The newspaper put this on T-shirts I could offer readers for tips that turned into the column items. The T-shirts became a collector's item, the most memorable thing about a forgettable column that didn't fit me. No one at the *Beacon Journal* knew this better than those who worked in the art department. My desk, in columnist corner with the late beloved Fran Murphey, who considered herself a reporter rather than a columnist since she offered the reader valued information more than opinion, abutted the artists' domain. Bud Morris ran a department that did not have anything inherently against me, since the artists were not writers who either wanted the column or didn't want me to have it. They adopted me. I think it was for the free labor. I became unofficial filler of the waxer. It proved an ice-breaker.

The art-department waxer was a gadget from the now-lost age of paste-up in cold type. [I'm so old that, when I began working for newspapers, they were still using hot lead type produced on Linotype machines.] After the artists drew a cartoon, produced an illustration, or created a map, they ran it through the waxer, which applied a thin coat of wax to the back and allowed it to be pasted onto a newspaper-size sheet of thin cardboard that was photographed to create a negative used to make a metal plate to attach to the printing press. My job, since I usually was one of the first in the office, was to drop a pellet of wax into the waxer to melt. Without the waxer, no newspaper for readers or friends for me.

One of those artists, Art Krummel and his wife, ace reporter/editor Charlene Nevada and early newsroom ally, became lifelong friends who warmed my cold *Beacon Journal* days. The art department—Walt Neal, Dennis Haas, Dennis Earlenbaugh, Deb Kauffman, and "Love in the Afternoon" artist Chuck Ayers—was warmer than hot wax. They stuck with me through my hardest times, perhaps as a result of eloquent waxing rather than any waxing eloquent in the column.

In the end, "Love in the Afternoon"—T-shirt excepted—failed. Which means I failed. Allen wanted to hear from the community what he heard when Stuart Warner replaced me and donned a big hat (which I don't remember him wearing as sports editor). It not only kept his head warm in the winter but also seemed to warm the hearts of the community, which responded to his humor and his sense of how far he could stretch truth in a fact-based medium. Allen wrote that people loved Stuart because he "seemed like one of them." And me? I was a "very serious guy" whose column "did not work well with his reporting or writing style." Ouch!

"While he had a sense of humor in casual conversation," Allen concluded about me, "it seldom found its way into his column. When it did make an appearance, it seemed forced." Good thing I had a fallback position as art-department waxer. Nevertheless, reading Dale's assessment—one with which I do not disagree—brought me low. It didn't help that he recognized his culpability in my failure. "My rather stern pronouncement about what the column should be was probably a big mistake from the git-go," he admitted. "Steve would have been better off left to his own considerable devices."

I returned to sports as a special-assignment writer and part-time columnist, and began an odyssey not of moving from newspaper to newspaper but from job to job at the *Beacon Journal*. At least this did not afflict my wife with another relocation; Jackie had established herself in an upward trajectory in the Hoover Company public relations department that would make her its director before the demise of North Canton's signature employer. It was during this period that I spent a fall inside the University of Akron football program that Gerry Faust had been hired to upgrade from what was then known as Division I-AA to the top level of the National Collegiate Athletic Association hierarchy (I-A). At the time, no university had pulled this off, and it became an important story in no small part because of Faust.

Faust had become an Ohio high school coaching legend with state championship after state championship at Cincinnati Moeller before what amounted to—no aspersion to religion intended—a near-holy ascension to Notre Dame, the collegiate football heaven in which he had prayed he might one day coach. It changed Faust's life, and, because he fell short in five years in South Bend, it also changed mine. To try to put his coaching career back together, he came to Akron in search of the success that had eluded him at Notre Dame. He let me dissect, from the inside, the beginning of a 10-year struggle during which he succeeded in lifting the Zips to I-A but not winning enough to satisfy even Akron.

I wrote a lengthy narrative of that first Akron season for *Beacon Magazine*, in which, along with my coverage as sports columnist from 1988 to 1993, Faust found enough he liked to invite me to collaborate on his memoir, *The Golden Dream*. It was my first book. The thing he liked most, he said, was that I got his "voice" right. I liked that, too, given I had not been able to find my own voice for "Love in the Afternoon." I kept trying, though. I may have set the record for writing columns for the most sections of a single newspaper—local, sports, at large, features, books, and editorial. Dale Allen said I had a "penchant for wanting to try new things."

What I could not seem to move on from was death, in both my professional and personal life. It was as if I were drawn to it—or it to me. It's sad and inexplicable but led to what was judged some of my best writing. It has been a serious subject for "a very serious guy." Though much pain remains, I recently contributed an essay to a collection about the *Beacon Journal* and Akron edited by Stuart Warner and wife Debbie Van Tassel for the University of Akron Press. I wrote about a seven-year-old first-grader, Charlie Wright, whom I never met but who yet is a part of me. Killed by a blow from his mother's live-in boyfriend, Charlie was silenced before he could tell anyone his story. I, and other *Beacon Journal* reporters, spoke for him. I'm still trying to do so. I cannot stop, give Charlie up, or let him go.

During the summer of 1983, three years before Charlie's murder, Jackie and I drove from Akron to Fort Wayne, Indiana, to visit Dan and Jane Osborne, our best friends from Tulsa who had migrated through Kansas City to Fort Wayne, where Dan became editorial-page editor of Knight-Ridder's *News-Sentinel*. It was a busman's holiday. We went for many reasons, especially the opportunity to meet the newest Osborne, two-year-old, cherubic Caroline. I wanted to talk with Dan about his job, one new to him, as the local column had been to me. Coming from the *Kansas City Star* business staff with no editorial-page experience, Dan, like me, had had to simultaneously learn job *and* city, about which he would craft the newspaper's opinions. I knew Dan would succeed; unlike mine, his job suited him.

We visited the *News-Sentinel* office, toured Fort Wayne with the Osbornes, ate, reminisced, laughed again in our jammies, and reveled in an idyllic new moment with old friends. It was our last. Back in Akron in September, a flurry in the *Beacon Journal* newsroom drew me to editor Tim Smith's desk to inquire about what was going on. He told me an editor and his family had been murdered in Fort Wayne. My heart sank. I asked for the wire-service story. It was Dan and Jane and Ben. My world again turned to black.

It remains a blur even now. I called the Hoover Company. How do I tell Jackie? No proper preamble to horror exists. The first story was sketchy. What I knew was that the three of them had been murdered in their home—the home we visited—over the weekend of September 17 and 18, 1983, and two-year-old Caroline had wandered this house so new to her for two days before being found. The scene had been first discovered by *News-Sentinel* associate editor Craig Ladwig, a close friend of Dan's, with whom he had worked in Kansas City. When Dan did not show up for work that Monday morning, Ladwig feared something was wrong. If Dan was not there to begin the week he planned to implement editorial-page changes months in the works, it bode ill. "We literally built the editorial page around him," Ladwig said.

After Ladwig knocked on the door, got no answer, and did not hear the Osborne dog barking, he peeked through a window and saw Jane sprawled on the floor, the first glimpse of a gruesome scene. Ladwig called police. When they arrived, Caroline told a female officer, "Daddy is asleep" and repeatedly said, "Mother is coming back." [In another version, Caroline reportedly said, "Mommy and daddy are sleeping." Whichever is correct, it broke my heart.]

I still cannot bear to open a box of newspaper stories that Norma Osborne, Dan's mother, collected and entrusted to me. Though I have written about the murders tangentially over the years—it is an obsession—it remains too close to my heart, the pain too everlasting, to dive deep into my friends' deaths. Jackie and I flew to Kansas City for a memorial service prior to the burial in Newton, Kansas, Jane's hometown. The underlying premise of such occasions is, of course, that a person should offer comfort to family and friends. We went for us, for Dan and Jane. We had to say goodbye. We were under no illusion our presence would help others. We hoped it might help us. Norma seemed pleased we had come, and Jane's sister, Margy, with whom Caroline would continue her life, allowed us to remain, in a small way, a part of that life for as long as Caroline wished; it was difficult to know if we served as a reminder of what had been taken from her or, as we hoped, that her mother's and father's friends loved them.

The many, many stories that tracked the police investigation conflicted in their details, but the underlying theme was the unspeakableness of the act. Andrew E. Stoner included it in his *Notorious 92: Indiana's Most Heinous Murders in All 92 Counties.* Nothing more hellish had ever occurred in Allen County, which includes Fort Wayne. The killer may have climbed in through an open kitchen window, a theory I found credible, given Dan and Jane's trusting nature. Their mid-twentieth-century home in Harrison Hill, a changing but well-kept neighborhood of attractive boulevards in southwestern Fort Wayne, looked inviting, which is what Dan had found the city to be when he visited to consider not only a job but also whether Fort Wayne would be a good fit for the family. "We were able to get him here to Fort Wayne," Ladwig said, "because he just liked the town for his family." Seeing the Osbornes in their new home, this was easy to understand—until it wasn't.

From his autopsies and the police investigation, Allen County Coroner Roland C. Ahlbrand concluded Dan and Ben and the family dog had been killed in an upstairs bedroom with a baseball bat the intruder found in the house. Ben had been in a sleeping bag in his parents' bedroom, and investigators speculated that he might not yet have been comfortable in his new home and that his parents allowed him to sleep in their room at times. A Fort Wayne detective called me at the *Akron Beacon Journal* after learning we had visited the Osbornes. He sought information about the visit, the Osbornes, and our relationship. He didn't say so, but he may have found our fingerprints—mine would have been part of my military records—in the house with others not identifiable early in the investigation. Had he asked why Ben might have been sleeping in his parents' room, I would have explained from our years in Tulsa and the visit in Fort Wayne that this would not have been unusual. Ben was a sensitive boy, and Dan and Jane tried to give him reassuring support when and however they could.

Ahlbrand's original assessment was, "The father and son were killed at the same time with the same instrument without awakening." He speculated that Jane may have been in the basement—something I originally believed but came to question—and went upstairs "to find out what was going on." When, four months later, police arrested Calvin D. Perry III after a similar home invasion in the Osbornes' neighborhood, the details changed, based on affidavits that resulted from Perry's videotaped confessions to other felonies. *The New York Times* reported a detective asked Perry if he had anything to add. He did.

"I know what you're talking about," eighteen-year-old Perry said, "the big one." He went on to confess killing the Osbornes, providing details only the killer could have known. Those details give me pause as I consider how much to share. They have not been as pertinent as my previous writings, in particular, why the fate of killers is better left to evidential and intellectual tools of the impartial rather than to those emotionally involved. (I would have killed the Osbornes' killer myself with the same weapon he'd used if I had had the opportunity.)

This juncture is different, a place to which Jane Osborne led me when I asked myself: What would Jane want? Would she share details of her moments of horror if she could? Would she think it gratuitous? I believe her first thought would be for how they would affect Caroline, her beloved daughter. Do the details serve a public good or merely fuel morbid interest? Jane was smart. Like Dan, she'd graduated from the University of Kansas, one of the few women in the business school. She respected knowledge and the writer's drive to understand the inexplicable.

I cannot know what Jane would have wanted. I do know she fought to live and endured the height of the horrors. If Jane didn't come upstairs from the basement, she may have been in bed, and based on what Perry told police, awoke when Perry hit the Osbornes' dog with the bat, killing it. He then took the bat to Dan and began to sexually assault Jane. Ben, still in his sleeping bag, pleaded with Perry not to hurt his parents, according to the affidavit. Perry said he hit Ben twice in the head and then returned to raping Jane, who fought back.

Jane was larger than Perry, if his mother's description of his size—"such a little thing"—was accurate. He responded, he told police, by hitting her in the head with the bat numerous times and continuing the rape until she lost consciousness. Originally, Coroner Ahlbrand had concluded that Jane died on the first floor, where she was found, and was struck with a blunter object, a portable radio on which her hair and blood were found. Despite the discrepancies between Ahlbrand's original reconstruction of events and the description Perry provided, one conclusion of the coroner remained inarguable: Jane "died after a vicious struggle."

Some of the disparities might have been resolved during a trial, but there was none. Eleven days after his arrest, Calvin D. Perry III hanged himself in his jail cell in such an unusual manner that it prompted skepticism about Perry's death, especially in Fort Wayne's African-American community. Officials said Perry, who, after his death, was linked to a dozen break-ins and at least six rapes on Fort Wayne's south side, pieced together material from a mattress cover in his cell to tie his feet to his bed and his neck to the cell bars. It stretched him into a human hammock. A note claimed, "I haven't killed nobody." Other messages, the sheriff said, were scrawled on the floor. The coroner revealed other notes, including one asking several people for forgiveness. None of those people was the Osbornes.

Attorneys representing Perry said there was no coercion and that his rights had not been violated. A ten-month U.S. Department of Justice investigation concluded: "There had been no foul play involved in Perry's death; it was a suicide."

In his videotaped confession, Perry told detectives he had chosen the Osborne house at random and that he had wanted a confrontation. He knew no one in the family, their house three blocks from where he, an unemployed high school dropout, lived with his mother. That fateful night ended Caroline Osborne's chance to live a life with her mother, father, and brother.

Jackie and I tried to share with Caroline what it had been like for us to live for a short time with Dan and Jane, and, of course, Jane's sister, Margaret (Margy) Porter, and her husband could and did tell Caroline much more about her parents. For a long time, a photo of the Osbornes sat on a shelf in our living room, reminding us every day of a great shared loss.

The Osborne deaths changed Fort Wayne. Fear enveloped Harrison Hill. Neighbors were stunned. In the four months between their deaths and Calvin Perry's arrest and subsequent suicide, gun and alarm-systems sales rose, and guard dogs appeared in manicured yards, one of which Ben Osborne had been mowing the evening Perry came calling. The south side was transformed; the pace of professional families moving to the suburbs accelerated. The promise that brought Dan Osborne to the city died with him and his family.

Cities change, of course, and change can feel like death of a different sort than that rent upon Fort Wayne's Harrison Hill. During the later stage of my *Akron Beacon Journal* career, Dale Allen approached me with what may have been the best idea he ever had, one Shirley Miller Albright, an Akron native living in Michigan, inspired when she sent Allen a letter. Her father, David Miller, had worked for General Tire and Rubber Company for 48 years as a rubber chemist. She had a question: "Has anyone bothered to do a history of any, or all, the tire companies?" Ideas do not have to be original to blossom. "Her letter proved to be the seed of an idea that grew into 'Wheels of Fortune,'" *Beacon Journal* Publisher John L. Dotson, Jr. would later explain in his Preface to a book of the same title, "a yearlong series of newspaper stories that tapped into a rich, but fading, era of Akron's history."

Tire manufacturing, except for racing tires, had disappeared from Rubber City. Foreign companies had bought Akron's tire companies, and all but one of the Big Four had been moved elsewhere. "By the mid-1990s," Dotson wrote, "the story had a beginning and an end," and, on dark days no longer caused by carbon black in the air from tire manufacturing, that end could feel like the end for Akron. It certainly felt that way to tens of thousands of rubber workers and many tangential companies that supported the industry.

No one had told Rubber City's story since World War II. Though it took a while—Shirley Miller Albright's letter arrived September 1993 and not until spring 1996 did Allen begin marshaling resources to tackle this Akron-centric story—we, indeed, "bothered" with it. It became the most important and best work of my career, a serious story for a serious writer.

As Dotson explained, the delay stemmed from the fact the *Beacon Journal* was busy in fall 1993 putting the finishing touches on another yearlong project—"A Question of Color," which addressed racial issues in Akron and would in spring 1994 win the Pulitzer Prize Gold

Medal, the Pulitzer of Pulitzers awarded for Public Service to a news organization rather than an individual. I had been enmeshed in my "chapter" of the series that, like three of the *Beacon*'s four Pulitzers, was a collective effort. The exception was John S. Knight's Pulitzer for "distinguished editorial writing" received for ten of his 1968 "Editor's Notebook" columns on the divisive Vietnam war. Knight opposed U.S. involvement and had since the French were defeated in Indochina in 1954. Fittingly, his was the *Beacon Journal's* first Pulitzer.

The Gold Medal, in a glass display case surrounded by reproductions of each page that made up the series chapters, commanded a visible place of honor near the elevator from which visitors disembarked into the newsroom. It was important to all of us. It must also have been coveted by others. When in 2019, to better accommodate its shrunken staff, the newspaper moved to a smaller space in a reimagined former Goodrich tire factory, someone stole the Gold Medal, briefly left behind during the transition.

Few medium-sized newspapers in the 1990s had the resources, human and financial, to devote to first "A Question of Color" and then "Wheels of Fortune." Fewer still would have expended them if they did. This was not just about money. Dotson noted that the imaginative idea also required a "grass-roots sense of community." When I consider this now, I am amazed that again Allen turned to a carpetbagger whose heart was in Oklahoma for an important job that required deep local knowledge and a feel for the city. Perhaps I had learned something in the 15 years that had passed since I first arrived there. There was, I think, a method to Allen's madness. He sold David Giffels on the idea of serving as the other principal writer. David was Akron to his core, a writer of prodigious talent. Before he joined the "Wheels" team, steered by editor Debbie Van Tassel, the best of choices, I had created an outline—a table of contents, if you will—that held up with comparatively few deletions or additions.

That is not to say there were no surprises along our yearlong reporting path, sideroads discovered, viewpoints reassessed and altered. That happens when some 350 people take time to share their stories and information.

When David and I began compiling a list of potential interviewees we called it—internally—The Drop-Dead List. It may sound irreverent but, in fact, sprung from deep respect. We targeted the Drop-Deads and prioritized interviews based on a regard for their knowledge and age: Oldest first, if possible. We did not want anyone to take their knowledge and story to the grave before adding it to that of rubber in Akron. One of my earliest interviews was with Waldo Semon, arguably Akron's most renowned rubber chemist and among those whom, it is not hyperbolic to conclude, helped America and its allies win World War II. For the development of the Ameripol synthetic rubber recipe and invention of polyvinyl chloride (vinyl), Semon joined Thomas Edison, Henry Ford, and other inventive geniuses in the Inventors Hall of Fame.

A former B.F. Goodrich research chemist with 116 patents, not the least of which was for a version of synthetic rubber that literally kept Allied Forces on track until the U.S. could create the hydrogen bombs that ended the war, the 98-year-old Semon was living in a Hudson retirement home when we talked. As a sports columnist, I had interviewed and written about some of the world's great athletes. Though Waldo belonged to a higher league (he even invented a type of golf ball), he was smart enough to be a team player who got the most out of those around him. He not only led the Goodrich team that created Ameripol, which means "a polymer of American materials" but also was chosen by representatives of the rubber, chemical, and petroleum industries to guide the choice of a synthetic rubber recipe for Government Rubber-Styrene (GR-S) and to set in motion its production. He immediately identified a problem: Too many egos and too many companies that believed their method for making synthetic rubber worked best. So Waldo Semon brought in a neutral decision-maker, Edward R. Weidlein, director of research for the Mellon Institute in Pittsburgh and of chemical research for the U.S. Office of Production Management, aka the War Production Board. It proved a stroke of humble genius. "I was more interested in doing a good job," Semon said, "than in the claim of who had done what."

If his philosophy helped to save the world, it also contributed to saving Akron, after the tire companies had moved on from the city and the workers who had made them great and prosperous—at a price. As Waldo Semon won acclaim, men such as Edgar Lyle went unnoticed and underappreciated. When I met Lyle, he was a retired Goodrich tire builder and manager who had made some of the first tires using Semon's version of synthetic rubber in the late 1930s. He was not in good health in no small part because of work building synthetic rubber tires that required softening with dangerous chemicals.

"The first synthetic rubber was real tough," Lyle said. "The only thing that would soften it enough to stick was ether." It could have been worse. In the early years of tire building, Diamond Rubber Co. chemist George Oenslager, with whom Waldo Semon later worked at Goodrich, discovered the first organic accelerator, aniline, a compound that sped the processing of rubber and strengthened the tire. "He tried the simplest and cheapest organic base available, which was aniline oil," Semon said. "And it worked. But aniline oil was volatile, and when he tried it in the factory, it turned the workers blue. It was poisonous." After 1916, aniline was no longer used to process rubber, but that did not mean Lyle and the next generation of rubber workers were safe working with ether.

"I had a machine by the windows that opened onto Bartges Street," Lyle said, "and to keep from going to sleep, I would stop after I put each ply on and stick my head out the window." Lyle faced a dilemma.

He had to keep from falling under ether's sleepy spell *and* maintain the quality of his work, which he cared about. Someone was always monitoring. "Inspectors used to stand around behind posts and watch you," he said. "If you didn't build that tire right, if there was a wrinkle, you were fired right then and there."

It was a tough life, but tire builders—rubber shop royalty—made some of the best wages in industrial America. The jobs provided a middle-class living for workers with high school educations and some without a diploma. When those jobs disappeared and students could no longer walk out the doors of their high schools and through those of the rubber shops, Akron changed irrevocably. Nevertheless, the city had something others across the upper Midwest's industrial corridor, disparagingly referred to as the Rust Belt, did not—seed corn.

Akron's seed corn fell from the rubber tree, from the city's long history with the substance and its rich knowledge of polymers, including natural and synthetic rubber, that took root at the University of Akron. Polymers are a series of linked molecules that resemble a chain, a characteristic that gives rubber its necessary elasticity. Similarly, a chain of knowledge linked the university and the rubber-company laboratories beginning in 1910, when Charles M. Knight taught a rubber-chemistry course in a lab in a new building at Buchtel College, UA's predecessor. Knight forged the first link, encouraging his students to step out of their college lab and apply their knowledge in Akron's industrial setting.

One of his students and first assistants, Hezzleton E. Simmons, succeeded Knight and extended the chain of knowledge that has become one of the more recognized and respected programs in polymer science and polymer engineering, attracting students worldwide. By 1991, the chemistry building had been superseded by a towering glass Polymer Science Building filled with polymer rock stars recruited by Frank Kelley, dean of what had become the College of Polymer

Science and Polymer Engineering. Kelley recruited scientists and engineers the way great football coaches recruited quarterbacks and linebackers. With the help of research vice presidents at Akron's four rubber companies, he lured James L. White from the University of Tennessee to form the polymer engineering department, and Akron had found its new way.

"In 1997," Goodyear Chairman Samir Gibara told us, "the city is much better off with a Polymer Institute that is world class than it would have been with another two plants here. I mean, everybody has plants." John Lutheran grew up in Youngstown, where steel was to that city what rubber had been to Akron. He more easily recognized this than a displaced worker from the rubber shops. He had come to Akron to earn his doctorate in polymer science and by 1997 was coordinating the university's polymer technology two-year associate degree program.

"There was little or no steel research going on in Youngstown," he said, "whereas the legacy here in Akron is the research in polymers."

Seed corn . . . a new row to hoe toward a future.

"If there is any reason why we feel very comfortable here in Akron," said Nissim Calderon, Goodyear's vice president for corporate research in 1997, "it is because of the polymer program. It's like a window to the world of polymers."

While researching and writing *Wheels of Fortune*, I learned more than I could have expected. Knowledge came from those who had worked the rubber-shop floors; those whose research transitioned old companies to new or refined products; executives, who occupied Mahogany Row of Goodyear, the one rubber company that stuck with Akron as the city had stuck with it through a takeover attempt. My one regret is never having had the opportunity to know F. A. "Frank" Seiberling, who with his brother Charlie, founded the company that refused to cut and run. I wrote so much about the Seiberlings, including a subsequent book, *Stan Hywet Hall and Gardens*, about the family and its landmark country home, that it *feels* as if I do know them. I would argue that of the original four barons of Akron's rubber industry—B.F. Goodrich, Frank Seiberling (Goodyear), Harvey Firestone Sr., and William O'Neil (General)—Seiberling left the most indelible personal mark on the city.

An inventive man with a fighting spirit, Seiberling perhaps inherited inventiveness from his father, John F. Seiberling, who created farm machinery, including the first reaper with a dropper that cut standing grain and left unbound bundles for tying. The equipment made John Seiberling rich. When the Seiberlings moved from the Norton countryside to Akron in 1865, son Frank, who was six, in not many years proved he was no one to be trifled with, even if he was only 5-foot-4. After Patsy McGinnis, leader of a gang of Irish lads, tied Frank's clothes and those of a friend in knots and heaved them into the Ohio & Erie Canal, where the boys had gone skinny-dipping, Frank confronted the bigger, older boy on his "Dublin" turf near the canal. Patsy and gang thumped Frank but good. Frank went home with a bloody nose, split lip, and in tears.

Sending his son back into the fray, as it were, his father asked Frank to go to the post office at Market and Howard streets, townie turf. There, he encountered Patsy. "Any Furnace Street boy [from the Irish section] was at a disadvantage up in our part of town, and Patsy knew it," said Frank, who went at Patsy again and, with improved odds, got the best of him.

"That was the last of my fights with Patsy McGinnis," Frank said, "but it was far from being the last of my fighting."

Frank Seiberling, known, respectfully, as "little Napoleon" of the rubber industry, would take the fight to his own, when necessary. He may have been imperfect as a businessman—critics believed he lived on the financial edge—but he fought to defend his own patents for rubber processes and vulcanization methods, not to mention those within Goodyear, the company he and Charlie founded in 1898. He was a little guy who stood up for the little guy.

Akron grew faster than any city in America between 1910 and 1920, its population erupting from 69,000 to 208,435. Drawn by rubber-shop jobs and those in supporting industries, workers had to sleep in shifts—if they could find a bed. Makeshift houses sprang up in backyards of other houses. Meanwhile, Frank Seiberling and wife, Gertrude, building a grand country home in west Akron, beyond tire-manufacturing odors and dirty air, appreciated both the need for housing and Goodyear's self-interest in creating it to retain workers.

The Seiberlings would have Stan Hywet (*hee-wit*), their sixty-five-room mansion, and the workers in east Akron near Goodyear, a neighborhood designed by Warren H. Manning, landscape architect of the Stan Hywet property. In early Goodyear days, workers lived near the factory in what daughter Irene Seiberling dubbed "Cinder World," charcoal ash-covered fields with rows of inflated boxes. "This bothered Father very, very much," Irene said. "There wasn't a single green tree or shrub or blade of grass." Goodyear's Board of Directors was less troubled. When Seiberling unveiled his plan for Goodyear Heights, the directors rejected it. Goodyear builds tires, they said, not neighborhoods. Their shortsightedness didn't stop Seiberling. "It seemed to me that if Goodyear wanted to avoid terrific labor problems," he said, "we would have to offer our workers more than just jobs."

Frank and Gertrude sat at their kitchen table and signed stock certificates as collateral to finance Goodyear Heights houses that employees could buy at cost—provided they were white. [Equality had not yet come to a city that in the 1920s became a hotbed of the Ku Klux Klan.] Goodyear's directors eventually conceded the wisdom of the project and supported Seiberling, whose idea proved good enough that Harvey Firestone borrowed it to create Firestone Park.

To be fair, the Goodyear directors' initial response could have been fueled by the belief that, as innovative and inventive as Frank Seiberling was, he was not a financial genius. Nevertheless, Seiberling's financial troubles during the 1920–21 recession, when his $15 million personal worth fell to nearly zero, resulted more from believing in his company so much that he invested nearly his entire fortune there. Goodyear stock dropped from more than $100 per share to $5.25, and New York financiers forced Seiberling out of Goodyear.

Forever the fighter—ask Patsy McGinnis—Frank Seiberling and brother Charlie, whom Frank credited with building more goodwill for the Seiberlings than he himself had, got off the canvas and launched another rubber company with the help of friends and former Goodyear workers, some of whom Charlie had lent money when they, too, lost what they had invested. Frank gathered at Stan Hywet Hall in 1921 those who would organize Seiberling Rubber, and, holding a silver spoon in his hand, told them: "Gentlemen, we are going to make the name Seiberling on rubber mean as much as the word sterling on silver." Seiberling, the industry's 364th company, ascended to seventh in annual sales, trailing only Akron's Big Four—Goodyear, Firestone, Goodrich, and General—and U.S. Rubber and Armstrong.

Along the way, Frank Seiberling repaid his creditors, in large part because Cyrus Eaton, Cleveland industrialist and friend, paid Frank a premium on 60,000 shares of Seiberling stock. Eaton resented New York financial interests forcing the Seiberlings out of Goodyear and knew what the company meant to them. "In losing Goodyear," Frank said, "I felt that I had lost something that was as much a part of me as my heart or lungs. Anyone misjudges me who supposes I busied myself all those years for money. The building was the exciting thing, and, of course, I liked to be captain." The term "captain of industry" fit Frank Seiberling perfectly.

While he was no beneficent captain like Frank Seiberling, I did meet another man who liked to be in charge and would let a person know it. This encounter of a scary kind occurred during my unending travels as sports columnist. The *Beacon Journal* literally covered the *world* of sports during the '80s to mid-'90s. Writers traveled with Cleveland's professional teams. The [pompous] Ohio State University was as much "local team" as the University of Akron, Kent State University, and Northeast Ohio small colleges. We went where the action was—Super Bowl, World Series, NBA playoffs (when the '90s Cavaliers were a force), and especially to major golf tournaments, where participants were among those who populated Akron's own annual event on the renowned South Course of Firestone Country Club. The only major tournament I never covered was the British Open. [I did, however, get to Great Britain—to write about a Cleveland Browns pre-season encounter in Wembley Stadium; the NFL was laying the groundwork for what became a series of games in London each season.]

Like golfers, the world's greatest bowlers came each year to Akron, home of the Professional Bowlers Association and the Firestone Tournament of Champions at Riviera Lanes. Akron's Eddie Elias founded the PBA, created its most prestigious tournament, and became its MVP. Akron was bowling's Mecca. Until it, like so much else associated with the rubber companies, abandoned the city, bowling had put Akron on the map and affected lives. If Eddie Elias was the biggest name behind the scenes, Fred Borden was the go-to guy for those who wanted to improve their games, from pros to top amateurs to some who just wanted to stay out of the gutter at Borden's Stonehedge Place and other bowling centers.

When Borden was chosen to guide the United States amateur bowling team in the Pan American Games in 1991, it created another good reason for me to attend them. Akron's Jeff Reynolds, brother of Butch, one of the world's greatest 400-meter runners, if not the greatest, was competing in the Pan Am Games, as was North Canton hammer thrower Jud Logan, America's best, who was warming up for the 1992 Barcelona Olympics. It was no challenge for the track and field athletes to get warm at the Pan Am Games in Havana, Cuba, in August.

As warm as Fidel Castro's island home was, aspects of it proved chilling for Borden, as well as some of us documenting his adventure on this island that Americans usually were not permitted to visit. Borden was an exception. He is special. He is so good he was asked to teach Cuban bowling coach Romero Rodriquez the game. And why not? Borden is the author of *Bowling: Knowledge Is the Key*, the bible on instruction. Borden is so good PBA champions turn to him when their games go south, and I don't mean to Cuba. Cuba was not the lap of luxury. In fact, with streets of cars from decades long gone, it resembled the 1950s. Don't even ask about the difficulties Cuba faced in building and equipping the Pan American Bowling Center.

Cuba's enemy to the north, the U.S.—as in us—did not extend a helping hand as readily as Borden had to Rodriquez. Borden was quick with bowling's version of humanitarian aid, "because," he explained, "[Rodriquez] wants to learn." American officials were less receptive. The United States Department of the Treasury decreed neither Brunswick nor AMF could supply dangerous capitalistic pinsetting equipment to socialist Cuba due to a trade embargo. When U.S. Tenpin Bowling Association officials appealed to John Sununu, President George H.W. Bush's chief of staff arranged for Cuba to get the needed equipment, with a proviso: It had to dismantle it and send it back after the games. Couldn't have that sneaky Fidel Castro, rumored to have in the palace his own lane with one of the few operative old hand-set pin machines, upgrading. Cuba officials said only six lanes remained on the island in 1991. Before completion of the Pan American Bowling Center, the Cuba team practiced on a gymnasium floor.

When the U.S. made it clear that it would provide nothing that could not be returned—a lane-preparation machine, for instance—Cuba looked elsewhere. It turned to Odin, a Japanese company that provided the lanes but whose equipment was not much used, even in Japan. The possibilities worried Borden. "We thought, *Oh, God—we'll be bowling on sandpaper*," Borden said. He was pleasantly surprised. "They could drop these lanes right in Akron and the city would be proud to have them." There could have been no stronger endorsement.

That didn't mean everything was peachy for the American bowlers and their coach. In the Athletes Village east of the capital, Borden discovered his toilet had no seat; a person had to sit on hard, cold porcelain. The bathroom did have one unexpected extra. "There's this electric wire that runs above the shower," Borden said. "If you touch it, you get it." Shocking! Borden forgave his hosts because they were advancing bowling's Olympic-sport chances.

When the big day arrived and Borden's U.S. team began rolling to six medals—three gold, a silver, and two bronze—I and three others from the American media contingent presented ourselves at the Pan American Bowling Center to bear witness and record the moment for posterity. Mark Purdy of the *San Jose Mercury News*, George Diaz of the *Orlando Sentinel*, Bill Conlin of the *Philadelphia Daily News*, and I, with Maureen Boyle, press officer for the U.S. Bowling team, were front and center in prime seats. "Don't move," Boyle instructed us. "They'll try to move you, but *don't* move." Got it. Sit tight. Be brave. Represent America.

We tried, with George Diaz carrying the flag. Born in Cuba and, of course, fluent in Spanish, Diaz told a female bowling center official who tried to shoo us from our front-row perch: "We're not moving." Having survived a recent bomb threat at America's preeminent bowling event, the Firestone Tournament of Champions, I suggested I was not about to move because of a little Cuban intimidation. She was not impressed, perhaps because she could not understand the language I was speaking. I think she asked if I lived in Nashville.

About the time Diaz suggested the woman consult Ms. Boyle, clapping and cheering erupted. I didn't think it was for our courage. We had learned at other venues such reaction meant only one thing: *El Presidente*, Fidel Castro, was in the building.

"Officials must sit here," the woman told us. She did not mean bowling officials. She also did not explain that the press section was about to become the presidential section. We had our pens and notebooks at the ready; Castro's entourage had their weapons. Seemed unfair.

Diaz, who carries U.S. and Cuban passports, said he was "sweating bullets."

Which is better than absorbing them.

Castro did not seem perturbed by our presence, but he did want action. "What do we have to do to get this going?" he inquired. "Let's bowl."

Julie Gardner, who would win individual silver and team gold medals, also was anxious. "I was really nervous," she admitted. But why? No one was pointing his weapon at her. "How often," she asked, "do you get to do what you do best in front of the president of a country?"

I had no answer to that rhetorical question. I was too busy scurrying out of *El Presidente*'s seat. *Muy pronto.* Castro's escorts made us most aware of their weapons. Diaz shared my concern. "We were close," he said, "to being in a monument." It would have made news: A monument at the Pan American Bowling Center with/to four dumb, dead journalists.

We were not close to death that day, even if it felt we were. This is a feeling sports journalists know well, especially columnists whose job it is to get behind and go beyond the action, find its significance/

meaning, and offer it to readers as a nugget of understanding wrapped in a smart package tied with a bright, attention-getting bow. This is easier said than done with the clock ticking like a time bomb on your deadline. Hearts race, especially when a late-night event takes a dramatic, 180-degree turn that makes what you have been writing irrelevant. An example of this occurred in Game One of the 1988 World Series between the Oakland Athletics and Los Angeles Dodgers in Dodgers Stadium in Chavez Ravine.

When the lame Kirk Gibson hit the two-strike, two-out, walk-off, pinch-hit home run, he did more than send a Dennis Eckersley slider over the right-field wall, beating baseball's best reliever and future Hall of Famer. He brought fiction (*The Natural*) to life and snuffed out the A's, the better team. It would require four more games, but the Dodgers were as good as champions. I did not know that when I decided to let my column stand as written and do a different take on Gibson the next day. It was a practical if unpleasant decision, a deadline danger. I was asking the reader to make an unstated connection and see emotion, generated by Gibson hippity-hopping around the bases on a bad right knee and a lousy left hamstring, fist raised in triumph, as the great leveler. I returned to the theme in my follow-up column, making a case that Gibson, former star wide receiver at Michigan State, played baseball with such toughness that he advanced the Hollywood take on Roy Hobbs rising from a hospital bed in *The Natural* to play in the Series. Gibson had climbed out of a tub of ice after having his leg injected with Xylocaine and cortisone, feel-better medicines.

When Gibson could not start the next day, or play thereafter, Mickey Hatcher, another former college receiver at Oklahoma, filled in nicely and bravely. "When I went out to left field," Hatcher said, "I was afraid that when people saw my number out there instead of Gibson, they'd throw stuff at me." They didn't, but if they had,

Hatcher could have handled it. He was Gibson's tough-guy soulmate. He spoke of his willingness to run through walls and just laugh.

"I think it's something I learned playing football," he said. "How to psych myself up. It's something you do when you know you're going to get crushed out there. You can see it in Kirk. Football mentally prepares you to play baseball hard. I play the game hard. He plays the game hard. We never give up." Hatcher sounded more like Knute Rockne than the Rock himself.

Only in Hollywood.

If Gibson's moment oozed the drama of fiction, the following year's Bay Bridge Series between the very same A's and the Giants, their San Francisco neighbor, turned frighteningly real. At 5:04 p.m. as I sat in a small interior room in Candlestick Park, writing a pre-game column before moving to my grandstand auxiliary press-box seat, the world came crashing down. This was The Big One, the 1989 Loma Prieta earthquake, a 6.9 magnitude nightmare.

The quake lasted only 17 seconds, rocked both sides of San Francisco Bay, and resulted in 63 deaths, nearly 3,800 injuries and more than $6 billion in damage. The lights went out at Candlestick, but an ESPN generator positioned beyond centerfield enabled it to remain on the air and provide early reports from a powerless, blacked-out city. Akron also played a role. The Goodyear Blimp, built near Wingfoot Lake, transitioned from aerial shots of the ballpark to documenting a disaster. San Francisco's Marina District burned. Part of the upper deck of the Bay Bridge collapsed onto the lower deck. A mile-long section of Interstate 880—the double-decked Cypress Structure—"pancaked during rush hour," as ESPN.com's Tim Keown wrote in a 25-years-later remembrance. With the highways impassable that we had taken from Oakland, where the Series began and our hotel was located, we had to drive an elongated route south, and then west and back north, to return there. Sheldon Ocker, *Beacon Journal* baseball writer, who, in 2018, was inducted into the writers section of the Baseball Hall of Fame, captained our ship back to Oakland. We found our hotel intact but not unaffected; the quake had wrenched the structure. My room's door barely closed and no longer locked.

The door created an inconvenience, and there would be others. What mattered is how Major League Baseball responded. The next day, as I wrote, new Commissioner Fay Vincent trod softly but surefootedly through the debris of more than the Bay Bridge Series. The quake night's game had been postponed, and the Series would not resume for ten days. The decision had as much to do with human values as with Candlestick Park structural damage. Baseball knew its place. Over the years, other sports often had not.

When Israeli athletes were massacred during the 1972 Munich Olympics, Avery Brundage, president of the International Olympic Committee, declared "the Games must go on." When in 1963 assassinated President John F. Kennedy lay in state in the Capitol Rotunda and a nation grieved, NFL Commissioner Pete Rozelle ordered games to be played. Vincent refused to allow his sport to display such callousness. In a hotel ballroom lit by candles, Vincent acknowledged the insignificance of "our modest little game" in the greater scope of life.

"We have a disaster in a community where we happen to be a guest," he explained. "If we play a game, we're going to be subtracting police and other government officials from higher priorities, and the fact is, I don't want to do that. We want to be sure that baseball does not intrude into a situation which is more serious and demanding of a higher degree of attention. We're mindful of the fact that we're part of a larger problem. We know our place."

And I knew mine. I was in the Bay Area because I was a sports columnist, sent to write about a World Series that suddenly wasn't. So in addition to chronicling and commenting on baseball's reaction to the devastating event—both its hierarchy and players—there was more important work to do. I could not hope to singlehandedly match the effort of an army of journalists from the *San Jose Mercury News*, a Knight-Ridder newspaper that produced stories to which Akron had access, but I could do what I could do; I'm not sure my editors were satisfied, but it was difficult to understand our circumstances from thousands of miles away.

While Sheldon Ocker concentrated on baseball, I wrote from other, less-familiar venues, including the collapsed Cypress Street Viaduct of the Nimitz Freeway in West Oakland. It may not have been the epicenter of the earthquake of '89, but it was the heart of its tragedy. I described it as a "concrete-and-steel layer cake with cars, bodies, and heartache between the layers." When President George H.W. Bush flew in by helicopter to tour the devastation of the worst Bay Area earthquake since 1906 and then flew away again, I stayed behind to talk with some of those he left to search for bodies, including construction worker Joe Carter, volunteer firefighter Bruce Andreozzi, and earthquake engineering researcher Ian Buckle.

"He reacted like he was in shock," Carter said of Bush. "It is the way we all reacted when we first got here. Now, we're numb." Carter and his men from MCM Construction in Sacramento, my former home, had worked 50 hours pounding through concrete, burning through steel, and then doing it all again to get beyond the second layer so that trained rescuers could go in. Every second mattered. The majority of deaths occurred where the men were working. At the time I wrote my column, 33 bodies had been found. Robert Best, director of the California Department of Transportation, said there might have been more but for the Series. Traffic was lighter than usual. People had wanted to be home by the 5:30 p.m. start of the game. Some of those still on the Cypress structure—the trees grow so close to the highway they seem part of it—thought they could make it even after the road began to dance.

Ian Buckle, deputy director of the National Center for Earthquake Engineering Research at the University of New York in Buffalo, said many roads are old and not built to withstand such stress. It takes vast sums to fix the problem or build new roads. "It is human nature," Buckle said, "to put it off," as he stood where nature had caught up with human nature.

After 12 days, I returned home without writing about the final two games. Sheldon Ocker saw the A's win the Series, 4–0. I had seen enough. Too much. What I had heard, however, from Oakland pitcher Dave Stewart, who won Game One, had provided a beacon in the darkness. He grew up in Oakland. In the faces of those from the city, he saw his own. He made a pledge. "I'm going down there," he said of the Cypress Street Viaduct. "If there is something I can do, I want to be part of it." He already had done something. He had stayed in Oakland. He was part of it, and it part of him. He did not bail. I could not say the same.

During more than 20 years in Akron, I flirted at least five times with leaving. For a person who had been irreparably altered by having to leave his Oklahoma hometown as a teenager when his family moved, I did a lot of leaving—or trying to leave. I interviewed for three sports columnist jobs [Fort Myers, Florida, Knoxville, Tennessee, and Kansas City; the latter I wanted badly, but it turned out I was only the token outside candidate brought in not to win the job but to confirm as genius management's preordained inside choice]. I also endured a ten-hour, dozen-interviews ordeal at the *Fort Worth Star-Telegram*—they did everything but waterboard me—after which I did not get so much as a Sorry-You-Stink rejection. After I finally wrote to inform my principal interrogator of this, I received an apology detailing how the newspaper would change its procedures. Small consolation, but, hey, glad to help.

If the Fort Worth dalliance proved a fiasco, it could not compare with my last. I thought I had found the ideal job at what seemed a perfect confluence of events. To reduce its largest expense—employees—the *Beacon Journal* offered what proved to be the most generous buyout in a series of them for those 55 or older who would accept early "retirement." I barely qualified in early 2001. I had a good position—chief editorial writer—working with an editorial-page editor whose opinions put us in close and necessary alignment.

I nevertheless had ambition to run an editorial page. This was not likely in Akron, where my boss, Michael Douglas, was younger and a force. So when I learned of the editorial-page-editor opening at the *Burlington Free Press*, a Gannett newspaper in Vermont's largest city—Bernie Sanders had been elected mayor in April 1981—I was interested. Geoff Gevalt, a former *Beacon Journal* editor who had moved to Vermont to become the *Free Press*'s managing editor, may have first told me of the opening, but when I began discussing the position via telephone, it was with Executive Editor Mickey Hirten. Jackie and I had fallen in love with Vermont vacationing in charming Woodstock, mostly in the off-season after leaf-peepers returned home and winter-sport devotees had yet to arrive. We preferred small places and smaller crowds, and found Vermont and its liberalism a match.

After I was invited to Burlington to interview for the job, unbeknownst to me, Mickey Hirten had accepted the executive editor's position at the *Lansing State Journal*, another Gannett newspaper in Michigan. The person whom I had come to believe might support my hiring and become an ally at the *Free Press*—Gevalt already was—had departed, and I was left to my own devices to convince the paper's conservative publisher that, even though I was what Vermonters refer to—and not fondly—as a flat-lander, I could be a fit.

I had come armed with an argument for my hiring. I could help the *Free Press* compete with Vermont editorial writing that had just been awarded a Pulitzer Prize for its "even-handed and influential series of editorials commenting on the divisive issues arising from civil unions for same-sex couples." *Rutland Herald* editorial-page editor David Moats received the honor for ten editorials written between January and May 2000, when the Vermont legislature was deciding how to comply after its Supreme Court ruled the law had to conform with a constitutional requirement for equal treatment, whether or not that required allowing civil unions, precursor to same-sex marriages. Moats established the parameters of the arguments and described the difficulties that a moral question infused with religiosity created for people functioning in a secular world that required resolution in the political arena. In his even-handedness, Moats acknowledged that "it is not as easy to counter that opposition [to same-sex marriage] on moral grounds as it was to counter racism in the civil rights era. The views of many opponents are shaped by ideas of sexuality taught by their religions. These moral teachings, even if one disagrees with them, have a legitimacy that racism does not." The point: Moats and the *Rutland Herald* engaged fully while the *Free Press* had not. I knew this could be poking a hornets' nest.

The safest course during my interviews, especially with publisher James M. Carey, would have been to respond only to questions regarding the responsibility of a newspaper and its editorial page in such consequential moments. Instead, I waded in. I did this not so much to make an impression as to find out if my commitment to a strong-voiced editorial page would be ill-placed. I wanted the job but not if it required cowering instead of courage and leadership.

As I listened to Carey, I began to understand that his own backstory informed his thinking more than others' rights. Even as I didn't appreciate his priorities, I understood and empathized. He had been adopted, and his gratitude both for his adoptive parents and the birth mother who gave him a chance at life dictated his thinking, which went like this: He would not have been where he was if not for his biological mother's willingness to give birth and allow him to be adopted and become part of a traditional family of a man and woman. These circumstances made him a staunch opponent of abortion and a firm believer in traditional marriage. Add a religious upbringing, and I understood that it would not benefit me to challenge the emphases of his life. I steered the conversation to professionalism.

Using his feelings about abortion as a totem, I suggested that, while my personal preference would be to stress a woman's right to choose, I knew well the difference between writing a personal column and the newspaper's opinion. As a professional, I could focus the argument not so much against the legal right to a safe abortion as set forth in *Roe v. Wade* as on the alternative of adoption. A newspaper could, with the appropriate agencies, campaign on its editorial page not only for choosing adoption over abortion but also to raise awareness of the steps in the process, detailing medical, financial, and personal help and how to obtain it. Instead of appreciating my professionalism, I got the feeling what Carey heard was potential conflict he wanted to avoid. It was easier to hire someone who thought like him. If I had detected that my views were out of sync with Carey and the editorial board in general on multiple topics, I would not have accepted the job had it been offered, no matter how much I might have coveted it. I would not have had the job long in such an environment.

I don't know if Mickey Hirten would have served as my advocate had he still been executive editor or if it might have made a difference. When I mentioned this to Geoff Gevalt years later at a memorial service for Dale Allen, he did not remember he had sat in on my interview with Carey, and I understood why. His position as managing editor was not one directly involved in hiring the editorial-page editor. While he would have been involved in the interview process, I assume he may not have been alongside Carey had Hirten been there.

The person hired to edit the editorial page did not remain in Burlington for long. By 2006 Aki Soga, business editor when I interviewed, had become editorial-page editor. Soga must have done well. He and Michael Townsend, the executive editor, were named finalists for the 2012 Pulitzer Prize for editorial writing for a campaign that led to Vermont's first reform of open-government laws in 35 years. For the ninth time in 95 years, the 18-member Pulitzer Prize board chose no winner. *Columbia Journalism Review* (*CJR*) pointed out the decision should not be taken as a comment on the finalists or the state of editorial writing; none of the finalists received the required majority vote after the editorial-writing jury recommended three of 44 entries. Neither Soga nor the other finalists whined, but he told *CJR*: "It does seem a little odd to be a finalist in a contest without a winner." He, other finalists, and editorial writing deserved better.

This left David Moats the only Vermont journalist ever to win a Pulitzer for editorial writing. Not only could he write, but he and the *Rutland Herald* also had the courage of their convictions and took on a far more controversial topic than open government. In the end, this did not save Moats from the fate that has befallen so many in journalism. In early 2018, the *Herald* and its sister newspaper, the *Barre-Montpelier Times Argus*, which were bought by out-of-state owners in 2016, eliminated the editorial-page-editor position. Editor Steve Pappas told *sevendaysvt.com* the emphasis had changed to "hyperlocal" and that "Moats' '20,000-foot view' of issues in a broad context [had become] less useful." John Walters, a political columnist with *sevendaysvt.com*, lamented the loss, even though Moats, who had been with the papers since 1982 and editorial-page editor since 1992, continued to work part-time. That is what journalism has come to: even a Pulitzer Prize editorialist who was "a beacon of quality" and "articulate voice of reason in Vermont's marketplace of ideas" is no longer valued. The same thing has happened in Akron, where the *Beacon Journal*, has become, like the diminished *Burlington Free Press*, a part of Gannett Newspapers. Because opinion seems boundless in new but not necessarily improved media, editorials and informed opinion matter less.

I did not anticipate the extent of decline of local small-to-midsize newspapers and editorial pages in particular in 2001, when the *Beacon Journal* began an inexorable slide from the mountaintop that had been the first Knight newspaper, foundation of the Knight-Ridder kingdom. By the time I had been spurned by the *Burlington Free Press*, I had decided to accept the *Beacon Journal* buyout despite efforts of my superiors to keep me. It allowed me to tiptoe in other waters—bookseller, college-newspaper adviser, adjunct journalism and writing instructor at three colleges, freelance writer, and author—but when Jackie lost her public relations director position (with our health insurance) in an end-time layoff at the Hoover Company, I returned to full-time work. I had always admired Hiram College, a small liberal arts institution off the beaten path in Northeast Ohio, and had written about it often for the *Beacon Journal.* So when I was offered the position of College Relations Director, I accepted, little knowing I would also become a graduate student and get a master's degree, the most enjoyable, rewarding experience in a lifetime of learning.

Mama would have been proud. I no longer was the least-educated Love. This doesn't mean that I wised up. If I had been able to do that, I would not have left unsaid so much that Mama longed to hear and that I am reduced to writing. In the summer of 1988, I visited Oklahoma, ostensibly to cover the PGA Championship at Oak Tree Golf Club in Edmond, north of Oklahoma City, where Mama and Daddy lived. I actually went for Mama.

Short of football, I enjoyed golf writing most, and this was a time when the *Beacon Journal* routinely covered the PGA Championship, as it fell so close on the pro-golf calendar to the tournament held each August on Firestone Country Club's South Course. The pros universally loved Firestone South, an exception being the late Seve

Ballesteros. For some reason, the Spanish major champion could not pass Firestone's straightforward test, with water on only two holes, one The Monster 16th. Sports Editor Tom Giffen would have sent me to Oak Tree anyway, but he knew I needed to visit Mama, who suffered from kidney disease. By 1988, it had worsened, and dialysis became ineffective in cleansing her blood. She was in an Oklahoma City hospital, the prognosis not good.

When I covered one of golf's Major Tournaments unaccompanied by the *Beacon Journal* golf writer—the case at Oak Tree—the workload increased. In addition to a column, I had to write a story of that day's round and usually notes. It did not leave much time for personal business, but my boss understood my circumstances. Mama came first.

I tried to arrive a day before a tournament began to write a preview and a column. I must have driven to Oklahoma City on Wednesday before Thursday's first round. I remember with stark clarity walking into Mama's hospital room. I had so much wanted to see her. When I did, it took all the self-control I had not to break down. She had lost weight as her kidney function worsened. A month from her 75th birthday, her appearance was not the worst of it. The room stank. She had soiled herself, and no one had noticed and cleaned her. I kissed her on the forehead and told her I would return.

Seeking an orderly, nurse's aide, or whomever I could find, I reminded myself it would not serve Mama well if I unleashed the rage I felt. I needed a scapegoat, someone I could blame for what was happening to Mama and the condition in which I found her. At the heart of it, I blamed myself for being so far away and unable to help her. I may have realized this was illogical, but Mama deserved better. I found help, explained the situation, and asked that it be addressed. I was assured it would be.

I returned to Mama's room to talk, but the circumstances were less than ideal. Mama was embarrassed. I almost had to stop breathing to keep from retching. We both held it together as best we could. I asked Mama about her care and what the doctors were telling her and told her about the tournament. Even as bad as she felt and in the condition she and her room were in, she was interested and wanted to know who I expected to win the PGA Championship. (I was not smart enough to suggest Jeff Sluman would win, crushing Oak Tree and third-round leader Paul Azinger with a six-under-par 65 final round. Sluman was best remembered to that point for losing the 1987 Tournament Players Championship on the third hole of a playoff after the distraction of a young fan jumping into a greenside lake as Sluman was about to putt.)

By the time I left Mama's room, no attendant had appeared. I kissed Mama goodbye and told her I would again seek assistance. I was not as polite the second time. I demanded someone accompany me to her room, and I did not leave until the person went in. It was so little to have done for the woman who had done so much for me.

Returning to Akron, I made a quick turnaround to Montreal, Canada, with Cleveland Browns writer Ed Meyer for a Thursday-night pre-season game. Such games reveal little about a team, and an 11–7 loss to the New York Jets was no exception. I might not have gone but for the unusual site, a test for NFL football in the land of the Canadian Football League and Sgt. Preston of the Yukon. I remember little of the Molson Brewery-sponsored game, with 39,112 ticket-buyers disguised as 20,154 empty yellow-and-blue seats. Postgame I remember all too well.

When Ed and I returned to our hotel, I had a message to call my father. It is the type of message a person never wants to receive. There could be only one reason Daddy had tracked me down in Montreal. Mama had gone home from the hospital and died there with Daddy and neighbor Bev Crowe beside her. [Bev, along with Jackie, was like a daughter to Mama.] That offered a moment of comfort, but had it not been for Ed's kindness, I don't know how I would have gotten through the night. I called Ed's room. When I told him of Mama's death, Ed said to meet him in the bar and that we would talk for as long as I wanted. He talked me through those terrible first hours and appreciated my stories about Mama and the whistle she used to call me home from those neighborhood football games. Now, here I was in another country the day she died, writing about the game she loved and, more than anyone, had taught me to love. She had indoctrinated me in the Nowata Ironmen from the time I was nine months old. She probably would have smiled at the memory. As for me, I thought I might never smile again.

As I write this, more than 31 years later, I remain unsmiling. I have just read the "Mother's Letter" Mama wrote in 1972, signed a year later, and placed in my "Log of Life" journal she kept so faithfully. It explains a number of things that influenced the way she and Daddy raised me but leaves me in pain to know her effort to help me become independent had been so successful that she felt it "disastrous" for her and Daddy. Instead of showing appreciation for all they had done for me—everything, except allow me to remain in Nowata, my home, until I finished high school—my behavior left Mama and Daddy believing I cared "nothing" about them except when I needed them. She went on to explain that her "dependent" life with her mother and Daddy's privation as part of a large family had led them to raise me to be excessively independent and to provide me the material possessions Daddy lacked.

The letter included a prophetic warning: "You take us so much for granted that you won't know what hit you when we are both gone." Mama, as usual, was right. But it did not take both of them being gone for me not to know what had hit me. When she died, Daddy already had begun a five-year slide into Alzheimer's—its loss of self and death. When he met Jackie and me at the Will Rogers Airport in Oklahoma City, before we drove to Nowata with Bev Crowe for Mama's funeral, Daddy's diminishment struck me. It would take more time and uncharacteristic behavior to reveal its full effects.

Daddy had preplanned for Mama's and his deaths. I will be forever grateful that included the purchase of four gravesites at Nowata Memorial Park Cemetery. It meant that, one day, all of us could go home to the place it killed me to leave. Time and circumstance eroded the response of those in Nowata who knew Mama. Because the *Nowata Daily Star* had become a weekly, it did not publish Mama's obituary until *after* her service at Benjamin Funeral Home. Only Uncle Elmer, Aunt Jewel, and my cousins attended. No one, it seemed, knew of her death.

As if that failure were not enough, the minister who conducted the service had not known Mama—she had not lived there for more than 26 years—and he had not spoken with anyone who might have told him what kind of person she had been and how much she had accomplished in her life. I contributed to the sad folly. Wrapped in my own loss, I failed to appreciate that I should have eulogized the most important person in my life. It was her only son's responsibility, even if just one person who was not a family member would have heard it. I doubt I would have made it through a eulogy. Sight of a small "Grandma" floral arrangement attached to her coffin lid had reduced me to a paroxysm of sobs and left me virtually paralyzed.

When the service mercifully ended—there won't be one after my death—I rose to leave the chapel and was surprised to discover a man behind where we had been seated. He rose, came forward, and extended a hand of comfort.

"Everett Sears," he said by way of introduction. "I don't know if you remember me."

I remembered. Everett Sears was the father of my classmate Alice and her older sister Rita. He remained a prominent member of the community, and, in this one instant, he could not have known how much it lifted me that he not only had somehow learned about Mama's service but also made time to come. Years later, when Mr. Sears died, I sent a donation in his name to the Nowata church we had both attended with a note explaining what his presence had meant at the time of Mama's death; in return I received kind notes from Alice and Rita.

The Love Columbarium awaits a homecoming in Nowata Memorial Park Cemetery. [*Photo courtesy the author*]

They buried Mama at the beginning of a new Nowata Ironmen football season, the unrelenting Oklahoma sun beating down, the hot breath of a ceaseless wind blowing still. It has dawned on me that I should have bought a new whistle and placed it in her coffin. Sometimes I hear her original whistle, though it grows fainter with the passing football seasons we loved to share. When I can no longer hear that whistle and my mind has grown dead quiet, I will be beside Mama again. How fortunate am I? I do wonder if the dead can see the Friday Night Lights of Ironman Memorial Stadium. Mama would like that, and—finally home—so would I.

I hope you enjoyed this book. Would you do me a favor?

Like all authors, I rely on online reviews to attract readers. Your opinion is invaluable. Would you take a few moments to share your assessment of my book on Amazon or any other book-review website you prefer? Your opinion will make the book marketplace more transparent and useful to all.

Thank you very much.

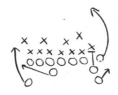

SOURCES

A SMALL-TOWN BACKYARD QUARTERBACK

Interviews

Chuck Berry (via email)

Douglas "Bucky" Buck

Charles Dugger

Newspapers, Magazines, Other Materials

Nowata Daily Star

Tulsa Tribune

Tulsa World

New York Times

Miami Herald

Sports Illustrated

The Coffin Corner (Professional Football Researchers Association)

Stephen H. Love Log of Life (a journal and scrapbook)

Websites

Maxine Bamburg, "Nowata," *The Encyclopedia of Oklahoma History and Culture*, https://www.okhistory.org/publications/enc/entry.php?entry=NO017.© Oklahoma Historical Society.

Gary L. Cheatham, "Nowata County," *The Encyclopedia of Oklahoma History and Culture*, https://www.okhistory.org/publications/enc/entry.php?entry=NO018.© Oklahoma Historical Society.

Donald E. Green, "Settlement Patterns," *The Encyclopedia of Oklahoma History and Culture*, https://www.okhistory.org/publications/enc/entry.php?entry=SE024.© Oklahoma Historical Society.

http://www.oklahomagenealogy.com/nowata/nowata-county-history.htm

http://www.oklahomagenealogy.com/nowata/index.htm

https://oklahoma.hometownlocator.com/ok/nowata/coodys-bluff.cfm

https://www.coffeyville.com/316/Dalton-Museum

https://www.history.com/this-day-in-history/the-dalton-gang-is-wiped-out-in-coffeyville-kansas

https://www.swt.usace.army.mil/Locations/Tulsa-District-Lakes/Oklahoma/Oologah-Lake/Oologah-Lake-Recreation/

https//nowataoklahoma.wordpress.com/2007/02/18/hello-world/ (. . . Where the origin of its name has many stories! Posted by an acre of Oklahoma)

https://nowatamuseum.org

http://sites.rootsweb.com/oknowata/Coody's%20Bluff%20Oklahoma.html

https://en.wikipedia.org/wiki/The_Last_Picture_Show

https://www.imdb.com/title/tt0067328/

http://ossaa.com (Oklahoma Secondary Schools Activities Association)

https://www.ancestry.com (AncestryDNA examined and provided results from my DNA test)

Books

Wilkinson, Jay with Gretchen Hirsch. *Bud Wilkinson: An Intimate Portrait of an American Legend.* Champaign, Illinois: Sagamore Publishing, 1994.

————. *Dear Jay, Love Dad: Bud Wilkinson's Letters to His Son.* Norman, Oklahoma: University of Oklahoma Press, 2012.

Keuffel, Kenneth W. *Winning Single Wing Football: A Simplified Guide for the Football Coach.* Lawrenceville, New Jersey: Swift Press, 2004.

Edmundson, Mark. *Why Football Matters: My Education in the Game.* New York: The Penguin Press, 2014.

Almond, Steve. *Against Football: One Fan's Reluctant Manifesto.* Brooklyn, NY: Melville House, 2014.

Griese, Bob and Dave Hyde. *Perfection: The Inside Story of the 1972 Dolphins' Perfect Season.* Hoboken, New Jersey: John Wiley & Sons, Inc., 2012.

Brooks, David. *The Second Mountain: The Quest for a Moral Life.* New York: Random House, 2019.

Articles

Campbell, Jim. "The Power and the Glory: Single-Wing Football," *The Coffin Corner* (PFRA), Vol. 14, No. 4 (1992).

ON BECOMING AN IRONMAN

Interviews

Chuck Berry (via email)

Douglas "Bucky" Buck

Charles Dugger

Newspapers, Other Materials

Nowata Daily Star

Stephen H. Love Log of Life (a journal and scrapbook)

Websites

https://www.history.com/topics/great-depression/dust-bowl

http://plainshumanities.unl.edu/encyclopedia/doc/egp.ii.044.xml

https://www.history.com/topics/native-american-history/trail-of-tears

https://www.goodreads.com/work/quotes/2933712-alice-in-wonderland

https://www.distancebetweencities.us

Books

Steinbeck, John. *The Grapes of Wrath.* New York: Book-of-the-Month Club by arrangement with Viking Penguin, 1995.

Carroll, Lewis. *Alice's Adventures in Wonderland and Other Stories.* San Diego, CA: Canterbury Classics/Baker & Taylor Publishing Group, 2013.

Articles

Frolund, Vic. "Ironmen . . .," *The Coffin Corner* (PFRA), Vol. 2, No. 9 (1980).

TORN BETWEEN TWO WORLDS

Interviews

Chuck Berry (via email)

Douglas "Bucky" Buck

Charles Dugger

Karolyn Pettingell (email)

Newspapers, Other Materials

Nowata Daily Star

New York Times

Nowata High School Yearbooks (1962, 1964)

Mira Loma High School Yearbooks (1963, 1964)

Mira Loma High School *Matador Capers* (student newspaper)

The Oklahoman (Oklahoma City, OK)

Tulsa World

Stephen H. Love Log of Life (a journal and scrapbook)

Websites

http://www.oklahomagenealogy.com/nowata/nowata-county-history.htm

Kenny A. Franks, "Petroleum Industry," *The Encyclopedia of Oklahoma History and Culture*, https://www.okhistory.org/publications/enc/entry.php?entry=PE023.© Oklahoma Historical Society.

Maxine Bamburg, "Nowata," *The Encyclopedia of Oklahoma History and Culture*, https://www.okhistory.org/publications/enc/entry.php?entry=NO017.© Oklahoma Historical Society.

https://www.harmonfnd.org/history

https://nowatamuseum.org

https://www.lasr.net/travel/city.php?Campbell+Hotel&TravelTo=OK0309035&VA=Y&Attraction_ID=OK0309035a004

http://www.designateddriving.net/historyofdesignateddriving.html

https://en.wikipedia.org/wiki/Nowata,_Oklahoma

https://en.wikipedia.org/wiki/Cruising_(driving)

https://en.wikipedia.org/wiki/American_Graffiti

https://www.imdb.com/title/tt0069704/

https://en.wikipedia.org/wiki/Marilyn_Monroe

https://www.vanityfair.com/culture/2010/11/marilyn-monroe-201011

https://www.sportsnaut.com

Books

Kreider, Tim. *We Learn Nothing: Essays*. New York: Simon & Schuster Paperbacks, 2012

Keith, Harold. *Forty-Seven Straight: The Wilkinson Era at Oklahoma*. Norman, Oklahoma: University of Oklahoma Press, 2003.

WHEN FOOTBALL IMITATES REEL LIFE

Newspapers, Magazines

Nowata Daily Star

(Nowata County Area) People

New York Times

The Oklahoman (Oklahoma City, OK)

Tulsa World

Sports Illustrated

Variety

Websites

http://www.permianpanthersfootball.com/WhatIsMOJO.html

https://www.imdb.com/title/tt0390022/

Kenny A. Franks, "Petroleum Industry," *The Encyclopedia of Oklahoma History and Culture*, https://www.okhistory.org/publications/enc/entry.php?entry=PE023.© Oklahoma Historical Society.

https://nowatamuseum.org

https://www.mentalfloss.com

https://en.wikipedia.org/wiki/Prattville,_Oklahoma

Books, Movies, Television

Bissinger, H. G. *Friday Night Lights: A Town, a Team, and a Dream.* Reading, Massachusetts: Addison-Wesley, 1990.

————. *After Friday Night Lights: When the Games Ended, Real Life Began. An Unlikely Love Story.* San Francisco: Byliner Originals, 2012.

Wilson, Leah, ed. *A Friday Night Lights Companion: Love, Loss, and Football in Dillon, Texas.* Dallas: Smart Pop, an Imprint of Bella Books, Inc., 2011.

Gent, Peter. *North Dallas Forty.* New York: William Morrow, 1973.

McCracken, Kirk. *Because of the Hate: The Murder of Jerry Bailey.* Amazon, 2018.

Friday Night Lights. 117 minutes. Universal: Imagine Entertainment, Beverly Hills, California. 2004.

Friday Night Lights (TV Series). 5 seasons. NBCUniversal. New York: 2006–2010.

Possums. 97 minutes. Monarch Home Video and HSX Films, 1998.

North Dallas Forty. 119 minutes. Paramount (Prime Home Video), Los Angeles. 1979.

STEVE DAVIS AND HIS HEAVENLY OPTION

Newspapers, Magazines

Lawton Morning Press; Lawton Constitution

The Oklahoman (Oklahoma City, OK)

Tulsa Tribune

Tulsa World

Sports Illustrated

Books

Jenkins, Dan. *Saturday's America.* New York: Berkley Medallion Books, 1973.

Switzer, Barry with Bud Shrake. *Bootlegger's Boy.* New York: William Morrow, 1990.

Cross, George Lynn. *Presidents Can't Punt.* Norman, Oklahoma: University of Oklahoma Press, 1977.

Fletcher, Jim. *The Die-Hard Fan's Guide to Sooner Football.* Washington, DC: Regnery Publishing, Inc., 2008.

Trotter, Jake. *I Love Oklahoma/I Hate Texas.* Chicago: Triumph Books, 2012.

Zimmerman, Paul. *The New Thinking Man's Guide to Pro Football.* New York: Simon & Schuster, Inc., 1984.

————. Peter King, ed. Dr. Z: *The Lost Memoirs of an Irreverent Football Writer.* Chicago: Triumph Books, 2017.

Upchurch, Jay C. *Tales from the Oklahoma Sooners Sideline.* New York: Sports Publishing, 2003, 2007, 2011.

Jefferson, Thomas, ed. *The Jefferson Bible: The Life and Morals of Jesus of Nazareth.* Washington, D.C. Smithsonian Books, 2011.

Video

OU Football Legends. DVD. 2003.

THE HARDEST GOODBYES

Interviews

Jewel Berry (1978)

Roy Berry (1978)

Chuck Berry (via email)

Douglas "Bucky" Buck

Charles Dugger

Erville Orndorff (email)

Margie Pierce (mail)

Leon Turman (phone, email)

Newspapers, Other Materials

Nowata Daily Star

Tulsa Tribune

Bartlesville Examiner-Entrprise

National Archives: National Personal Records Center (Military Records)

The Oklahoman (Oklahoma City, OK)

Websites

http://www.VirtualWall.org

http://www.warmemorial.us/mediawiki3/index.php?title=Vietnam_(Nowata,_Oklahoma)

https://vvmf.org/Wall-of-Faces/3783/KENNETH-B-BERRY/

https://www.vietnam.ttu.edu/exhibits/helicopter/

https://www.archives.gov/research/military/vietnam-war/casualty-statistics

https://www.archives.gov/research/vietnam-war

Books

Chinnery, Philip D. *Vietnam: The Helicopter War*. Annapolis, Maryland: Naval Institute Press, 1991.

FOLLOWING THE BREADCRUMBS OF JOURNALISM

Newspapers, Magazines, Other Materials

Virginia Military Institute Yearbook (1965)

Woodland (California) *Daily Democrat*

National Archives: National Personal Records Center (Military Records)

Lawton Morning Press; Lawton Constitution

The Oklahoman (Oklahoma City, OK)

Tulsa Tribune

Websites

https://www.vmi.edu/cadet-life/

https://history.oa-bsa.org/node/3142

https://www.wlu.edu

https://www.goodreads.com/quotes/434971-the-heart-wants-what-it-wants---or-else-it

http://content.time.com/time/magazine/article/0,9171,160439,00.html

https://newspaperarchive.com/woodland-daily-democrat-apr-13–1968-p-1/

https://en.wikipedia.org/wiki/Salinas,_California

https://www.cityofsalinas.org

https://www.salinasuhsd.org/Domain/4

https://salinaspubliclibrary.org/about/john-steinbeck-library

https://www.findagrave.com/memorial/88442496/charles-leighton-housh

https://okjournalismhalloffame.com/2008/bill-harper/

https://oklahoman.com/article/5631450/oklahoma-officials-association-announces-2019-hall-of-fame-class

https://okjournalismhalloffame.com/2014/jay-cronley/

https://en.wikipedia.org/wiki/Jay_Cronley

https://okjournalismhalloffame.com/1974/john-cronley/

https://www.notablebiographies.com/newsmakers2/2006-Ei-La/Hunter-Evan.html

http://www.tasteofcinema.com/2015/the-20-best-movies-about-divorce/

Books

Bryson, Bill. *The Life and Times of the Thunderbolt Kid: A Memoir.* New York: Broadway Books, 2006.

RUBBER CITY PEAKS AND VALLEYS

Newspapers, Magazines, Other Media and Materials

Akron Beacon Journal

Fort Wayne (Indiana) *News-Sentinel*

Fort Wayne Journal Gazette

New York Times

Kansas City Star

Associated Press

United Press International

Burlington (Vermont) *Free Press*

Columbia Journalism Review

Stephen H. Love Log of Life (a journal and scrapbook)

Books

Allen, Dale. An unpublished memoir.

Faust, Gerry and Steve Love. *The Golden Dream.* Champaign, Illinois: Sagamore Publishing, 1997.

Stoner, Andrew E. *Notorious 92: Indiana's Most Heinous Murders in All 92 Counties.* Indianapolis, Indiana: Rooftop Press, 2007 and subsequently by Blue River Press, 2017.

Love, Steve and David Giffels. *Wheels of Fortune: The Story of Rubber in Akron.* Akron, Ohio: University of Akron Press, 1999.

Websites

https://en.wikipedia.org/wiki/Paste_up

https://news.ycombinator.com/item?id=2186871

http://www.forgottenartsupplies.com/?what=artifacts&image_id=46&cat=53

https://www.findagrave.com/memorial/26796035/ralph-daniel-osborne

https://www.espn.com/espn/print?id=11712653&type=Columnist&imagesPrint=off

https://baseballhall.org/discover/awards/j-g-taylor-spink/sheldon-ocker

https://www.encyclopedia.com/people/sports-and-games/sports-biographies/avery-brundage

https://www.pulitzer.org/winners/david-moats

https://www.pulitzer.org/finalists/aki-soga-and-michael-townsend

https://www.cjr.org/behind_the_news/pulitzer_editorial_writing_fin.php

https://www.sevendaysvt.com/OffMessage/archives/2018/02/27/media-note-david-moats-out-at-herald-times-argus?mode=print

Made in the USA
Coppell, TX
15 May 2021

55750617R00187